797,885 Books
are available to read at

www.ForgottenBooks.com

Forgotten Books' App
Available for mobile, tablet & eReader

ISBN 978-0-282-25242-7
PIBN 10845411

This book is a reproduction of an important historical work. Forgotten Books uses state-of-the-art technology to digitally reconstruct the work, preserving the original format whilst repairing imperfections present in the aged copy. In rare cases, an imperfection in the original, such as a blemish or missing page, may be replicated in our edition. We do, however, repair the vast majority of imperfections successfully; any imperfections that remain are intentionally left to preserve the state of such historical works.

Forgotten Books is a registered trademark of FB &c Ltd.
Copyright © 2015 FB &c Ltd.
FB &c Ltd, Dalton House, 60 Windsor Avenue, London, SW19 2RR.
Company number 08720141. Registered in England and Wales.

For support please visit www.forgottenbooks.com

1 MONTH OF FREE READING

at

www.ForgottenBooks.com

By purchasing this book you are eligible for one month membership to ForgottenBooks.com, giving you unlimited access to our entire collection of over 700,000 titles via our web site and mobile apps.

To claim your free month visit:
www.forgottenbooks.com/free845411

* Offer is valid for 45 days from date of purchase. Terms and conditions apply.

English
Français
Deutsche
Italiano
Español
Português

www.forgottenbooks.com

Mythology Photography **Fiction** Fishing Christianity **Art** Cooking Essays Buddhism Freemasonry Medicine **Biology** Music **Ancient Egypt** Evolution Carpentry Physics Dance Geology **Mathematics** Fitness Shakespeare **Folklore** Yoga Marketing **Confidence** Immortality Biographies Poetry **Psychology** Witchcraft Electronics Chemistry History **Law** Accounting **Philosophy** Anthropology Alchemy Drama Quantum Mechanics Atheism Sexual Health **Ancient History Entrepreneurship** Languages Sport Paleontology Needlework Islam **Metaphysics** Investment Archaeology Parenting Statistics Criminology **Motivational**

SELECT WORKS

OF

PORPHYRY;

CONTAINING

HIS FOUR BOOKS ON
ABSTINENCE FROM ANIMAL FOOD;

HIS TREATISE ON
THE HOMERIC CAVE OF THE NYMPHS;

AND HIS
AUXILIARIES
TO THE
PERCEPTION OF INTELLIGIBLE NATURES.

TRANSLATED FROM THE GREEK

BY

THOMAS TAYLOR.

WITH

AN APPENDIX,
EXPLAINING THE ALLEGORY OF THE WANDERINGS OF ULYSSES.
BY THE TRANSLATOR.

Και ουτω θεων και ανθρωπων θειων και ευδαιμονων βιος, απαλλαγη των αλλων των τηδε, απηδονος των τηδε, φυγη μονου προς μονον.—PLOTINI Op. p. 771.

LONDON:
PRINTED FOR
THOMAS RODD, 17, GREAT NEWPORT STREET.
1823.

888
P75d
+T25

LONDON:
PRINTED BY J. MOYES, GREVILLE STREET.

TO

THE REV. WILLIAM JOHN JOLLIFFE,

AS A TESTIMOMY OF GREAT ESTEEM FOR HIS
TALENTS AND WORTH,

AND A TRIBUTE OF THE WARMEST GRATITUDE FOR
HIS PATRONAGE,

THIS WORK IS DEDICATED

BY THE TRANSLATOR,

THOMAS TAYLOR.

INTRODUCTION.

Porphyry, the celebrated author of the treatises translated in this volume, was dignified by his contemporaries, and by succeeding Platonists, with the appellation of *the philosopher*, on account of his very extraordinary philosophical attainments. He is likewise called by Simplicius, *the most learned of the philosophers*, and is praised by Proclus for his ιεροπρεπη νοηματα, or *conceptions adapted to sanctity;* the truth of all which appellations is by the following treatises most abundantly and manifestly confirmed.

A few biographical particulars only have been transmitted to us respecting this great man, and these are as follow. He was born at Tyre, in the twelfth year of the reign of the Emperor Alexander Severus, and in the two hundred and thirty-third of the Christian era; and he died at Rome, when he was more than seventy years old, in the latter part of the Emperor Dioclesian's reign. He was also a disciple first of Longinus, and afterwards of the great Plotinus, with whom he became acquainted in the thirtieth year of his age; and it is to Porphyry we are indebted for the publication of the inestimable and uncommonly profound works of that most extraordinary man. For, as I have observed in my History of the Restoration of the Platonic Theology, it was a long time before Plotinus committed his thoughts to writing, and gave the world a copy of his inimitable mind. That light which was destined to illuminate the philosophical world, as yet shone with solitary splendour, or beamed only on a beloved few; and it was through Porphyry alone that it at length emerged from its sanctuary, and displayed its radiance in full perfection, and with unbounded diffusion. For Porphyry, in the language of Eunapius, "like a Mercurial chain let down for the benefit of mortals, unfolded every thing with accuracy and clearness, by the assistance of universal erudition."

We are likewise informed, by the same Eunapius, that Porphyry, when he first associated with Plotinus, bade farewell to all his other preceptors, and totally applied himself to the friendship of that wonderful man. Here he filled his mind with science, as from a perennial and never-satiating fount. But afterwards, being conquered, as it were, by the magnitude of his doctrines, he conceived a hatred of body, and could no longer endure the fetters of mortality. —

"Hence," says he[a], "I formed an intention of destroying myself, which Plotinus wonderfully perceived; and as I was walking home, stood before me, and said, *Your present design, O Porphyry, is not the dictate of a sound intellect, but rather of a soul raging with an atrabilarious fury.* In consequence of this he ordered me to depart from Rome; and accordingly I went to Sicily, having heard that a certain worthy and elegant man dwelt at that time about Lilybæum. And thus, indeed, I was liberated from this perturbation of soul; but was, in the meantime, hindered from being with Plotinus till his death."

Porphyry also maintains a very distinguished rank among those great geniuses who contributed to the development of the genuine dogmas of Plato, after they had been lost for upwards of five hundred years; as I have shown in my abovementioned History of the Restoration of the Platonic Theology. Among these dogmas, that which is transcendently important is this,—that the ineffable principle of things, which is denominated by Plato *the good* and *the one*, is something superior to intellect and being itself. This, as we are informed by Proclus, was demonstrated by Porphyry, by many powerful and beautiful arguments, in his treatise Concerning Principles,

[a] In Vit. Plotin.

which is unfortunately lost. And this dogma, which was derived principally from the 6th book of the Republic, and the Parmenides, of Plato, and was adopted by all succeeding Platonists, is copiously unfolded, and the truth of it supported by reasoning replete with what Plato calls geometrical necessities, by those two great philosophical luminaries Proclus and Damascius[b]; the former of whom was the Coryphæus of the Platonists, and the latter possessed a profoundly investigating mind.

Of the disciples of Porphyry the most celebrated was Iamblichus, a man of an uncommonly penetrating genius, and who, like his master Plato, on account of the sublimity of his conceptions, and his admirable proficiency in theological learning, was surnamed *the divine*. This extraordinary man, though zealously attached to the Platonic philosophy, yet explored the wisdom of other sects, particularly of the Pythagoreans, Egyptians, and Chaldeans; and formed one beautiful system of recondite knowledge, from their harmonious conjunction[c].

[b] See the 2d book of my translation of Proclus on the Theology of Plato, and the Introduction to my translation of Plato, and notes on the 3d volume of that translation.

[c] See my translation of his Life of Pythagoras, and also of his treatise on the Mysteries. The Emperor Julian says of Iamblichus, " that he was posterior in time, but not in genius, to Plato himself."

INTRODUCTION. ix

With respect to the works of Porphyry which are translated in this volume, the first, which is *On Abstinence from Animal Food,* is a treatise not only replete with great erudition, but is remarkable for the purity of life which it inculcates, and the sanctity of conception with which it abounds. At the same time it must be remembered, that it was written solely, as Porphyry himself informs us, with a view to the man who wishes in the present life to liberate himself as much as possible from the fetters of the corporeal nature, in order that he may elevate his intellectual eye to the contemplation of *truly-existing being* (το οντως ον,) and may establish himself in deity as in his paternal port [d]. But such a one, as

---

[d] Such a man as this, is arranged by Plotinus in the class of *divine men*, in the following extract from my translation of his treatise on Intellect, Ideas, and Real Being, Ennead V. 9. The extract, which is uncommonly beautiful in the original, forms the beginning of the treatise. " Since all men, from their birth, employ sense prior to intellect, and are necessarily first conversant with sensibles, some, proceeding no farther, pass through life, considering these as the first and last of things, and apprehending, that whatever is painful among these, is evil, and whatever is pleasant, is good; thus, thinking it sufficient to pursue the one and avoid the other. Those, too, among them, who pretend to a greater share of reason than others, esteem this to be wisdom; being affected in a manner similar to more heavy birds, who, collecting many things from the earth, and being oppressed with the weight, are unable to fly on high,

he beautifully observes, must divest himself of every thing of a mortal nature which he has assumed, must withdraw himself from sense and imagination, and the irrationality with which they are attended, and from an adhering affection and passion towards them; and must enter the stadium naked and unclothed, striving for the most glorious of all prizes, the Olympia of the soul[e]. Hence, says he, " my discourse is not directed to those who are occupied in sordid mechanical arts, nor to those who are engaged in athletic exercises; neither to soldiers nor sailors, nor rhetoricians, *nor to those who lead an active*

though they have received wings for this purpose from nature. But others are in a small degree elevated from things subordinate, the more excellent part of the soul recalling them from pleasure to a more worthy pursuit. As they are, however, unable to look on high, and as not possessing any thing else which can afford them rest, they betake themselves, together with the name of virtue, to actions and the election of things inferior, from which they at first endeavoured to raise themselves, though in vain. *In the third class is the race of divine men*, who through a more excellent power, and with piercing eyes, acutely perceive supernal light, to the vision of which they raise themselves, above the clouds and darkness, as it were, of this lower world, and there abiding, despise every thing in these regions of sense; being no otherwise delighted with the place which is truly and properly their own, than he who, after many wanderings, is at length restored to his lawful country."

[e] Page 23.

life[f]*;* but I write to the man who considers what he is, whence he came, and whither he ought to tend, and who, in what pertains to nutriment and other necessary concerns, is different from those who propose to themselves other kinds of life; *for to none but such as these do I direct my discourse*[g]." This treatise, also, is highly valuable for the historical information which it contains, independently of the philosophical beauties with which it abounds.

The *Explanation of the Homeric Cave of the Nymphs*, which follows next, is not only remarkable for the great erudition which it displays, but also for containing some profound arcana of the mythology and symbolical theology of the Greeks.

And the third treatise, which is denominated

---

[f] The translator of this work, and of the other treatises contained in this volume, having been so circumstanced, that he has been obliged to mingle the active with the contemplative life (μετα θεωρητικου του πολιτευομενος) in acquiring for himself a knowledge of the philosophy of Plato, and disseminating that philosophy for the good of others, has also found it expedient to make use of a fleshy diet. Nothing, however, but an imperious necessity, from causes which it would be superfluous to detail at present, could have induced him to adopt animal, instead of vegetable nutriment. But though he has been nurtured in Eleatic and Academic studies, yet it has not been in Academic bowers.

[g] Page 19.

Auxiliaries to the Perception of Intelligibles, may be considered as an excellent introduction to the works of Plotinus in general, from which a great part of it is extracted, and in particular, to the following books of that most sublime genius, viz. On the Virtues[h]; On the Impassivity of Incorporeal Natures[i]; and On Truly-Existing Being, in which it is demonstrated that such being is every where one and the same whole[k]. This Porphyrian treatise, also, is admirably calculated to afford assistance to the student of the Theological Elements of Proclus, a work never to be sufficiently praised for the scientific accuracy, profundity of conception, and luminous development of the most important dogmas, which it displays.

In the fourth place, Porphyry, in his treatise On the Cave of the Nymphs, having informed us, that Numenius, the Pythagorean, considered the person of Ulysses, in the Odyssey, as the image of a man who passes in a regular manner over the stormy sea of generation, or a sensible life, and thus at length arrives at a region where tempest and seas are unknown, and finds a nation

" Who ne'er new salt, or heard the billows roar :"

I have endeavoured, by the assistance of this

---

[h] Ennead I. 2.   [i] Ennead III. 6.
[k] Ennead VI. lib. 4, 5.

intimation, to unfold, in the Appendix which concludes the work, the secret meaning of the allegory; and, I trust, in a way which will not be deemed by the intelligent reader either visionary or vain.

With respect to the translation of the treatises, I have endeavoured faithfully to preserve both the matter and manner of the author; and have availed myself of the best editions of them, and, likewise, of all the information which appeared to me to be most important, and most appropriate, from the remarks of critics and philologists, but especially from the elucidations of philosophers. This, I trust, will be evident from a perusal of the notes which accompany the translation.

Of all the other writings of Porphyry, besides those translated in this volume, few unfortunately have been preserved entire[1], the greater part of what remains of them being fragments. Among these fragments, however, there is one very important, lately found by Angelus Maius, and published by him, Mediol. 1816, 8vo. It is nearly the whole of the Epistle of Porphyry to his wife Marcella, in which I have discovered the

[1] For even with respect to the treatise On Abstinence from Animal Food, there is every reason to believe that something is wanting at the end of it.

original of many of the Sentences of the celebrated Sextus Pythagoricus[m], which have been

[m] See the Latin translation of these Sentences by Ruffinus, in the Opuscula Mythologica of Gale. The Sentences which are to be found in this Epistle of Porphyry, were published by me, with some animadversions, in the Classical Journal, about two years ago; but on account of the great importance of these Sentences, and for the sake of those who may not have this Journal in their possession, I shall here repeat what I have there said on this subject.

After having premised that great praise is due to the editor for the publication of this Epistle, but that, as he has taken no notice of the sources whence most of the beautiful moral sentences with which this Epistle abounds, are derived, it becomes necessary to unfold them to the reader, particularly as by this means several of the Sentences of Sextus Pythagoricus may be obtained in the original Greek; — I then observe:

" Previous, however, to this development, I shall present the reader with the emendation of the following defective sentence in p. 19: Το δε πεπαιδευσθαι ουκ εν πολυμαθειας αναληψει * * * * παλαξει δε των ψυχικων παθων εθεωρειτο. The editor, not being an adept in the philosophy of Pythagoras and Plato, conceived that παλαξει was a genuine word; for he remarks, " Nota vocabulum παλαξις," whereas it is only a part of a word, *i.e.* it is a part of απαλλαξει. Hence, if after αναληψει, the words εν απαλλαξει are inserted, the sentence of Porphyry will be perfect both in its construction and meaning, and will be in English, " Erudition does not consist in the resumption of polymathy, but is to be surveyed in a liberation from the passions pertaining to the soul." The editor, not perceiving the necessity of this emendation, has, by the following version, totally mistaken the meaning of the sentence: " Bonam autem institutionem nun-

hitherto supposed to be alone extant in the fraudulent Latin version of the Presbyter Ruf-

quam æstimem, quæ cum eruditionis copia, animalium quoque passionum contaminatione sordescat."

The first sentence of which I have discovered the source, is from Sextus, and is the following, in p. 23: θεος μεν γαρ δειται ουδενος· σοφος δε μονου θεου: *i. e.* "For God is not in want of any thing; but the wise man is alone in want of God." This, in the version of Ruffinus, is: "Deus quidem nullius eget, fidelis autem Dei solius." (Vid. Opusc. Mytholog. 8vo. 1688, p. 646.)

2: Πασης πραξεως και παντος εργου και λογου θεος εποπτης παριστω και εφορος, (p. 24): *i. e.* "Of every action, and of every deed and word, God is present as the scrutator and inspector." This is evidently derived from the following sentence of Demophilus, (Opusc. Mythol. p. 621): Εαν αει μνημονευης, οτι οπου αν ἦ η ψυχη σου, και το σωμα εργον αποτελει, θεος εφιστηκεν εφορος, εν πασαις σου ταις ευχαις και πραξεσιν, αιδεσθηση μεν του θεωρου το αληστον, εξεις δε τον θεον συνοικον, *i. e.* "If you always remember, that wherever your soul, or your body, performs any deed, God is present as an inspector, in all your prayers and actions, you will reverence the nature of an inspector, from whom nothing can be concealed, and will have God for a cohabitant." What immediately follows in this paragraph is from Sextus, viz. και παντων ων πραττομεν αγαθων τον θεον αιτιον ηγωμεθα: *i. e.* "Of all the good that we do, we should consider God as the cause." And Sextus says, p. 648. "Deus in bonis actibus hominibus dux est." Porphyry adds: Των δε κακων αιτιοι ημεις εσμεν οι ελομενοι, θεος δε αναιτιος. And the latter part is evidently from Sextus, who says, p. 648, "Mali nullius autor est Deus." Porphyry further adds: Οθεν και ευκταιον τα αξια θεου· και αιτωμεθα ἃ μη λαβοιμεν αν παρ' ετερου· και ων ηγεμονες οι μετ' αρετης πονοι, ταυτα ευχομεθα γενεσθαι μετα τους πονους: *i. e.* "Hence we should ask of God things which are worthy of him, and which we cannot

finus. And for an account of the other entire works and fragments that are extant, and also

receive from any other. The goods also, of which labours are the leaders, in conjunction with virtue, we should pray that we may obtain after the labours [are accomplished]." All this is from Sextus. For, in p. 648, he says: " Hæc posce à Deo, quæ dignum est præstare Deum. Ea pete à Deo, quæ accipere ab homine non potes. In quibus præcedere debet labor, hæc tibi opta evenire post laborem." Only, in this last sentence, Ruffinus has omitted to add, after *labor*, the words *cum virtute*. What Porphyry says, almost immediately after this, is precisely the first of the Sentences of Demophilus, (Opusc. Mythol. p. 626), viz. Ἁ δε κτησαμενος ου καθεξεις, μη αιτου παρα θεου· δωρον γαρ θεου παν αναφαιρετον· ωστε ου δωσει ὁ μη καθεξεις: i. e. " Do not ask of God that which, when you have obtained, you cannot preserve. For every gift of God is incapable of being taken away; so that he will not give that which you cannot retain." The sentence immediately following this is ascribed to Pythagoras, and is to be found in the Sentences of Stobæus, (edit. 1609, p. 65): viz. Ων δε του σωματος απαλλαγεισα ου δεηθηση, εκεινων καταφρονει· και ων αν απαλλαγεισα δεη, εις ταυτα συ ασκουμενη τον θεον παρεκαλει γενεσθαι συλληπτορα. In Stobæus, however, there is some difference, so as to render the sentence more complete. For immediately after καταφρονει, there is παντων; for δεηθηση there is δεηση; for δεη, δεηση; for τον θεον, τους θεους; for συ ασκουμενη, σοι ασκουμενῳ; and instead of γενεσθαι συλληπτορα, γενεσθαι σοι συλληπτορα. This, therefore, translated, will be: " Despise all those things which, when liberated from the body, you will not want; and exercising yourself in those things, of which, when liberated from the body, you will be in want, invoke the Gods to become your helpers." In pp. 27 and 28, Porphyry says, αιρετωτερου σοι οντος [χρηματα] εικη

of the lost writings of Porphyry, I refer the reader to the Bibliotheca Græca of Fabricius, and

βαλειν ἢ λογον· και το ηττασθαι τ' αληθη λεγοντα, ἢ νικᾳν απατωντα: *i. e.* "It should be more eligible to you carelessly to throw away riches than reason; and to be vanquished when speaking the truth, than to vanquish by deception." And the latter part of this sentence is to be found in Sextus: for in p. 649 he says, "Melius est vinci vera dicentem, quam vincere, mentientem." Almost immediately after Porphyry adds, Αδυνατον τον αυτον φιλοθεον τε ειναι και φιληδονον και φιλοσωματον· ο γαρ φιληδονος και φιλοσωματος παντως και φιλοχρηματος· ο δὲ φιλοχρηματος, εξ αναγκης αδικος· ο δε αδικος, και εις θεον και εις πατερας ανοσιος, και εις τους αλλους παρανομος· ωστε καν εκατομβας θυῃ, και μυριοις αναθημασι νεως αγαλλῃ, ασεβης εστι και αθεος και τῃ προαιρεσει ιεροσυλος· διο και παντα φιλοσωματον ως αθεον και μιαρον εκτρεπεσθαι χρη. This sentence is the last of the Sentences of Demophilus, (Opusc. Mythol. p. 625); but in Porphyry it is in one part defective, and in another is fuller than in Demophilus. For in the first colon, φιλοχρηματον is wanting: in the second colon, after ο γαρ φιληδονος και φιλοσωματος, the words ο δε φιλοσωματος are wanting. And in Demophilus, instead of ο δε αδικος και εις θεον και εις πατερας ανοσιος, και εις τους αλλους παρανομος, there is nothing more than ο δε αδικος, εις μεν θεον ανοσιος, εις δε ανθρωπους παρανομος. In Demophilus also, after ωστε καν εκατομβας θυῃ the words και μυριοις αναθημασι τους νεως αγαλλῃ, are wanting. And in Porphyry, after νεως αγαλλῃ, the words πολυ μαλλον ανοσιωτερος εστι, και, are wanting. This sentence therefore, thus amended, will be in English, "It is impossible for the same person to be a lover of God, a lover of pleasure, a lover of body, and a lover of riches. For a lover of pleasure is also a lover of body; but a lover of body is entirely a lover of riches; and a

to my before-mentioned History of the Restoration of the Platonic Theology; in which latter

lover of riches is necessarily unjust. But he who is unjust is impious towards God and his parents, and lawless towards others. So that, though he should sacrifice hecatombs, and adorn temples with ten thousand gifts, he will be much more unholy, impious, atheistical, and sacrilegious in his deliberate choice. Hence it is necessary to avoid every lover of body, as one who is without God, and is defiled."

3. The following passages in the epistle of Porphyry, are from Sextus: Ο δε αξιος ανθρωπος θεου, θεος αν ειη, (p. 30,) *i. e.* "The man who is worthy of God, will be himself a God." And Sextus says, "Dignus Deo homo, deus est et in hominibus." (p. 654.) Porphyry says, Και τιμησεις μεν αριστα τον θεον, οταν τῳ θεῳ την σαυτης διανοιαν ομοιωσεις, (p. 30,) *i. e.* "And you will honour God in the best manner, when you assimilate your reasoning power to God." Thus also Sextus, "Optime honorat Deum ille, qui mentem suam, quantum fieri potest, similem Deo facit," (p. 655.) Again, Porphyry says, Θεος δε ανθρωπον βεβαιοι πρασσοντα καλα· κακων δε πραξεων κακος δαιμων ηγεμων, (p. 31): *i. e.* "God corroborates man when he performs beautiful deeds; but an evil dæmon is the leader of bad actions." And Sextus says, "Deus bonos actus hominum confirmat. Malorum actuum, malus dæmon dux est." (p. 653). Porphyry adds, Ψυχη δε σοφου αρμοζεται προς θεον, αει θεον ορα, συνεστιν αει θεῳ, (p. 31,) *i. e.* "The soul of the wise man is adapted to God; it always beholds God, and is always present with God." Thus, too, Sextus, "Sapientis anima audit Deum, sapientis anima aptatur à Deo, sapientis anima semper est cum Deo, (p. 655). There is, however, some difference between the original and the Latin version, which is most probably owing to the fraud of Ruffinus. And in

work, in speaking of Porphyry's lost treatise on the Reascent of the Soul, I have given a

the last place, Porphyry says, Αλλα κρηπις ευσεβειας σοι νομιζισθω η φιλανθρωπια, (p. 58,) *i. e.* "Philanthropy should be considered by you as the foundation of piety." And Sextus says, "Fundamentum et initium est cultûs Dei, amare Dei homines." (p. 654). Ruffinus, however, in this version, fraudulently translates φιλανθρωπια, *amare Dei homines*, in order that this sentence, as well as the others, might appear to be written by Sixtus the bishop!

4. The learned reader will find the following passages in the Epistle of Porphyry, to be sentences of Demophilus, viz. Λογον γαρ θεου τοις υπο δοξης διεφθαρμενοις λεγειν, κ.τ.λ. usque ad ισον φερει, (p. 29). Ουχ η γλωττα του σοφου τιμιον παρα θεω, κ.τ.λ. usque ad μονος ειδως ευξασθαι, (p. 32). Ου χολωθεντες ουν οι θεοι βλαπτουσι, κ.τ.λ. usque ad θεω δε ουδεν αβουλητον, (p. 35). Ουτε δακρυα και ικετειαι θεον επιστρεφουσι, ουτε θυηπολια θεον τιμωσιν, ουτε αναθηματων πληθος κοσμουσι θεον, κ.τ.λ. usque ad ιεροσυλοις χορηγια, (p. 36). In which passage, however, there is a remarkable difference, as the learned reader will find, between the text of Porphyry and that of Demophilus. Εαν ουν αει μνημονευης, οτι οπου αν η ψυχη σου περιπατη, και το σωμα ενεργον (lege εργον,) αποτελη, κ.τ.λ. usque ad τον θεον συνοικον, (p. 37). Ο συνετος ανηρ και θεοφιλης, κ.τ.λ. usque ad σπουδαζεται πονησας, (p. 54). Γυμνος δε αποσταλεις [σοφος] κ.τ.λ. usque ad επηκοος ο θεος, (p. 54.) Χαλεπωτερον δουλευειν παθεσιν η τυραννοις. And οσα γαρ παθη ψυχης, τοσουτοι και ωμοι δεσποται, (p. 57). And lastly, πολλω γαρ κρειττον τεθναναι η δι' ακρασιαν την ψυχην αμαυρωσαι, (p. 58). In all these passages, it will be found, by comparing them with Porphyry, that they occasionally differ from the text of Demophilus, yet not so as to alter the sense.

long and most interesting extract relative to that treatise, from Synesius on Dreams.

I only add, that many of the Sentences of Demophilus will be found among those of Sextus. Nor is this at all wonderful, as it was usual with the Pythagoreans, from their exalted notions of friendship, to consider the work of one of them as the production of all.

THE SELECT WORKS OF PORPHYRY.

ON ABSTINENCE FROM ANIMAL FOOD.

BOOK THE FIRST.

1. Hearing from some of our acquaintance, O Firmus[*], that you, having rejected a fleshless diet, have again returned to animal food, at first I did not credit the report, when I considered your temperance, and the reverence which you have been taught to pay to those ancient and pious men from whom we have received the precepts of philosophy. But when others who came after these confirmed this report, it appeared to me that it would be too rustic and remote from the rational method of persuasion to reprehend you, who neither, according to the proverb, flying from evil have found something better, nor according to Empedocles, having lamented your former life, have converted yourself to one that is more excellent. I have therefore thought it worthy of the friendship which subsists between us, and also adapted to those who have arranged their life con-

[*] Porphyry elsewhere calls this Firmus Castricius his friend and fellow disciple. See more concerning him in Porphyry's Life of Plotinus.

formably to truth, to disclose your errors through a confutation derived from an argumentative discussion.

2. For when I considered with myself what could be the cause of this alteration in your diet, I could by no means suppose that it was for the sake of health and strength, as the vulgar and idiots would say; since, on the contrary, you yourself, when you were with us, confessed that a fleshless diet contributed both to health and to the proper endurance of philosophic labours; and experience testifies, that in saying this you spoke the truth. It appears, therefore, that you have returned to your former illegitimate[b] conduct, either through deception[c], because you think it makes no difference with respect to the acquisition of wisdom whether you use this or that diet; or perhaps through some other cause of which I am ignorant, which excited in you a greater fear than that which could be produced by the impiety of transgression. For I should not say that you have despised the philosophic laws which we derived from our ancestors, and which you have so much admired, through intemperance, or for the sake of voracious gluttony; or that you are naturally inferior to some of the vulgar, who, when they have assented to laws, though contrary to those under which they formerly lived, will suffer amputation [rather than violate them], and will abstain from certain animals on which they before fed, more than they would from human flesh.

3. But when I was also informed by certain persons that you even employed arguments against those who abstained from animal food, I not only pitied, but was

---

[b] παρανομημματα. Porphyry calls the conduct of Firmus *illegitimate*, because the feeding on flesh is for the most part contrary to the laws of genuine philosophy.

[c] The original in this place is, ἡ δι απατην ουν, ἡ το μηδεν διαφερειν ηγεισθαι προς φρονησιν, κ.τ.λ.; but, for ἡ το μηδεν διαφερειν, I read δια το μηδεν διαφερειν. And this appears to have been the reading which Felicianus found in his MS.; for his version of this passage is, "Vel igitur deceptione inductus, quod sive hoc sive illo modo vescaris, &c."

indignant with you, that, being persuaded by certain frigid and very corrupt sophisms, you have deceived yourself, and have endeavoured to subvert a dogma which is both ancient and dear to the Gods. Hence it appeared to me to be requisite not only to show you what our own opinion is on this subject, but also to collect and dissolve the arguments of our opponents, which are much stronger than those adduced by you in multitude and power, and every other apparatus; and thus to demonstrate, that truth is not vanquished even by those arguments which seem to be weighty, and much less by superficial sophisms. For you are perhaps ignorant, that not a few philosophers are adverse to abstinence from animal food, but that this is the case with those of the Peripatetic and Stoic sects, and with most of the Epicureans; the last of whom have written in opposition to the philosophy of Pythagoras and Empedocles, of which you once were studiously emulous. To this abstinence, likewise, many philologists are adverse, among whom Clodius the Neapolitan wrote a treatise against those who abstain from flesh. Of these men I shall adduce the disquisitions and common arguments against this dogma, at the same time omitting those reasons which are peculiarly employed by them against the demonstrations of Empedocles.

The Arguments of the Peripatetics and Stoics, from Heraclides Ponticus[d].

4. OUR opponents therefore say, in the first place, that justice will be confounded, and things immoveable be moved, if we extend what is just, not only to the rational, but also to the irrational nature; conceiving that not only Gods and men pertain to us, but that there is likewise an alliance between us and brutes, who [in reality] have no conjunction with us. Nor shall we employ some of them in laborious works, and use others for food, from a conviction that the association which is

---

[d] This philosopher was an auditor of Plato and Speusippus.

between us and them, in the same manner as that of some foreign polity, pertains to a tribe different from ours, and is dishonourable. For he who uses these as if they were men, sparing and not injuring them, thus endeavouring to adapt to justice that which it cannot bear, both destroys its power, and corrupts that which is appropriate, by the introduction of what is foreign. For it necessarily follows, either that we act unjustly by sparing them, or if we spare and do not employ them, that it will be impossible for us to live. We shall also, after a manner, live the life of brutes, if we reject the use which they are capable of affording.

5. For I shall omit to mention the innumerable multitude of Nomades and Troglodytæ, who know of no other nutriment than that of flesh; but to us who appear to live mildly and philanthropically, what work would be left for us on the earth or in the sea, what illustrious art, what ornament of our food would remain, if we conducted ourselves innoxiously and reverentially towards brutes, as if they were of a kindred nature with us? For it would be impossible to assign any work, any medicine, or any remedy for the want which is destructive of life, or that we can act justly, unless we preserve the ancient boundary and law.

> To fishes, savage beasts, and birds, devoid
> Of justice, Jove to devour each other
> Granted; but justice to mankind he gave [*].

i. e. towards each other.

6. But it is not possible for us to act unjustly towards those to whom we are not obliged to act justly. Hence, for those who reject this reasoning, no other road of justice is left, either broad or narrow, into which they can enter. For, as we have already observed, our nature, not being sufficient to itself, but indigent of many things, would be entirely destroyed, and enclosed in a life involved in difficulties, unorganic, and deprived of neces-

---

[*] Hesiod. Op. et Di. lib. I. v. 275, &c.

saries, if excluded from the assistance derived from animals. It is likewise said, that those first men did not live prosperously; for this superstition did not stop at animals, but compelled its votaries even to spare plants. For, indeed, what greater injury does he do, who cuts the throat of an ox or a sheep, than he who cuts down a fir tree or an oak? since, from the doctrine of transmigration, a soul is also implanted in these. These therefore are the principal arguments of the Stoics and Peripatetics.

The Arguments of the Epicureans, from Hermachus[f].

7. THE Epicureans, however, narrating, as it were, a long genealogy, say, that the ancient legislators, looking to the association of life, and the mutual actions of men, proclaimed that manslaughter was unholy, and punished it with no casual disgrace. Perhaps, indeed, a certain natural alliance which exists in men towards each other, through the similitude of form and soul, is the reason why they do not so readily destroy an animal of this kind, as some of the other animals which are conceded to our use. Nevertheless, the greatest cause why manslaughter was considered as a thing grievous to be borne, and impious, was the opinion that it did not contribute to the whole nature and condition of human life. For, from a principle of this kind, those who are capable of perceiving the advantage arising from this decree, require no other cause of being restrained from a deed so dire. But those who are not able to have a sufficient perception of this, being terrified by the magnitude of the punishment, will abstain from readily destroying each other. For those, indeed, who survey the utility of the before-mentioned ordinance, will promptly observe it; but those who are not able to perceive the benefit with which it is attended, will obey the mandate,

---

[f] This philosopher was a Mitylenæan, and is said to have been an auditor of, and also the successor of, Epicurus.

in consequence of fearing the threatenings of the laws; which threatenings certain persons ordained for the sake of those who could not, by a reasoning process, infer the beneficial tendency of the decree, at the same time that most would admit this to be evident.

8. For none of those legal institutes which were established from the first, whether written or unwritten, and which still remain, and are adapted to be transmitted, [from one generation to another] became lawful through violence, but through the consent of those that used them. For those who introduced things of this kind to the multitude, excelled in wisdom, and not in strength of body, and the power which subjugates the rabble. Hence, through this, some were led to a rational consideration of utility, of which before they had only an irrational sensation, and which they had frequently forgotten; but others were terrified by the magnitude of the punishments. For it was not possible to use any other remedy for the ignorance of what is beneficial, than the dread of the punishment ordained by law. For this alone even now keeps the vulgar in awe, and prevents them from doing any thing, either publicly or privately, which is not beneficial [to the community]. But if all men were similarly capable of surveying and recollecting what is advantageous, there would be no need of laws, but men would spontaneously avoid such things as are prohibited, and perform such as they were ordered to do. For the survey of what is useful and detrimental, is a sufficient incentive to the avoidance of the one and the choice of the other. But the infliction of punishment has a reference to those who do not foresee what is beneficial. For impendent punishment forcibly compels such as these to subdue those impulses which lead them to useless actions, and to do that which is right.

9. Hence also, legislators ordained, that even involuntary manslaughter should not be entirely void of punishment; in order that they might not only afford no pretext for the voluntary imitation of those deeds which

were involuntarily performed, but also that they might prevent many things of this kind from taking place, which happen, in reality, involuntarily. For neither is this advantageous through the same causes by which men were forbidden voluntarily to destroy each other. Since, therefore, of involuntary deeds, some proceed from a cause which is unstable, and which cannot be guarded against by human nature; but others are produced by our negligence and inattention to different circumstances; hence legislators, wishing to restrain that indolence which is injurious to our neighbours, did not even leave an involuntary noxious deed without punishment, but, through the fear of penalties, prevented the commission of numerous offences of this kind. I also am of opinion, that the slaughters which are allowed by law, and which receive their accustomed expiations through certain purifications, were introduced by those ancient legislators, who first very properly instituted these things for no other reason than that they wished to prevent men as much as possible from voluntary slaughter. For the vulgar every where require something which may impede them from promptly performing what is not advantageous [to the community]. Hence those who first perceived this to be the case, not only ordained the punishment of fines, but also excited a certain other irrational dread, through proclaiming those not to be pure who in any way whatever had slain a man, unless they used purifications after the commission of the deed. For that part of the soul which is void of intellect, being variously disciplined, acquired a becoming mildness, certain taming arts having been from the first invented for the purpose of subduing the irrational impulses of desire, by those who governed the people. And one of the precepts promulgated on this occasion was, that men should not destroy each other without discrimination.

10. Those, however, who first defined what we ought to do, and what we ought not, very properly did not forbid us to kill other animals. For the advantage

arising from these is effected by a contrary practice, since it is not possible that men could be preserved, unless they endeavoured to defend those who are nurtured with themselves from the attacks of other animals. At that time, therefore, some of those, of the most elegant manners, recollecting that they abstained from slaughter because it was useful to the public safety, they also reminded the rest of the people in their mutual associations of what was the consequence of this abstinence; in order that, by refraining from the slaughter of their kindred, they might preserve that communion which greatly contributes to the peculiar safety of each individual. But it was not only found to be useful for men not to separate from each other, and not to do any thing injurious to those who were collected together in the same place, for the purpose of repelling the attacks of animals of another species; but also for defence against men whose design was to act nefariously. To a certain extent, therefore, they abstained from the slaughter of men, for these reasons, viz. in order that there might be a communion among them in things that are necessary, and that a certain utility might be afforded in each of the above-mentioned incommodities. In the course of time, however, when the offspring of mankind, through their intercourse with each other, became more widely extended, and animals of a different species were expelled, certain persons directed their attention in a rational way to what was useful to men in their mutual nutriment, and did not alone recal this to their memory in an irrational manner.

11. Hence they endeavoured still more firmly to restrain those who readily destroyed each other, and who, through an oblivion of past transactions, prepared a more imbecile defence. But in attempting to effect this, they introduced those legal institutes which still remain in cities and nations; the multitude spontaneously assenting to them, in consequence of now perceiving, in a greater degree, the advantage arising from an association with

each other. For the destruction of every thing noxious, and the preservation of that which is subservient to its extermination, similarly contribute to a fearless life. And hence it is reasonable to suppose, that one of the above-mentioned particulars was forbidden, but that the other was not prohibited. Nor must it be said, that the law allows us to destroy some animals which are not corruptive of human nature, and which are not in any other way injurious to our life. For, as I may say, no animal among those which the law permits us to kill is of this kind; since, if we suffered them to increase excessively, they would become injurious to us. But through the number of them which is now preserved, certain advantages are imparted to human life. For sheep and oxen, and every such like animal, when the number of them is moderate, are beneficial to our necessary wants; but if they become redundant in the extreme, and far exceed the number which is sufficient, they then become detrimental to our life; the latter by employing their strength, in consequence of participating of this through an innate power of nature, and the former, by consuming the nutriment which springs up from the earth for our benefit alone. Hence, through this cause, the slaughter of animals of this kind is not prohibited, in order that as many of them as are sufficient for our use, and which we may be able easily to subdue, may be left. For it is not with horses, oxen, and sheep, and with all tame animals, as it is with lions and wolves, and, in short, with all such as are called savage animals, that, whether the number of them is small or great, no multitude of them can be assumed, which, if left, would alleviate the necessity of our life. And on this account, indeed, we utterly destroy some of them; but of others, we take away as many as are found to be more than commensurate to our use.

12. On this account, from the above-mentioned causes, it is similarly requisite to think, that what pertains to the eating of animals, was ordained by those who

from the first established the laws; and that the advantageous and the disadvantageous were the causes why some animals were permitted to be eaten and others not. So that those who assert, that every thing beautiful and just subsists conformably to the peculiar opinions of men respecting those who established the laws, are full of a certain most profound stupidity. For it is not possible that this thing can take place in any other way than that in which the other utilities of life subsist, such as those that are salubrious, and an innumerable multitude of others. Erroneous opinions, however, are entertained in many particulars, both of a public and private nature. For certain persons do not perceive those legal institutes, which are similarly adapted to all men; but some, conceiving them to rank among things of an indifferent nature, omit them; while others, who are of a contrary opinion, think that such things as are not universally profitable, are every where advantageous. Hence, through this cause, they adhere to things which are unappropriate; though in certain particulars they discover what is advantageous to themselves, and what contributes to general utility. And among these are to be enumerated the eating of animals, and the legally ordained destructions which are instituted by most nations on account of the peculiarity of the region. It is not necessary, however, that these institutes should be preserved by us, because we do not dwell in the same place as those did by whom they were made. If, therefore, it was possible to make a certain compact with other animals in the same manner as with men, that we should not kill them, nor they us, and that they should not be indiscriminately destroyed by us, it would be well to extend justice as far as to this; for this extent of it would be attended with security. But since it is among things impossible, that animals which are not recipients of reason should participate with us of law, on this account, utility cannot be in a greater degree procured by security from other animals, than from inanimate natures. But we can alone obtain security from the liberty which we now possess of putting them to death. And such are the arguments of the Epicureans.

The Arguments of Claudius the Neapolitan, who published a Treatise against Abstinence from Animal Food.

13. It now remains, that we should adduce what plebeians and the vulgar are accustomed to say on this subject. For they say, that the ancients abstained from animals, not through piety, but because they did not yet know the use of fire; but that as soon as they became acquainted with its utility, they then conceived it to be most honourable and sacred. They likewise called it Vesta, and from this the appellation of *convestals* or companions was derived; and afterwards they began to use animals. For it is natural to man to eat flesh, but contrary to his nature to eat it raw. Fire, therefore, being discovered, they embraced what is natural, and admitted the eating of boiled and roasted flesh. Hence lynxes are [said by Homer[g] to be] *crudivorous*, or *eaters of raw flesh*; and of Priam, also, he says, as a disgraceful circumstance,

   Raw flesh by you, O Priam, is devoured[h].

And,

   Raw flesh, dilacerating, he devoured[i].

And this is said, as if the eating of raw flesh pertained to the impious. Telemachus, also, when Minerva was his guest, placed before her not raw, but roasted flesh. At first, therefore, men did not eat animals, for man is not [naturally] a devourer of raw flesh. But when the use of fire was discovered, fire was employed not only for the cooking of flesh, but also for most other eatables. For that man is not [naturally] adapted to eat

---

[g] Iliad, XI. v. 479.   [h] Iliad, IV. v. 35.
[i] Iliad, XXII. v. 347.

raw flesh, is evident from certain nations that feed on fishes. For these they roast, some upon stones that are very much heated by the sun; but others roast them in the sand. That man, however, is adapted to feed on flesh, is evident from this, that no nation abstains from animal food. Nor is this adopted by the Greeks through depravity, since the same custom is admitted by the barbarians.

14. But he who forbids men to feed on animals, and thinks it is unjust, will also say that it is not just to kill them, and deprive them of life. Nevertheless, an innate and just war is implanted in us against brutes. For some of them voluntarily attack men, as, for instance, wolves and lions; others not voluntarily, as serpents, since they bite not, except they are trampled on. And some, indeed, attack men; but others destroy the fruits of the earth. From all these causes, therefore, we do not spare the life of brutes; but we destroy those who commence hostilities against us, as also those who do not, lest we should suffer any evil from them. For there is no one who, if he sees a serpent, will not, if he is able, destroy it, in order that neither it, nor any other serpent, may bite a man. And this arises, not only from our hatred of those that are the destroyers of our race, but likewise from that kindness which subsists between one man and another. But though the war against brutes is just, yet we abstain from many which associate with men. Hence, the Greeks do not feed either on dogs, or horses, or asses, because of these, those that are tame are of the same species as the wild. Nevertheless, they eat swine and birds. For a hog is not useful for any thing but food. The Phœnicians, however, and Jews, abstain from it, because, in short, it is not produced in those places. For it is said, that this animal is not seen in Ethiopia even at present. As, therefore, no Greek sacrifices a camel or an elephant to the Gods, because Greece does not produce these animals, so neither is a hog sacrificed to the Gods in Cyprus or Phœnicia, because it is not

indigenous in those places. And, for the same reason, neither do the Egyptians sacrifice this animal to the Gods. In short, that some nations abstain from a hog, is similar to our being unwilling to eat the flesh of camels.

15. But why should any one abstain from animals? Is it because feeding on them makes the soul or the body worse? It is, however, evident, that neither of these is deteriorated by it. For those animals that feed on flesh are more sagacious than others, as they are venatic, and possess an art, by which they supply themselves with food, and acquire power and strength; as is evident in lions and wolves. So that the eating of flesh neither injures the soul nor the body. This likewise is manifest, both from the athletæ, whose bodies become stronger by feeding on flesh, and from physicians, who restore bodies to health by the use of animal food. For this is no small indication that Pythagoras did not think sanely, that none of the wise men embraced his opinion; since neither any one of the seven wise men, nor any of the physiologists who lived after them, nor even the most wise Socrates, or his followers, adopted it.

16. Let it, however, be admitted that all men are persuaded of the truth of this dogma, respecting abstinence from animals. But what will be the boundary of the propagation of animals? For no one is ignorant how numerous the progeny is of the swine and the hare. And to these add all other animals. Whence, therefore, will they be supplied with pasture? And what will husbandmen do? For they will not destroy those who destroy the fruits of the earth. And the earth will not be able to bear the multitude of animals. Corruption also will be produced from the putridity of those that will die. And thus, from pestilence taking place, no refuge will be left. For the sea, and rivers, and marshes, will be filled with fishes, and the air with birds, but the earth will be full of reptiles of every kind.

17. How many likewise will be prevented from having their diseases cured, if animals are abstained from?

For we see that those who are blind recover their sight by eating a viper. A servant of Craterus, the physician, happening to be seized with a new kind of disease, in which the flesh fell away from the bones, derived no benefit from medicines; but by eating a viper prepared after the manner of a fish, the flesh became conglutinated to the bones, and he was restored to health. Many other animals also, and their several parts, cure diseases when they are properly used for that purpose; of all which remedies he will be frustrated who rejects animal food.

18. But if, as they say, plants also have a soul, what will become of our life if we neither destroy animals nor plants? If, however, he is not impious who cuts off plants, neither will he who kills animals.

19. But some one may, perhaps, say it is not proper to destroy that which belongs to the same tribe with ourselves; if the souls of animals are of the same essence with ourselves. If, however, it should be granted that souls are inserted in bodies voluntarily, it must be said that it is through a love of juvenility: for in the season of youth there is an enjoyment of all things. Why, therefore, do they not again enter into the nature of man? But if they enter voluntarily, and for the sake of juvenility, and pass through every species of animals, they will be much gratified by being destroyed. For thus their return to the human form will be more rapid. The bodies also which are eaten will not produce any pain in the souls of those bodies, in consequence of the souls being liberated from them; and they will love to be implanted in the nature of man. Hence, as much as they are pained on leaving the human form, so much will they rejoice when they leave other bodies. For thus they will more swiftly become man again, who predominates over all irrational animals, in the same manner as God does over men. There is, therefore, a sufficient cause for destroying other animals, viz. their acting unjustly in destroying men. But if the souls of men are immortal, but those of irrational animals mortal, men

will not act unjustly by destroying irrational animals. And if the souls of brutes are immortal, we shall benefit them by liberating them from their bodies. For, by killing them, we shall cause them to return to the human nature.

20. If, however, we [only] defend ourselves [in putting animals to death], we do not act unjustly, but we take vengeance on those that injure us. Hence, if the souls of brutes are indeed immortal, we benefit them by destroying them. But if their souls are mortal, we do nothing impious in putting them to death. And if we defend ourselves against them, how is it possible that in so doing we should not act justly. For we destroy, indeed, a serpent and a scorpion, though they do not attack us, in order that some other person may not be injured by them; and in so doing we defend the human race in general. But shall we not act justly in putting those animals to death, which either attack men, or those that associate with men, or injure the fruits of the earth?

21. If, however, some one should, nevertheless, think it is unjust to destroy brutes, such a one should neither use milk, nor wool, nor sheep, nor honey. For, as you injure a man by taking from him his garments, thus, also, you injure a sheep by shearing it. For the wool which you take from it is its vestment. Milk, likewise, was not produced for you, but for the young of the animal that has it. The bee also collects honey as food for itself; which you, by taking away, administer to your own pleasure. I pass over in silence the opinion of the Egyptians, that we act unjustly by meddling with plants. But if these things were produced for our sake, then the bee, being ministrant to us, elaborates honey, and the wool grows on the back of sheep, that it may be an ornament to us, and afford us a bland heat.

22. Co-operating also with the Gods themselves in what contributes to piety, we sacrifice animals: for, of the Gods, Apollo, indeed, is called λυκοκτονος, *the slayer of wolves;* and Diana, θηρκτονος, *the destroyer of wild beasts.*

Demi-gods likewise, and all the heroes who excel us both in origin and virtue, have so much approved of the slaughter of animals, that they have sacrificed to the Gods *Dodeceïdes*[k] and *Hecatombs*. But Hercules, among other things, is celebrated for being an *ox-devourer*.

23. It is, however, stupid to say that Pythagoras exhorted men to abstain from animals, in order that he might, in the greatest possible degree, prevent them from eating each other. For, if all men at the time of Pythagoras were anthropophagites, he must be delirious who drew men away from other animals, in order that they might abstain from devouring each other. For, on this account, he ought rather to have exhorted them to become anthropophagites, by showing them that it was an equal crime to devour each other, and to eat the flesh of oxen and swine. But if men at that time did not eat each other, what occasion was there for this dogma? And if he established this law for himself and his associates, the supposition that he did so is disgraceful. For it demonstrates that those who lived with Pythagoras were anthropophagites.

24. For we say that the very contrary of what he conjectured would happen. For, if we abstained from animals, we should not only be deprived of pleasure and riches of this kind, but we should also lose our fields, which would be destroyed by wild beasts; since the whole earth would be occupied by serpents and birds, so that it would be difficult to plough the land; the scattered seeds would immediately be gathered by the birds; and all such fruits as had arrived at perfection, would be consumed by quadrupeds. But men being oppressed by such a want of food, would be compelled, by bitter necessity, to attack each other.

25. Moreover, the Gods themselves, for the sake of a remedy, have delivered mandates to many persons about sacrificing animals. For history is full of instances of

---

[k] *i. e.* Sacrifices from twelve animals.

the Gods having ordered certain persons to sacrifice animals, and, when sacrificed, to eat them. For, in the return of the Heraclidæ, those who engaged in war against Lacedæmon, in conjunction with Eurysthenes and Proscles, through a want of necessaries, were compelled to eat serpents, which the land at that time afforded for the nutriment of the army. In Libya, also, a cloud of locusts fell for the relief of another army that was oppressed by hunger. The same thing likewise happened at Gades. Bogus was a king of the Mauritanians, who was slain by Agrippa in Mothone. He in that place attacked the temple of Hercules, which was most rich. But it was the custom of the priests daily to sprinkle the altar with blood. That this, however, was not effected by the decision of men, but by that of divinity, the occasion at that time demonstrated. For, the siege being continued for a long time, victims were wanting. But the priest being dubious how he should act, had the following vision in a dream. He seemed to himself to be standing in the middle of the pillars of the temple of Hercules, and afterwards to see a bird sitting opposite to the altar, and endeavouring to fly to it, but which at length flew into his hands. He also saw that the altar was sprinkled with its blood. Seeing this, he rose as soon as it was day, and went to the altar, and standing on the turret, as he thought he did in his dream, he looked round, and saw the very bird which he had seen in his sleep. Hoping, therefore, that his dream would be fulfilled, he stood still, saw the bird fly to the altar and sit upon it, and deliver itself into the hands of the high priest. Thus the bird was sacrificed, and the altar sprinkled with blood. That, however, which happened at Cyzicus, is still more celebrated than this event. For Mithridates having besieged this city, the festival of Proserpine was then celebrated, in which it was requisite to sacrifice an ox. But the sacred herds, from which it was necessary the victim should be taken, fed opposite to the city, on the continent[1]: and one of them was already marked for this purpose. When, therefore, the hour demanded the sacrifice, the ox lowed, and swam over the sea, and the guards of the city opened the gates to it. Then the ox directly ran into the city, and stood at the altar, and was sacrificed to the Goddess. Not unreasonably, therefore, was it thought to be most pious to sacrifice many animals, since it appeared that the sacrifice of them was pleasing to the Gods.

26. But what would be the condition of a city, if all the citizens were of this opinion, [viz. that they should abstain from destroying animals?] For how would they repel their enemies, when they were attacked by them, if they were careful in the extreme not to kill any one of them? In this case, indeed, they must be immediately destroyed. And it would be too prolix to narrate other difficulties and inconveniences, which would necessarily take place. That it is not, however, impious to slay and feed on animals, is evident from this, that Pythagoras himself, though those prior to him permitted the athletæ to drink milk, and to eat cheese, irrigated with water; but others, posterior to him, rejecting this diet, fed them with dry figs; yet he, abrogating the ancient custom, allowed them to feed on flesh, and found that such a diet greatly increased their strength. Some also relate, that the Pythagoreans themselves did not spare animals when they sacrificed to the gods. Such, therefore, are the arguments of Clodius, Heraclides Ponticus, Hermachus the Epicurean, and the Stoics and Peripatetics, [against abstinence from animal food]: among which also are comprehended the arguments which were sent to us by you, O Castricius. As, however, I intend to oppose these opinions, and those of the multitude, I may reasonably premise what follows.

27. In the first place, therefore, it must be known

---

[1] For Cyzicus was situated in an island.

that my discourse does not bring with it an exhortation to every description of men. For it is not directed to those who are occupied in sordid mechanical arts, nor to those who are engaged in athletic exercises; neither to soldiers, nor sailors, nor rhetoricians, nor to those who lead an active life. But I write to the man who considers what he is, whence he came, and whither he ought to tend, and who, in what pertains to nutriment, and other necessary concerns, is different from those who propose to themselves other kinds of life; for to none but such as these do I direct my discourse. For, neither in this common life can there be one and the same exhortation to the sleeper, who endeavours to obtain sleep through the whole of life, and who, for this purpose, procures from all places things of a soporiferous nature, as there is to him who is anxious to repel sleep, and to dispose every thing about him to a vigilant condition. But to the former it is necessary to recommend intoxication, surfeiting, and satiety, and to exhort him to choose a dark house, and

> A bed luxuriant, broad, and soft,—

as the poets say; and that he should procure for himself all such things as are of a soporiferous nature, and which are effective of sluggishness and oblivion, whether they are odours, or ointments, or are liquid or solid medicines. And to the latter it is requisite to advise the use of a drink sober and without wine, food of an attenuated nature, and almost approaching to fasting; a house lucid, and participating of a subtle air and wind, and to urge him to be strenuously excited by solicitude and thought, and to prepare for himself a small and hard bed. But, whether we are naturally adapted to this, I mean to a vigilant life, so as to grant as little as possible to sleep, since we do not dwell among those who are perpetually vigilant, or whether we are designed to be in a soporiferous state of existence, is the business of another discussion, and is a subject which requires very extended demonstrations.

28. To the man, however, who once suspects the enchantments attending our journey through the present life, and belonging to the place in which we dwell; who also perceives himself to be naturally vigilant, and considers the somniferous nature of the region which he inhabits;—to this man addressing ourselves, we prescribe food consentaneous to his suspicion and knowledge of this terrene abode, and exhort him to suffer the somnolent to be stretched on their beds, dissolved in sleep. For it is requisite to be cautious, lest as those who look on the blear-eyed contract an ophthalmy, and as we gape when present with those who are gaping, so we should be filled with drowsiness and sleep, when the region which we inhabit is cold, and adapted to fill the eyes with rheum, as being of a marshy nature, and drawing down all those that dwell in it to a somniferous and oblivious condition. If, therefore, legislators had ordained laws for cities, with a view to a contemplative and intellectual life, it would certainly be requisite to be obedient to those laws, and to comply with what they instituted concerning food. But if they established their laws, looking to a life according to nature, and which is said to rank as a medium, [between the irrational and the intellectual life,] and to what the vulgar admit, who conceive externals, and things which pertain to the body to be good or evil, why should any one, adducing their laws, endeavour to subvert a life, which is more excellent than every law which is written and ordained for the multitude, and which is especially conformable to an unwritten and divine law? For such is the truth of the case.

29. The contemplation which procures for us felicity, does not consist, as some one may think it does, in a multitude of discussions and disciplines; nor does it receive any increase by a quantity of words. For if this were the case, nothing would prevent those from being

happy by whom all disciplines are collected together [and comprehended]. Now, however, every discipline by no means gives completion to this contemplation, nor even the disciplines which pertain to truly existing beings, unless there is a conformity to them of our nature[m] and life. For since there are, as it is said, in every purpose three[n] ends, the end with us is to obtain the contemplation of real being, the attainment of it procuring, as much as it is possible for us, a conjunction of the contemplator with the object of contemplation. For the reascent of the soul is not to any thing else than true being itself, nor is its conjunction with any other thing. But intellect is truly-existing being; so that the end is to live according to intellect. Hence such discussions and exoteric disciplines as impede our purification, do not give completion to our felicity. If, therefore, felicity consisted in literary attainments, this end might be obtained by those who pay no attention to their food and their actions. But since for this purpose it is requisite to exchange the life which the multitude lead for another, and to become purified both in words and deeds, let us consider what reasonings and what works will enable us to obtain this end.

30. Shall we say, therefore, that they will be such as separate us from sensibles, and the passions which pertain to them, and which elevate us as much as possible to an intellectual, unimaginative, and impassive life; but that the contraries to these are foreign, and deserve to be rejected? And this by so much the more, as they separate us from a life according to intellect. But, I think, it must be admitted, that we should follow the object to which intellect attracts us. For we resemble those who enter into, or depart from a foreign region,

---

[m] In the original εαν μη προση και η κατ' αυτα φυσιωσις και ζωη; but it is obviously necessary for φυσιωσις to read φυσις.

[n] viz. As it appears to me, a pleasurable, a profitable, and a virtuous end, which last is a truly beautiful and good end.

not only because we are banished from our intimate associates, but in consequence of dwelling in a foreign land, we are filled with barbaric passions, and manners, and legal institutes, and to all these have a great propensity. Hence, he who wishes to return to his proper kindred and associates, should not only with alacrity begin the journey, but, in order that he may be properly received, should meditate how he may divest himself of every thing of a foreign nature which he has assumed, and should recall to his memory such things as he has forgotten, and without which he cannot be admitted by his kindred and friends. After the same manner, also, it is necessary, if we intend to return to things which are truly our own, that we should divest ourselves of every thing of a mortal nature which we have assumed, together with an adhering affection towards it, and which is the cause of our descent [into this terrestrial region;] and that we should excite our recollection of that blessed and eternal essence, and should hasten our return to the nature which is without colour and without quality, earnestly endeavouring to accomplish two things; one, that we may cast aside every thing material and mortal; but the other, that we may properly return, and be again conversant with our true kindred, ascending to them in a way contrary to that in which we descended hither. For we were intellectual natures, and we still are essences purified from all sense and irrationality; but we are complicated with sensibles, through our incapability of eternally associating with the intelligible, and through the power of being conversant with terrestrial concerns. For all the powers which energize in conjunction with sense and body, are injured, in consequence of the soul not abiding in the intelligible; (just as the earth, when in a bad condition, though it frequently receives the seed of wheat, yet produces nothing but tares), and this is through a certain depravity of the soul, which does not indeed destroy its essence from the generation of irrationality, but through this is conjoined with a mortal nature, and is drawn down from its own proper to a foreign condition of being.

31. So that, if we are desirous of returning to those natures with which we formerly associated, we must endeavour to the utmost of our power to withdraw ourselves from sense and imagination, and the irrationality with which they are attended, and also from the passions which subsist about them, as far as the necessity of our condition in this life will permit. But such things as pertain to intellect should be distinctly arranged, procuring for it peace and quiet from the war with the irrational part; that we may not only be auditors of intellect and intelligibles, but may as much as possible enjoy the contemplation of them, and, being established in an incorporeal nature, may truly live through intellect; and not falsely in conjunction with things allied to bodies. We must therefore divest ourselves of our manifold garments, both of this visible and fleshly vestment, and of those with which we are internally clothed, and which are proximate to our cutaneous habiliments; and we must enter the stadium naked and unclothed, striving for [the most glorious of all prizes] the Olympia of the soul. The first thing, however, and without which we cannot contend, is to divest ourselves of our garments. But since of these some are external and others internal, thus also with respect to the denudation, one kind is through things which are apparent, but another through such as are more unapparent. Thus, for instance, not to eat, or not to receive what is offered to us, belongs to things which are immediately obvious; but not to desire is a thing more obscure; so that, together with deeds, we must also withdraw ourselves from an adhering affection and passion towards them. For what benefit shall we derive by abstaining from deeds, when at the same time we tenaciously adhere to the causes from which the deeds proceed?

32. But this departure [from sense, imagination, and

irrationality,] may be effected by violence, and also by persuasion and by reason, through the wasting away, and, as it may be said, oblivion and death of the passions; which, indeed, is the best kind of departure, since it is accomplished without oppressing that from which we are divulsed. For, in sensibles, a divulsion by force is not effected without either a laceration of a part, or a vestige of avulsion. But this separation is introduced by a continual negligence of the passions. And this negligence is produced by an abstinence from those sensible perceptions which excite the passions, and by a persevering attention to intelligibles. And among these passions or perturbations, those which arise from food are to be enumerated.

33. We should therefore abstain, no less than from other things, from certain food, viz. such as is naturally adapted to excite the passive part of our soul, concerning which it will be requisite to consider as follows: There are two fountains whose streams irrigate the bond by which the soul is bound to the body; and from which the soul being filled as with deadly potions, becomes oblivious of the proper objects of her contemplation. These fountains are pleasure and pain; of which sense indeed is preparative, and the perception which is according to sense, together with the imaginations, opinions, and recollections which accompany the senses. But from these, the passions being excited, and the whole of the irrational nature becoming fattened, the soul is drawn downward, and abandons its proper love of true being. As much as possible, therefore, we must separate ourselves from these. But the separation must be effected by an avoidance of the passions which subsist through the senses and the irrational part. But the senses are employed either on objects of the sight, or of the hearing, or of the taste, or of the smell, or of the touch; for sense is as it were the metropolis of that foreign colony of passions which we contain. Let us, therefore, consider how much fuel of the passions enters into us through each of

the senses. For this is effected partly by the view of the contests of horses and the athletæ, or those whose bodies are contorted in dancing; and partly from the survey of beautiful women. For these, ensnaring the irrational nature, attack and subjugate it by all-various deceptions.

34. For the soul, being agitated with Bacchic fury through all these by the irrational part, is made to leap, to exclaim and vociferate, the external tumult being inflamed by the internal, and which was first enkindled by sense. But the excitations through the ears, and which are of a passive nature, are produced by certain noises and sounds, by indecent language and defamation, so that many through these being exiled from reason, are furiously agitated, and some, becoming effeminate, exhibit all-various convolutions of the body. And who is ignorant how much the use of fumigations, and the exhalations of sweet odours, with which lovers supply the objects of their love, fatten the irrational part of the soul? But what occasion is there to speak of the passions produced through the taste? For here, especially, there is a complication of a twofold bond; one which is fattened by the passions excited by the taste; and the other, which we render heavy and powerful, by the introduction of foreign bodies [*i. e.* of bodies different from our own]. For, as a certain physician said, those are not the only poisons which are prepared by the medical art; but those likewise which we daily assume for food, both in what we eat, and what we drink, and a thing of a much more deadly nature is imparted to the soul through these, than from the poisons which are compounded for the purpose of destroying the body. And as to the touch, it does all but transmute the soul into the body, and produces in it certain inarticulate sounds, such as frequently take place in inanimate bodies. And from all these, recollections, imaginations, and opinions being collected together, excite a swarm of passions, viz. of

fear, desire, anger, love, voluptuousness*, pain, emulation, solicitude, and disease, and cause the soul to be full of similar perturbations.

35. Hence, to be purified from all these is most difficult, and requires a great contest, and we must bestow much labour both by night and by day to be liberated from an attention to them, and this, because we are necessarily complicated with sense. Whence, also, as much as possible, we should withdraw ourselves from those places in which we may, though unwillingly, meet with this hostile crowd. From experience, also, we should avoid a contest with it, and even a victory over it, and the want of exercise from inexperience.

36. For we learn, that this conduct was adopted by some of the celebrated ancient Pythagoreans and wise men; some of whom dwelt in the most solitary places; but others in temples and sacred groves, from which, though they were in cities, all tumult and the multitude were expelled. But Plato chose to reside in the Academy, a place not only solitary and remote from the city, but which was also said to be insalubrious. Others have not spared even their eyes, through a desire of not being divulsed from the inward contemplation [of reality]. If some one, however, at the same time that he is conversant with men, and while he is filling his senses with the passions pertaining to them, should fancy that he can remain impassive, he is ignorant that he both deceives himself and those who are persuaded by him, nor does he see that we are enslaved to many passions, through not alienating ourselves from the multitude. For he did not speak vainly, and in such a way as to falsify the nature of [the Coryphæan] philosophers, who said of them, " These, therefore, from their youth, neither know the way to the forum, nor where the court of justice or senate-house is situated, or any common place of assembly belonging to the city. They likewise neither hear nor

---

* For φιλτρων here, I read φιληδονιων.

see laws, or decrees, whether orally promulgated or written. And as to the ardent endeavours of their companions to obtain magistracies, the associations of these, their banquets and wanton feastings, accompanied by pipers, these they do not even dream of accomplishing. But whether any thing in the city has happened well or ill, or what evil has befallen any one from his progenitors, whether male or female, these are more concealed from such a one, than, as it is said, how many measures called choes the sea contains. And besides this, he is even ignorant that he is ignorant[p] of all these particulars. For he does not abstain from them for the sake of renown, but, in reality, his body only dwells, and is conversant in the city; but his reasoning power considering all these as trifling and of no value, " he is borne away," according to Pindar, "on all sides, and does not apply himself to any thing which is near."

37. In what is here said, Plato asserts, that the Coryphæan philosopher, by not at all mingling himself with the above-mentioned particulars, remains impassive to them. Hence, he neither knows the way to the court of justice nor the senate-house, nor any thing else which has been before enumerated. He does not say, indeed, that he knows and is conversant with these particulars, and that, being conversant, and filling his senses with them, yet does not know any thing about them; but, on the contrary, he says, that abstaining from them, he is ignorant that he is ignorant of them. He also adds, that this philosopher does not even dream of betaking himself to banquets. Much less, therefore, would he be indignant, if deprived of broth, or pieces of flesh; nor, in short, will he admit

---

[p] The multitude are ignorant that they are ignorant with respect to objects of all others the most splendid and real; but the Coryphæan philosopher is ignorant that he is ignorant with respect to objects most unsubstantial and obscure. The former ignorance is the consequence of a defect, but the latter of a transcendency of gnostic energy. What Porphyry here says of the Coryphæan philosopher, is derived from the Theætetus of Plato.

things of this kind. And will he not rather consider the abstinence from all these as trifling, and a thing of no consequence, but the assumption of them to be a thing of great importance and noxious? For since there are two paradigms in the order of things, one of a divine nature, which is most happy, the other of that which is destitute of divinity, and which is most miserable [q]; the Coryphæan philosopher will assimilate himself to the one, but will render himself dissimilar to the other, and will lead a life conformable to the paradigm to which he is assimilated, viz. a life satisfied with slender food, and sufficient to itself, and in the smallest degree replete with mortal natures.

38. Hence, as long as any one is discordant about food, and contends that this or that thing should be eaten, but does not conceive that, if it were possible, we should abstain from all food, assenting by this contention to his passions, such a one forms a vain opinion, as if the subjects of his dissension were things of no consequence. He, therefore, who philosophizes, will not separate himself [from his terrestrial bonds] by violence; for he who is compelled to do this, nevertheless remains there from whence he was forced to depart. Nor must it be thought, that he who strengthens these bonds, effects a thing of small importance. So that only granting to nature what is necessary, and this of a light quality, and through more slender food, he will reject whatever exceeds this, as only contributing to pleasure. For he will be persuaded of the truth of what Plato says, that sense is a nail by which the soul is fastened to bodies [r], through the agglutination of the passions, and the enjoyment of corporeal delight. For if sensible perceptions were no impediment to the pure energy of the soul, why would it be a thing of a dire nature to be in body, while

---

[q] See p. 52 of my translation of the Theætetus of Plato, from which Dialogue, what Porphyry here says, as well as what he a little before said, is derived.

[r] See the Phædo of Plato, where this is asserted.

at the same time the soul remained impassive to the motions of the body?

39. How is it, also, that you have decided and said, that you are not passive to things which you suffer, and that you are not present with things by which you are passively affected? For intellect, indeed, is present with itself, though we are not present with it. But he who departs from intellect, is in that place to which he departs; and when, by discursive energies, he applies himself upwards and downwards by his apprehension of things, he is there where his apprehension is. But it is one thing not to attend to sensibles, in consequence of being present with other things, and another for a man to think, that though he attends to sensibles yet he is not present with them. Nor can any one show that Plato admits this, without at the same time demonstrating himself to be deceived. He, therefore, who submits to the assumption of [every kind of] food, and voluntarily betakes himself to [alluring] spectacles, to conversation with the multitude, and laughter; such a one, by thus acting, is there where the passion is which he sustains. But he who abstains from these in consequence of being present with other things, he it is who, through his unskilfulness, not only excites laughter in Thracian maid-servants, but in the rest of the vulgar, and when he sits at a banquet, falls into the greatest perplexity, not from any defect of sensation, or from a superior accuracy of sensible perception, and energizing with the irrational part of the soul alone; for Plato does not venture to assert this; but because, in slanderous conversation, he has nothing reproachful to say of any one, as not knowing any evil of any one, because he has not made individuals the subject of his meditation. Being in such perplexity, therefore, he appears, says Plato, to be ridiculous; and in the praises and boastings of others, as he is manifestly seen to laugh, not dissemblingly, but, in reality, he appears to be delirious.

40. So that, through ignorance of, and abstaining

from sensible concerns, he is unacquainted with them. But it is by no means to be admitted, that though he should be familiar with sensibles, and should energize through the irrational part, yet it is possible for him [at the same time] genuinely to survey the objects of intellect. For neither do they who assert that we have two souls, admit that we can attend at one and the same time to two different things. For thus they would make a conjunction of two animals, which being employed in different energies, the one would not be able to perceive the operations of the other.

41. But why would it be requisite that the passions should waste away, that we should die with respect to them, and that this should be daily the subject of our meditation, if it was possible for us, as some assert, to energize according to intellect, though we are at the same time intimately connected with mortal concerns, and this without the intuition of intellect? For intellect sees, and intellect hears [as Epicharmus says]. But if, while eating luxuriously, and drinking the sweetest wine, it were possible to be present with immaterial natures, why may not this be frequently effected while you are present with, and are performing things which it is not becoming even to mention? For these passions every where proceed from the boy* which is in us. And you certainly will admit that the baser these passions are, the more we are drawn down towards them. For what will be the distinction which ought here to be made, if you admit that to some things it is not possible to be passive, without being present with them, but that you may accomplish other things, at the same time that you are surveying intelligibles? For it is not because some things are apprehended to be base by the multitude, but others not. For all the above mentioned passions are base. So that to the attainment of a life according to intellect,

---

* Sense, and that which is beautiful in the energies of sense, are thus denominated by Plato.

it is requisite to abstain from all these, in the same manner as from venereal concerns. To nature therefore, but little food must be granted, through the necessity of generation [or of our connexion with a flowing condition of being.] For, where sense and sensible apprehension are, there a departure and separation from the intelligible take place; and by how much stronger the excitation is of the irrational part, by so much the greater is the departure from intellection. For it is not possible for us to be borne along to this place and to that, while we are *here*, and yet be *there*, [i. e. be present with an intelligible essence.] For our attentions to things are not effected with a part, but with the whole of ourselves.

42. But to fancy that he who is passively affected according to sense, may, nevertheless, energize about intelligibles, has precipitated many of the Barbarians to destruction; who arrogantly assert, that though they indulge in every kind of pleasure, yet they are able to convert themselves to things of a different nature from sensibles, at the same time that they are energizing with the irrational part. For I have heard some persons patronizing their infelicity after the following manner. " We are not," say they, " defiled by food, as neither is the sea by the filth of rivers. For we have dominion over all eatables, in the same manner as the sea over all humidity. But if the sea should shut up its mouth, so as not to receive the streams that now flow into it, it would be indeed, with respect to itself, great; but, with respect to the world, small, as not being able to receive dirt and corruption. If, however, it was afraid of being defiled, it would not receive these streams; but knowing its own magnitude, it receives all things, and is not averse to any thing which proceeds into it. In like manner, say they, we also, if we were afraid of food, should be enslaved by the conception of fear. But it is requisite that all things should be obedient to us. For, if we collect a little water, indeed, which has received any filth, it becomes immediately defiled and oppressed

by the filth; but this is not the case with the profound sea. Thus, also, aliments vanquish the pusillanimous; but where there is an immense liberty with respect to food, all things are received for nutriment, and no defilement is produced." These men, therefore, deceiving themselves by arguments of this kind, act in a manner conformable to their deception. But, instead of obtaining liberty, being precipitated into an abyss of infelicity, they are suffocated. This, also, induced some of the Cynics to be desirous of eating every kind of food, in consequence of their pertinaciously adhering to the cause of errors, which we are accustomed to call a thing of an indifferent nature.

43. The man, however, who is cautious, and is suspicious of the enchantments of nature, who has surveyed the essential properties of body, and knows that it was adapted as an instrument to the powers of the soul, will also know how readily passion is prepared to accord with the body, whether we are willing or not, when any thing external strikes it, and the pulsation at length arrives at perception. For perception is, as it were, an answer [to that which causes the perception.] But the soul cannot answer unless she wholly converts herself to the sound, and transfers her animadversive eye to the pulsation. In short, the irrational part not being able to judge to what extent, how, whence, and what thing ought to be the object of attention, but of itself being inconsiderate, like horses without a charioteer[t]; whither it verges downward, thither it is borne along, without any power of governing itself in things external. Nor does it know the fit time or the measure of the food which should be taken, unless the eye of the charioteer is attentive to it, which regulates and governs the motions of irrationality, this part of the soul being essentially blind.

---

[t] The rational part of the soul is assimilated by Plato, in the Phædrus, to a charioteer, and the two irrational parts, *desire* and *anger*, to two horses. See my translation of that Dialogue.

But he who takes away from reason its dominion over the irrational part, and permits it to be borne along, conformably to its proper nature: such a one, yielding to desire and anger, will suffer them to proceed to whatever extent they please. On the contrary, the worthy man will so act that his deeds may be conformable to presiding reason, even in the energies of the irrational part.

44. And in this the worthy appears to differ from the depraved man, that the former has every where reason present, governing and guiding, like a charioteer, the irrational part; but the latter performs many things without reason for his guide. Hence the latter is said to be most irrational, and is borne along in a disorderly manner by irrationality; but the former is obedient to reason, and superior to every irrational desire. This, therefore, is the cause why the multitude err in words and deeds, in desire and anger, and why, on the contrary, good men act with rectitude, viz. that the former suffer the boy within them to do whatever it pleases; but the latter give themselves up to the guidance of the tutor of the boy, [*i. e.* to reason] and govern what pertains to themselves in conjunction with it. Hence in food, and in other corporeal energies and enjoyments, the charioteer being present, defines what is commensurate and opportune. But when the charioteer is absent, and, as some say, is occupied in his own concerns, then, if he also has with him our attention, he does not permit it to be disturbed, or at all to energize with the irrational power. If, however, he should permit our attention to be directed to the boy, unaccompanied by himself, he would destroy the man, who would be precipitately borne along by the folly of the irrational part.

45. Hence, to worthy men, abstinence in food, and in corporeal enjoyments and actions, is more appropriate than abstinence in what pertains to the touch; because though, while we touch bodies, it is necessary we should descend from our proper manners to the instruction of

that which is most irrational in us; yet this is still more necessary in the assumption of food. For the irrational nature is incapable of considering what will be the effect of it, because this part of the soul is essentially ignorant of that which is absent. But, with respect to food, if it were possible to be liberated from it, in the same manner as from visible objects, when they are removed from the view; for we can attend to other things when the imagination is withdrawn from them; — if this were possible, it would be no great undertaking to be immediately emancipated from the necessity of the mortal nature, by yielding, in a small degree, to it. Since, however, a prolongation of time in cooking and digesting food, and together with this the co-operation of sleep and rest, are requisite, and, after these, a certain temperament from digestion, and a separation of excrements, it is necessary that the tutor of the boy within us should be present, who, selecting things of a light nature, and which will be no impediment to him, may concede these to nature, in consequence of foreseeing the future, and the impediment which will be produced by his permitting the desires to introduce to us a burden not easily to be borne, through the trifling pleasure arising from the deglutition of food.

46. Reason, therefore, very properly rejecting the much and the superfluous, will circumscribe what is necessary in narrow boundaries, in order that it may not be molested in procuring what the wants of the body demand, through many things being requisite; nor being attentive to elegance, will it need a multitude of servants; nor endeavour to receive much pleasure in eating, nor, through satiety, to be filled with much indolence; nor by rendering its burden [the body] more gross, to become somnolent; nor through the body being replete with things of a fattening nature, to render the bond more strong, but himself more sluggish and imbecile in the performance of his proper works. For, let any man show us who endeavours as much as possible to live according

to intellect, and not to be attracted by the passions of the body, that animal food is more easily procured than the food from fruits and herbs; or that the preparation of the former is more simple than that of the latter, and, in short, that it does not require cooks, but, when compared with inanimate nutriment, is unattended by pleasure, is lighter in concoction, and is more rapidly digested, excites in a less degree the desires, and contributes less to the strength of the body than a vegetable diet.

47. If, however, neither any physician, nor philosopher, nor wrestler, nor any one of the vulgar, has dared to assert this, why should we not willingly abstain from this corporeal burden? Why should we not, at the same time, liberate ourselves from many inconveniences by abandoning a fleshly diet? For we should not be liberated from one only, but from myriads of evils, by accustoming ourselves to be satisfied with things of the smallest nature; viz. we should be freed from a superabundance of riches, from numerous servants, a multitude of utensils, a somnolent condition, from many and vehement diseases, from medical assistance, incentives to venery, more gross exhalations, an abundance of excrements, the crassitude of the corporeal bond, from the strength which excites to [base] actions, and, in short, from an Iliad of evils. But from all these, inanimate and slender food, and which is easily obtained, will liberate us, and will procure for us peace, by imparting salvation to our reasoning power. For, as Diogenes says, thieves and enemies are not found among those that feed on maize[u], but sycophants and tyrants are produced from those who feed on flesh. The cause, however, of our being in want of many things being taken away, together with the multitude of nutriment introduced into the body, and also the weight of digestibles being lightened, the eye of the soul will become free, and will be established as in

---

[u] A kind of bread made of milk and flour.

a port beyond the smoke and the waves of the corporeal nature.

48. And this neither requires monition, nor demonstration, on account of the evidence with which it is immediately attended. Hence, not only those who endeavour to live according to intellect, and who establish for themselves an intellectual life, as the end of their pursuits, have perceived that this abstinence was necessary to the attainment of this end; but, as it appears to me, nearly every philosopher, preferring frugality to luxury, has rather embraced a life which is satisfied with a little, than one that requires a multitude of things. And, what will seem paradoxical to many, we shall find that this is asserted and praised by men who thought that pleasure is the end of those that philosophize. For most of the Epicureans, beginning from the Corypheus of their sect, appear to have been satisfied with maize and fruits, and have filled their writings with showing how little nature requires, and that its necessities may be sufficiently remedied by slender and easily-procured food.

49. For the wealth, say they, of nature is definite, and easily obtained; but that which proceeds from vain opinions, is indefinite, and procured with difficulty. For things which may be readily obtained, remove in a beautiful and abundantly sufficient manner that which, through indigence, is the cause of molestation to the flesh; and these are such as have the simple nature of moist and dry aliments. But every thing else, say they, which terminates in luxury, is not attended with a necessary appetition, nor is it necessarily produced from a certain something which is in pain; but partly arises from the molestation and pungency solely proceeding from something not being present; partly from joy; and partly from vain and false dogmas, which neither pertain to any natural defect, nor to the dissolution of the human frame, those not being present. For things which may every where be obtained, are sufficient for those purposes

which nature necessarily requires. But these, through their simplicity and paucity, may be easily procured. And he, indeed, who feeds on flesh, requires also inanimate natures; but he who is satisfied with things inanimate, is easily supplied from the half of what the other wants, and needs but a small expense for the preparation of his food.

50. They likewise say, it is requisite that he who prepares the necessaries of life, should not afterwards make use of philosophy as an accession; but, having obtained it, should, with a confident mind, thus genuinely endure[x] the events of the day. For we shall commit what pertains to ourselves to a bad counsellor, if we measure and procure what is necessary to nature, without philosophy. Hence it is necessary that those who philosophize should provide things of this kind, and strenuously attend to them as much as possible. But, so far as there is a dereliction from thence, [*i. e.* from philosophizing], which is not capable of effecting a perfect purification[y], so far we should not endeavour to procure either riches or nutriment. In conjunction, therefore, with philosophy, we should engage in things of this kind, and be immediately persuaded that it is much better to pursue what is the least, the most simple, and light in nutriment. For that which is least, and is unattended with molestation, is derived from that which is least[z].

51. The preparation also of these things, draws along

---

[x] In the original, αλλα παρασκευασαμενον το θαρρειν τη ψυχη γνησιως ουτως αντιχεσθαι των καθ' ημεραν. But the editor of the quarto edition of this work, who appears to have been nothing more than a mere verbal critic, says, in a note on this passage, that the word αντιχεσθαι, signifies *pertinacissime illis inhærere, nihil ultra studere;* whereas it must be obvious to any man who understands what is here said, that in this place it signifies *to endure.*

[y] In the original, ο μη κυριευσι της τελειας εκθαρρησεως; but for εκθαρρησεως I read with Felicianus εκκαθαρσεως.

[z] In the original, ελαχιστον γαρ και το οχληρον εκ του ελαχιστου. But it is obviously necessary for οχληρον to read ανοχληρον, and yet this was not perceived by the German editor of this work, Jacob Rhoer.

with it many impediments, either from the weight of the body, [which they are adapted to increase,] or from the difficulty of procuring them, or from their preventing the continuity of the energy of our most principal reasonings[a], or from some other cause. For this energy then becomes immediately useless, and does not remain unchanged by the concomitant perturbations. It is necessary, however, that a philosopher should hope that he may not be in want of any thing through the whole of life. But this hope will be sufficiently preserved by things which are easily procured; while, on the other hand, this hope is frustrated by things of a sumptuous nature. The multitude, therefore, on this account, though their possessions are abundant, incessantly labour to obtain more, as if they were in want. But the recollection that the greatest possible wealth has no power worth mentioning of dissolving the perturbations of the soul, will cause us to be satisfied with things easily obtained, and of the most simple nature. Things also, which are very moderate and obvious, and which may be procured with the greatest facility, remove the tumult occasioned by the flesh. But the deficiency of things of a luxurious nature will not disturb him who meditates on death. Farther still, the pain arising from indigence is much milder than that which is produced by repletion, and will be considered to be so by him who does not deceive himself with vain opinions. Variety also of food not only does not dissolve the perturbations of the soul, but does not even increase the pleasure which is felt by the flesh. For this is terminated as soon as pain is removed[b]. So that the feeding on flesh does not remove any thing which is troublesome to nature, nor effect any thing which, unless it is accomplished, will end in pain.

[a] i. e. Of our reasonings about intelligible objects.

[b] Conformable to this, it is beautifully observed by Aristotle, in his Nicomachean Ethics, that corporeal pleasures are the remedies of pain, and that they fill up the indigence of nature, but do not perfect any energy of the [rational] soul.

But the pleasantness with which it is attended is violent, and, perhaps, mingled with the contrary. For it does not contribute to the duration of life, but to the variety of pleasure; and in this respect resembles venereal enjoyments, and the drinking of foreign wines, without which nature is able to remain. For those things, without which nature cannot last, are very few, and may be procured easily, and in conjunction with justice, liberty, quiet, and abundant leisure.

52. Again, neither does animal food contribute, but is rather an impediment to health. For health is preserved through those things by which it is recovered. But it is recovered through a most slender and fleshless diet; so that by this also it is preserved. If, however, vegetable food does not contribute to the strength of Milo, nor, in short, to an increase of strength, neither does a philosopher require strength, or an increase of it, if he intends to give himself up to contemplation, and not to an active and intemperate life. But it is not at all wonderful, that the vulgar should fancy that animal food contributes to health; for they also think that sensual enjoyments and venery are preservative of health, none of which benefit any one; and those that engage in them must be thankful if they are not injured by them. And if many are not of this opinion, it is nothing to us. For neither is any fidelity and constancy in friendship and benevolence to be found among the vulgar; nor are they capable of receiving these, nor of participating of wisdom, or any portion of it which deserves to be mentioned. Neither do they understand what is privately or publicly advantageous; nor are they capable of forming a judgment of depraved and elegant manners, so as to distinguish the one from the other. And, in addition to these things, they are full of insolence and intemperance. On this account, there is no occasion to fear that there will not be those who will feed on animals.

53. For if all men conceived rightly, there would be no need of fowlers, or hunters, or fishermen, or swine-

herds. But animals governing themselves, and having no guardian and ruler, would quickly perish, and be destroyed by others, who would attack them and diminish their multitude, as is found to be the case with myriads of animals on which men do not feed. But all-various folly incessantly dwelling with mankind, there will be an innumerable multitude of those who will voraciously feed on flesh. It is necessary however to preserve health; not by the fear of death, but for the sake of not being impeded in the attainment of the good which is derived from contemplation. But that which is especially preservative of health, is an undisturbed state of the soul, and a tendency of the reasoning power towards truly existing being. For much benefit is from hence derived to the body, as our associates have demonstrated from experience. Hence some who have been afflicted with the gout in the feet and hands, to such a degree as to be infested with it for eight entire years, have expelled it through abandoning wealth, and betaking themselves to the contemplation of divinity[c]. At the same time, therefore, that they have abandoned riches, and a solicitude about human concerns, they have also been liberated from bodily disease. So that a certain state of the soul greatly contributes both to health and to the good of the whole body. And to this also, for the most part, a diminution of nutriment contributes. In short, as Epicurus likewise has rightly said, that food is to be avoided, the enjoyment of which we desire and pursue, but which, after we have enjoyed, we rank among things of an unacceptable nature. But of this kind is every thing luxuriant and gross. And in this manner those are affected, who are vehemently desirous of such nutriment, and through it are involved either in great expense, or in disease, or repletion, or the privation of leisure[d].

[c] This is said by Porphyry, in his Life of Plotinus, to have been the case with the senator Rogatianus.

[d] And leisure, to those who know how rightly to employ it, is, as Socrates said, καλλιστον κτηματων, "*the most beautiful of possessions.*"

54. Hence also, in simple and slender food, repletion is to be avoided, and every where we should consider what will be the consequence of the possession or enjoyment of it, what the magnitude of it is, and what molestation of the flesh or of the soul it is capable of dissolving. For we ought never to act indefinitely, but in things of this kind we should employ a boundary and measure; and infer by a reasoning process, that he who fears to abstain from animal food, if he suffers himself to feed on flesh through pleasure, is afraid of death. For immediately, together with a privation of such food, he conceives that something indefinitely dreadful will be present, the consequence of which will be death. But from these and similar causes, an insatiable desire is produced of riches, possessions, and renown, together with an opinion that every good is increased with these in a greater extent of time, and the dread of death as of an infinite evil. The pleasure however which is produced through luxury, does not even approach to that which is experienced by him who lives with frugality. For such a one has great pleasure in thinking how little he requires. For luxury, astonishment about venereal occupations, and ambition about external concerns, being taken away, what remaining use can there be of idle wealth, which will be of no advantage to us whatever, but will only become a burden, no otherwise than repletion?—while, on the other hand, the pleasure arising from frugality is genuine and pure. It is also necessary to accustom the body to become alienated, as much as possible, from the pleasure of the satiety arising from luxurious food, but not from the fulness produced by a slender diet, in order that moderation may proceed through all things, and that what is necessary, or what is most excellent, may fix a boundary to our diet. For he who thus mortifies his body will receive every possible good, through being sufficient to himself, and an assimilation to divinity. And thus also, he will not desire a greater extent of time, as if it would bring with it an augmentation of good. He will

likewise thus be truly rich, measuring wealth by a natural bound, and not by vain opinions. Thus too, he will not depend on the hope of the greatest pleasure, the existence of which is incredible, since this would be most troublesome. But he will remain satisfied with his present condition, and will not be anxious to live for a longer period of time.

55. Besides this also, is it not absurd, that he who is in great affliction, or is in some grievous external calamity, or is bound with chains, does not even think of food, nor concern himself about the means of obtaining it; but when it is placed before him, refuses what is necessary to his subsistence; and that the man who is truly in bonds, and is tormented by inward calamities, should endeavour to procure a variety of eatables, paying attention to things through which he will strengthen his bonds? And how is it possible that this should be the conduct of men who know what they suffer, and not rather of those who are delighted with their calamities, and who are ignorant of the evils which they endure? For these are affected in a way contrary to those who are in chains, and who are conscious of their miserable condition; since these, experiencing no gratification in the present life, and being full of immense perturbation, insatiably aspire after another life. For no one who can easily liberate himself from all perturbations, will desire to possess silver tables and couches, and to have ointments and cooks, splendid vessels and garments, and suppers remarkable for their sumptuousness and variety; but such a desire arises from a perfect uselessness to every purpose of the present life, from an indefinite generation of good, and from immense perturbation. Hence some do not remember the past, the recollection of it being expelled by the present; but others do not inquire about the present, because they are not gratified with existing circumstances.

56. The contemplative philosopher, however, will invariably adopt a slender diet. For he knows the particulars in which his bond consists, so that he is not

capable of desiring luxuries. Hence, being delighted with simple food, he will not seek for animal nutriment, as if he was not satisfied with a vegetable diet. But if the nature of the body in a philosopher was not such as we have supposed it to be, and was not so tractable, and so adapted to have its wants satisfied through things easily procured, and it was requisite to endure some pains and molestations for the sake of true salvation, ought we not [willingly] to endure them? For when it is requisite that we should be liberated from disease, do we not voluntarily sustain many pains, viz. while we are cut, covered with blood, burnt, drink bitter medicines, and are purged through the belly, through emetics, and through the nostrils, and do we not also reward those who cause us to suffer in this manner? And this being the case, ought we not to sustain every thing, though of the most afflictive nature, with equanimity, for the sake of being purified from internal disease, since our contest is for immortality, and an association with divinity, from which we are prevented through an association with the body? By no means, therefore, ought we to follow the laws of the body, which are violent and adverse to the laws of intellect, and to the paths which lead to salvation. Since, however, we do not now philosophize about the endurance of pain, but about the rejection of pleasures which are not necessary, what apology can remain for those, who impudently endeavour to defend their own intemperance?

57. For if it is requisite not to dissemble any thing through fear, but to speak freely, it is no otherwise possible to obtain the end [of a contemplative life], than by adhering to God, as if fastened by a nail, being divulsed from body, and those pleasures of the soul which subsist through it; since our salvation is effected by deeds, and not by a mere attention to words. But as it is not possible with any kind of diet, and, in short, by feeding on flesh, to become adapted to an union with even some partial deity, much less is this possible with

that God who is beyond all things, and is above a nature simply incorporeal; but after all-various purifications, both of soul and body, he who is naturally of an excellent disposition, and lives with piety and purity, will scarcely be thought worthy to perceive him. So that, by how much more the Father of all things excels in simplicity, purity, and sufficiency to himself, as being established far beyond all material representation, by so much the more is it requisite, that he who approaches to him should be in every respect pure and holy, beginning from his body, and ending internally, and distributing to each of the parts, and in short to every thing which is present with him, a purity adapted to the nature of each. Perhaps, however, these things will not be contradicted by any one. But it may be doubted, why we admit abstinence from animal food to pertain to purity, though in sacrifices we slay sheep and oxen, and conceive that these immolations are pure and acceptable to the Gods. Hence, since the solution of this requires a long discussion, the consideration of sacrifices must be assumed from another principle.

ON

ABSTINENCE FROM ANIMAL FOOD.

BOOK THE SECOND.

1. Pursuing therefore the inquiries pertaining to simplicity and purity of diet, we have now arrived, O Castricius, at the discussion of sacrifices; the consideration of which is difficult, and at the same time requires much explanation, if we intend to decide concerning it in such a way as will be acceptable to the Gods. Hence, as this is the proper place for such a discussion, we shall now unfold what appears to us to be the truth on this subject, and what is capable of being narrated, correcting what was overlooked in the hypothesis proposed from the beginning.

2. In the first place therefore we say, it does not follow because animals are slain that it is necessary to eat them. Nor does he who admits the one, I mean that they should be slain, entirely prove that they should be eaten. For the laws permit us to defend ourselves against enemies who attack us [by killing them]; but it did not seem proper to these laws to grant that we should eat them, as being a thing contrary to the nature of man. In the second place, it does not follow, that because it is proper to sacrifice certain animals to dæmons, or Gods, or certain powers, through causes either known or unknown to men, it is therefore necessary to feed on animals. For it may be shown, that men assumed animals in sacrifices, which no one even of those who

introduced, we do not rightly interpret; since we call the worship of the Gods through the immolation of animals θυσια, *thusia*. But so careful were the ancients not to transgress this custom, that against those who, neglecting the pristine, introduced novel modes of sacrificing, they employed *execrations*[b], and therefore they now denominate the substances which are used for fumigations αρωματα, *aromata*, i. e. *aromatics*, [or things of an execrable nature.] The antiquity, however, of the before-mentioned fumigations may be perceived by him who considers that many now also sacrifice certain portions of odoriferous wood. Hence, when after grass, the earth produced trees, and men at first fed on the fruits of the oak, they offered to the Gods but few of the fruits on account of their rarity, but in sacrifices they burnt many of its leaves. After this, however, when human life proceeded to a milder nutriment, and sacrifices from nuts were introduced, they said *enough of the oak*.

6. But as barley first appeared after leguminous substances, the race of men used it in primitive sacrifices, moistening it for this purpose with water. Afterwards, when they had broken and bruised it, so as to render it eatable, as the instruments of this operation afforded a divine assistance to human life, they concealed them in an arcane place, and approached them as things of a sacred nature. But esteeming the food produced from it when bruised to be blessed, when compared with their former nutriment, they offered, in fine, the first-fruits of it to the Gods. Hence also now, at the end of the sacrifices, we use fruits that are bruised or ground; testifying by this how much fumigations have departed from their ancient simplicity; at the same time not perceiving on what account we perform each of these. Proceeding, however, from hence, and being more abundantly sup-

---

[b] In the original αρασαμενους, which is derived from the verb αραομαι, *imprecor, maledico*; and from hence, according to Porphyry, came the word αρωματα.

plied, both with other fruits and wheat, the first-fruits of cakes, made of the fine flour of wheat, and of every thing else, were offered in sacrifices to the Gods; many flowers being collected for this purpose, and with these all that was conceived to be beautiful, and adapted, by its odour, to a divine sense, being mingled. From these, also, some were used for garlands, and others were given to the fire. But when they had discovered the use of the divine drops of wine, and honey, and likewise of oil, for the purposes of human life, then they sacrificed these. to their causes, the Gods.

7. And these things appear to be testified by the splendid procession in honour of the Sun and the Hours, which is even now performed at Athens, and in which there were other herbs besides grass, and also acorns, the fruit of the crab tree, barley, wheat, a heap of dried figs, cakes made of wheaten and barley flour; and, in the last place, an earthen pot. This mode, however, of offering first-fruits in sacrifices, having, at length, proceeded to great illegality, the assumption of immolations, most dire and full of cruelty, was introduced; so that it would seem that the execrations which were formerly uttered against us, have now received their consummation, in consequence of men slaughtering animals, and defiling altars with blood; and this commenced from that period in which mankind tasted of blood, through having experienced the evils of famine and war. Divinity, therefore, as Theophrastus says, being indignant, appears to have inflicted a punishment adapted to the crime. Hence some men became atheists; but others, in consequence of forming erroneous conceptions of a divine nature, may be more justly called κακοφρονες, *kakophrones*, than κακοθεοι, *kakothevi*[c], because they think that the Gods are depraved, and in no respect naturally more excellent than we are. Thus, therefore, some were seen to live without

---

[c] *i. e.* May be rather called *malevolent* than *unhappy.*

sacrificing any thing, and without offering the first-fruits of their possessions to the Gods; but others sacrificed improperly, and made use of illegal oblations.

8. Hence the Thoes[d], who dwell in the confines of Thrace, as they neither offered any first-fruits, nor sacrificed to the Gods, were at that time suddenly taken away from the rest of mankind; so that neither the inhabitants, nor the city, nor the foundations of the houses, could by any one be found.

> " Men prone to ill, denied the Gods their due,
> And by their follies made their days but few.
> The altars of the bless'd neglected stand,
> Without the offerings which the laws demand;
> But angry Jove in dust this people laid,
> Because no honours to the Gods they paid."
>
> HESIOD. Op. et Di. lib. i. v. 133.

Nor did they offer first-fruits to the Gods, as it was just that they should. But with respect to the Bassarians, who formerly were not only emulous of sacrificing bulls, but also ate the flesh of slaughtered men, in the same manner as we now do with other animals; for we offer to the Gods some parts of them as first-fruits, and eat the rest;—with respect to these men, who has not heard, that insanely rushing on and biting each other, and in reality feeding on blood, they did not cease to act in this manner till the whole race was destroyed of those who used sacrifices of this kind?

9. The sacrifice, therefore, through animals is posterior and most recent, and originated from a cause which is not of a pleasing nature, like that of the sacrifice from fruits, but received its commencement either from famine, or some other unfortunate circumstance. The causes, indeed, of the peculiar mactations among the

---

[d] Fabricius is of opinion that these *Thoes* are the same with the Acrothoitæ, mentioned by Simplicius in his Comment. in Epictet. from Theophrastus.

Athenians, had their beginning either in ignorance, or anger, or fear. For the slaughter of swine is attributed to an involuntary error of Clymene, who, by unintentionally striking, slew the animal. Hence her husband, being terrified as if he had perpetrated an illegal deed, consulted the oracle of the Pythian God about it. But as the God did not condemn what had happened, the slaughter of animals was afterwards considered as a thing of an indifferent nature. The inspector, however, of sacred rites, who was the offspring of prophets, wishing to make an offering of first-fruits from sheep, was permitted to do so, it is said, by an oracle, but with much caution and fear. For the oracle was as follows:—

> " Offspring of prophets, sheep by force to slay,
> The Gods permit not thee; but with wash'd hands
> For thee 'tis lawful any sheep to kill,
> That dies a voluntary death."

10. But a goat was first slain in Icarus, a mountain of Attica, because it had cropped a vine. And Diomus, who was a priest of Jupiter Polieus, was the first that slew an ox; because, when the festival sacred to Jupiter, and called Diipolia, was celebrated, and fruits were prepared after the ancient manner, an ox approaching tasted the sacred cake. But the priest, being aided by others who were present, slew the ox. And these are the causes, indeed, which are assigned by the Athenians for this deed; but by others, other causes are narrated. All of them, however, are full of explanations that are not holy. But most of them assign famine, and the injustice with which it is attended, as the cause. Hence men having tasted of animals, they offered them in sacrifice, as first-fruits, to the Gods; but prior to this, they were accustomed to abstain from animal food. Whence, since the sacrifice of animals is not more ancient than necessary food, it may be determined from this circumstance what ought to be the nutriment of men. But it does not follow, because men have tasted of and offered animals in

sacrifices as first-fruits, that it must necessarily be admitted to be pious to eat that which was not piously offered to the Gods.

11. But what especially proves that every thing of this kind originated from injustice, is this, that the same things are neither sacrificed nor eaten in every nation, but that they conjecture what it is fit for them to do from what they find to be useful to themselves. With the Egyptians, therefore, and Phœnicians, any one would sooner taste human flesh than the flesh of a cow. The cause, however, is, that this animal being useful, is also rare among them. Hence, though they eat bulls, and offer them in sacrifice as first-fruits, yet they spare cows for the sake of their progeny, and ordain that, if any one kill them, it shall be considered as an expiation. And thus, for the sake of utility in one and the same genus of animals, they distinguish what is pious, and what is impious. So that these particulars subsisting after this manner, Theophrastus reasonably forbids those to sacrifice animals who wish to be truly pious; employing these, and other similar arguments, such as the following.

12. In the first place, indeed, because we sacrificed animals through the occurrence, as we have said, of a greater necessity. For pestilence and war were the causes that introduced the necessity of eating them. Since, therefore, we are supplied with fruits, what occasion is there to use the sacrifice of necessity? In the next place, the remunerations of, and thanks for benefits, are to be given differently to different persons, according to the worth of the benefit conferred; so that the greatest remunerations, and from things of the most honourable nature, are to be given to those who have benefited us in the greatest degree, and especially if they are the causes of these gifts. But the most beautiful and honourable of those things, by which the Gods benefit us, are the fruits of the earth. For through these they preserve us, and enable us to live legitimately; so that, from

these we ought to venerate them. Besides, it is requisite to sacrifice those things by the sacrifice of which we shall not injure any one. For nothing ought to be so innoxious to all things as sacrifice. But if some one should say, that God gave animals for our use, no less than the fruits of the earth, yet it does not follow that they are, therefore, to be sacrificed, because in so doing they are injured, through being deprived of life. For *sacrifice* is, as the name implies, something *holy*[*]. But no one is holy who requites a benefit from things which are the property of another, whether he takes fruits or plants from one who is unwilling to be deprived of them. For how can this be holy, when those are injured from whom they are taken? If, however, he who takes away fruits from others does not sacrifice with sanctity, it cannot be holy to sacrifice things taken from others, which are in every respect more honourable than the fruits of the earth. For a more dire deed is thus perpetrated. But soul is much more honourable than the vegetable productions of the earth, which it is not fit, by sacrificing animals, that we should take away.

13. Some one, however, perhaps may say, that we also take away something from plants [when we eat, and sacrifice them to the Gods]. But the ablation is not similar; since we do not take this away from those who are unwilling that we should. For, if we omitted to gather them, they would spontaneously drop their fruits. The gathering of the fruits, also, is not attended with the destruction of the plants, as it is when animals lose their animating principle. And, with respect to the fruit which we receive from bees, since this is obtained by our labour, it is fit that we should derive a common benefit from it. For bees collect their honey from plants; but we carefully attend to them. On which account it is requisite that such a division should be made [of our attention and their labour] that they may suffer no injury.

[*] In the original, η γαρ θυσια, ωσια τις εστιν κατα τουνομα.

But that which is useless to them, and beneficial to us, will be the reward which we receive from them [of our attention to their concerns]. In sacrifices, therefore, we should abstain from animals. For, though all things are in reality the property of the Gods, yet plants appear to be our property; since we sow and cultivate them, and nourish them by other attentions which we pay to them. We ought to sacrifice, therefore, from our own property, and not from the property of others; since that which may be procured at a small expense, and which may easily be obtained, is more holy, more acceptable to the Gods, and better adapted to the purposes of sacrifice, and to the exercise of continual piety. Hence, that which is neither holy, nor to be obtained at a small expense, is not to be offered in sacrifice, even though it should be present.

14. But that animals do not rank among things which may be procured easily, and at a small expense, may be seen by directing our view to the greater part of our race: for we are not now to consider that some men abound in sheep, and others in oxen. In the first place, therefore, there are many nations that do not possess any of those animals which are offered in sacrifice, some ignoble animals, perhaps, excepted. And, in the second place, most of those that dwell in cities themselves, possess these but rarely. But if some one should say that the inhabitants of cities have not mild fruits in abundance; yet, though this should be admitted, they are not in want of the other vegetable productions of the earth; nor is it so difficult to procure fruits as it is to procure animals. Hence an abundance of fruits, and other vegetables, is more easily obtained than that of animals. But that which is obtained with facility, and at a small expense, contributes to incessant and universal diety.

15. Experience also testifies that the Gods rejoice in this more than in sumptuous offerings. For when that Thessalian sacrificed to the Pythian deity oxen with gilt

horns, and hecatombs, Apollo said, that the offering of Hermioneus was more gratifying to him, though he had only sacrificed as much meal as he could take with his three fingers out of a sack. But when the Thessalian, on hearing this, placed all the rest of his offerings on the altar, the God again said, that by so doing his present was doubly more unacceptable to him than his former offering. Hence the sacrifice which is attended with a small expense is pleasing to the Gods, and divinity looks more to the disposition and manners of those that sacrifice, than to the multitude of the things which are sacrificed.

16. Theopompus likewise narrates things similar to these, viz. that a certain Magnesian came from Asia to Delphi; a man very rich, and abounding in cattle, and that he was accustomed every year to make many and magnificent sacrifices to the Gods, partly through the abundance of his possessions, and partly through piety and wishing to please the Gods. But being thus disposed, he came to the divinity at Delphi, bringing with him a hecatomb for the God, and magnificently honouring Apollo, he consulted his oracle. Conceiving also that he worshipped the Gods in a manner more beautiful than that of all other men, he asked the Pythian deity who the man was that, with the greatest promptitude, and in the best manner, venerated divinity, and made the most acceptable sacrifices, conceiving that on this occasion the God would deem him to be pre-eminent. The Pythian deity however answered, that Clearchus, who dwelt in Methydrium, a town of Arcadia, worshipped the Gods in a way surpassing that of all other men. But the Magnesian being astonished, was desirous of seeing Clearchus, and of learning from him the manner in which he performed his sacrifices. Swiftly, therefore, betaking himself to Methydrium, in the first place, indeed, he despised the smallness and vileness of the town, conceiving that neither any private person, nor even the whole city, could

honour the Gods more magnificently and more beautifully than he did. Meeting, however, with the man, he thought fit to ask him after what manner he reverenced the Gods. But Clearchus answered him, that he diligently sacrificed to them at proper times in every month at the new moon, crowning and adorning the statues of Hermes and Hecate, and the other sacred images which were left to us by our ancestors, and that he also honoured the Gods with frankincense, and sacred wafers and cakes. He likewise said, that he performed public sacrifices annually, omitting no festive day; and that in these festivals he worshipped the Gods, not by slaying oxen, nor by cutting victims into fragments, but that he sacrificed whatever he might casually meet with, sedulously offering the first-fruits to the Gods of all the vegetable productions of the seasons, and of all the fruits with which he was supplied. He added, that some of these he placed before the [statues of the] Gods[f], but that he burnt others on their altars; and that, being studious of frugality, he avoided the sacrificing of oxen.

17. By some writers, also, it is related, that certain tyrants, after the Carthaginians were conquered, having, with great strife among themselves, placed hetacombs before Apollo, afterwards inquired of the God with which of the offerings he was most delighted; and that he answered, contrary to all their expectation, that he was most pleased with the cakes of Docimus. But this Docimus was an inhabitant of Delphi, and cultivated some rugged and stony land. Docimus, therefore, coming on that day from the place which he cultivated, took from a bag which was fastened round him a few handfuls of meal, and sacrificed them to the God, who was more delighted with his offering than with the magnificent

---

[f] In the original, και τα μεν παρατιθεναι, which Felicianus very erroneously renders, "alius siquidem mihi ad vescendem sumo;" but Valentinus rightly, " et horum aliqua coram illis apponere."

sacrifices of the tyrants. Hence, also, a certain poet, because the affair was known, appears to have asserted things of a similar kind, as we are informed by Antiphanes in his Mystics:

> In simple offerings most the Gods delight:
> For though before them hecatombs are placed,
> Yet frankincense is burnt the last of all.
> An indication this that all the rest,
> Preceding, was a vain expense, bestowed
> Through ostentation, for the sake of men;
> But a small offering gratifies the Gods.

Menander likewise, in the comedy called the Morose, says,

> Pious th' oblation which with frankincense
> And *popanum*[g] is made; for in the fire
> Both these, when placed, divinity accepts.

18. On this account also, earthen, wooden, and wicker vessels were formerly used, and especially in public sacrifices, the ancients being persuaded that divinity is delighted with things of this kind. Whence, even now, the most ancient vessels, and which are made of wood, are thought to be more divine, both on account of the matter and the simplicity of the art by which they were fashioned. It is said, therefore, that Æschylus, on his brother's asking him to write a Pæan in honour of Apollo, replied, that the best Pæan was written by Tynnichus[h]; and that if his composition were to be compared with that of Tynnichus, the same thing would take place as if new were compared with ancient statues. For the latter, though they are simple in their formation, are conceived to be divine; but the former, though they are most accurately elaborated, produce indeed admiration, but are not believed to possess so much of a divine

[g] A round, broad, and thin cake, which was offered in sacrifice to the Gods.
[h] Tynnichus, the Chalcidensian, is mentioned by Plato in his Io.

nature. Hence Hesiod, praising the law of ancient sacrifices, very properly says,

> Your country's rites in sacrifice observe:
> [In pious works] the ancient law is best[1].

19. But those who have written concerning sacred operations and sacrifices, admonish us to be accurate in preserving what pertains to the *popana*, because these are more acceptable to the Gods than the sacrifice which is performed through the mactation of animals. Sophocles also, in describing a sacrifice which is pleasing to divinity, says in his Polyidus:

> The skins of sheep in sacrifice were used,
> Libations too of wine, grapes well preserved,
> And fruits collected in a heap of every kind;
> The olive's pinguid juice, and waxen work
> Most variegated, of the yellow bee.

Formerly, also, there were venerable monuments in Delos of those who came from the Hyperboreans, bearing handfuls [of fruits]. It is necessary, therefore, that, being purified in our manners, we should make oblations, offering to the Gods those sacrifices which are pleasing to them, and not such as are attended with great expense. Now, however, if a man's body is not pure and invested with a splendid garment, he does not think it is qualified for the sanctity of sacrifice. But when he has rendered his body splendid, together with his garment, though his soul at the same time is not purified from vice, yet he betakes himself to sacrifice, and thinks that it is a thing of no consequence; as if divinity did not especially rejoice in that which is most divine in our nature, when it is in a pure condition, as being allied to his essence. In Epidaurus, therefore, there was the following inscription on the doors of the temple:

> Into an odorous temple, he who goes
> Should pure and holy be; but to be wise
> In what to sanctity pertains, is to be pure.

---

[1] Vid. Hesiod. Fragm. v. 169.

20. But that God is not delighted with the amplitude of sacrifices, but with any casual offering, is evident from this, that of our daily food, whatever it may be that is placed before us, we all of us make an offering to the Gods, before we have tasted it ourselves; this offering being small indeed, but the greatest testimony of honour to divinity. Moreover, Theophrastus shows, by enumerating many of the rites of different countries, that the sacrifices of the ancients were from fruits, and he narrates what pertains to libations in the following manner: "Ancient sacrifices were for the most part performed with sobriety. But those sacrifices are sober in which the libations are made with water. Afterwards, however, libations were made with honey. For we first receive this liquid fruit prepared for us by the bees. In the third place, libations were made with oil; and in the fourth and last place with wine."

21. These things, however, are testified not only by the pillars which are preserved in Cyrbe[k], and which contain, as it were, certain true descriptions of the Cretan sacred rites of the Corybantes; but also by Empedocles, who, in discussing what pertains to sacrifices and theogony, or the generation of the Gods, says:

> With them nor Mars nor tumult dire was found,
> Nor Saturn, Neptune, or the sovereign Jove,
> But Venus [beauty's] queen.

And Venus is friendship. Afterwards he adds,

> With painted animals, and statues once
> Of sacred form, with unguents sweet of smell,
> The fume of frankincense and genuine myrrh,
> And with libations poured upon the ground
> Of yellow honey, Venus was propitious made.

Which ancient custom is still even now preserved by some persons as a certain vestige of the truth. And in the last place, Empedocles says,

> Nor then were altars wet with blood of bulls
> Irrationally slain.

[k] A city of Crete.

22. For, as it appears to me, when friendship and a proper sense of the duties pertaining to kindred natures, was possessed by all men, no one slaughtered any living being, in consequence of thinking that other animals were allied to him. But when strife and tumult, every kind of contention, and the principle of war, invaded mankind, then, for the first time, no one in reality spared any one of his kindred natures. The following particulars, likewise, ought to be considered: For, as though there is an affinity between us and noxious men, who, as it were, by a certain impetus of their own nature and depravity, are incited to injure any one they may happen to meet, yet we think it requisite that all of them should be punished and destroyed; thus also, with respect to those irrational animals that are naturally malefic and unjust, and who are impelled to injure those that approach them, it is perhaps fit that they should be destroyed. But with respect to other animals who do not at all act unjustly, and are not naturally impelled to injure us, it is certainly unjust to destroy and murder them, no otherwise than it would be to slay men who are not iniquitous. And this seems to evince, that the justice between us and other animals does not arise from some of them being naturally noxious and malefic, but others not, as is also the case with respect to men.

23. Are therefore those animals to be sacrificed to the Gods which are thought to be deserving of death? But how can this be possible, if they are naturally depraved? For it is no more proper to sacrifice such as these, than it would be to sacrifice mutilated animals. For thus, indeed, we shall offer the first-fruits of things of an evil nature, but we shall not sacrifice for the sake of honouring the Gods. Hence, if animals are to be sacrificed to the Gods, we should sacrifice those that are perfectly innoxious. It is however acknowledged, that those animals are not to be destroyed who do not at all injure us, so that neither are they to be sacrificed to the Gods. If, therefore, neither these, nor those that are noxious,

are to be sacrificed, is it not evident that we should abstain from them more than from any thing else, and that we should not sacrifice any one of them, though it is fit that some of them should be destroyed?

24. To which may be added, that we should sacrifice to the Gods for the sake of three things, viz. either for the sake of honouring them, or of testifying our gratitude, or through our want of good. For, as we offer first-fruits to good men, thus also we think it is necessary that we should offer them to the Gods. But we honour the Gods, either exploring the means of averting evils and obtaining good, or when we have been previously benefited, or in order that we may obtain some present advantage and assistance, or merely for the purpose of venerating the goodness of their nature. So that if the first-fruits of animals are to be offered to the Gods, some of them for the sake of this are to be sacrificed. For whatever we sacrifice, we sacrifice for the sake of some one of the above-mentioned particulars. Is it therefore to be thought that God is honoured by us, when we are directly seen to act unjustly through the first-fruits which we offer to him? Or will he not rather think that he is dishonoured by such a sacrifice, in which, by immolating animals that have not at all injured us, we acknowledge that we have acted unjustly. So that no one of other animals is to be sacrificed for the sake of honouring divinity. Nor yet are they to be sacrificed for the purpose of testifying our gratitude to the Gods. For he who makes a just retribution for the benefits he has received, ought not to make it by doing an injury to certain other animals. For he will no more appear to make a retribution than he who, plundering his neighbour of his property, should bestow it on another person for the sake of honour. Neither are animals to be sacrificed for the sake of obtaining a certain good of which we are in want. For he who endeavours to be benefited by acting unjustly, is to be suspected as one who would not be grateful even when he is benefited. So that animals are not to be

sacrificed to the Gods through the expectation of deriving advantage from the sacrifice. For he who does this, may perhaps elude men, but it is impossible that he can elude divinity. If, therefore, we ought to sacrifice for the sake of a certain thing, but this is not to be done for the sake of any of the before mentioned particulars, it is evident that animals ought not to be sacrificed.

25. For, by endeavouring to obliterate the truth of these things through the pleasures which we derive from sacrifices, we deceive ourselves, but cannot deceive divinity. Of those animals, therefore, which are of an ignoble nature, which do not impart to our life any superior utility, and which do not afford us any pleasure, we do not sacrifice any one to the Gods. For who ever sacrificed serpents, scorpions, and apes, or any one of such like animals? But we do not abstain from any one of those animals which afford a certain utility to our life, or which have something in them that contributes to our enjoyments; since we, in reality, cut their throats, and excoriate them, under the patronage of divinity[1]. For we sacrifice to the Gods oxen and sheep, and besides these, stags and birds, and fat hogs, though they do not at all participate of purity, but afford us delight. And of these animals, indeed, some, by co-operating with our labours, afford assistance to our life, but others supply us with food, or administer to our other wants. But those which effect neither of these, yet, through the enjoyment which is derived from them, are slain by men in sacrifices similarly with those who afford us utility. We do not, however, sacrifice asses or elephants, or any other of those animals that co-operate with us in our labours, but are not subservient to our pleasure; though, sacrificing being excepted, we do not abstain from such like animals, but we cut their throats on account of the delight with which the deglutition of them is attended; and of those which are fit to be sacrificed, we do not sacrifice such

---

[1] *i. e.* Under the pretext of being patronized by divinity in so doing.

as are acceptable to the Gods, but such as in a greater degree gratify the desires of men; thus testifying against ourselves, that we persist in sacrificing to the Gods, for the sake of our own pleasure, and not for the sake of gratifying the Gods.

26. But of the Syrians, the Jews indeed, through the sacrifice which they first made, even now, says Theophrastus, sacrifice animals, and if we were persuaded by them to sacrifice in the same way that they do, we should abstain from the deed. For they do not feast on the flesh of the sacrificed animals, but having thrown the whole of the victims into the fire, and poured much honey and wine on them during the night, they swiftly consume the sacrifice, in order that the all-seeing sun may not become a spectator of it. And they do this, fasting during all the intermediate days, and through the whole of this time, as belonging to the class of philosophers, and also discourse with each other about the divinity[n]. But in the night, they apply themselves to the theory of the stars, surveying them, and through prayers invoking God. For these make offerings both of other animals and themselves, doing this from necessity, and not from their own will. The truth of this, however, may be learnt by any one who directs his attention to the Egyptians, the most learned of all men; who are so far from slaying other animals, that they make the images of these to be imitations of the Gods; so adapted and allied do they conceive these to be both to Gods and men.

27. For at first, indeed, sacrifices of fruits were made to the Gods; but, in the course of time, men becoming negligent of sanctity, in consequence of fruits being scarce, and, through the want of legitimate nutriment, being impelled to eat each other; then supplicating divinity with many prayers, they first began to make oblations of themselves to the Gods, not only conse-

---

[n] Porphyry, in what he here says of the Jews, alludes to that sect of them called Essæans; concerning whom, see the 4th book of this work.

crating to the divinities whatever among their possessions was most beautiful, but, proceeding beyond this, they sacrificed those of their own species. Hence, even to the present time, not only in Arcadia, in the Lupercal festivals, and in Carthage, men are sacrificed in common to Saturn, but periodically, also, for the sake of remembering the legal institute, they sprinkle the altars of those of the same tribe with blood, although the rites of their sacrifices exclude, by the voice of the crier, him from engaging in them who is accused of human slaughter. Proceeding therefore from hence, they made the bodies of other animals supply the place of their own in sacrifices, and again, through a satiety of legitimate nutriment, becoming oblivious of piety, they were induced by voracity to leave nothing untasted, nothing undevoured. And this is what now happens to all men with respect to the aliment from fruits. For when, by the assumption of them, they have alleviated their necessary indigence, then searching for a superfluity of satiety, they labour to procure many things for food which are placed beyond the limits of temperance. Hence, as if they had made no ignoble sacrifices to the Gods, they proceeded also to taste the animals which they immolated; and from this, as a principle of the deed, the eating of animals became an addition to men to the nutriment derived from fruits. As, therefore, antiquity offered the first produce of fruits to the Gods, and gladly, after their pious sacrifice, tasted what they offered, thus also, when they sacrificed the firstlings of animals to the divinities, they thought that the same thing ought to be done by them, though ancient piety did not ordain these particulars after this manner, but venerated each of the Gods from fruits. For with such oblations, both nature, and every sense of the human soul, are delighted.

> No altar then was wet with blood of bulls
> Irrationally slain; but this was thought
> To be of every impious deed the worst,
> Limbs to devour of brutes deprived of life.

28. The truth of this may also be perceived from the altar which is even now preserved about Delos, which, because no animal is brought to, or is sacrificed upon it, is called the altar of the pious. So that the inhabitants not only abstain from sacrificing animals, but they likewise conceive, that those who established, are similarly pious with those who use the altar. Hence, the Pythagoreans having adopted this mode of sacrifice, abstained from animal food through the whole of life. But when they distributed to the Gods a certain animal instead of themselves, they merely tasted of it, living in reality without touching other animals. We, however, do not act after this manner; but being filled with animal diet, we have arrived at this manifold illegality in our life by slaughtering animals, and using them for food. For neither is it proper that the altars of the Gods should be defiled with murder, nor that food of this kind should be touched by men, as neither is it fit that men should eat one another; but the precept which is still preserved at Athens, should be obeyed through the whole of life.

29. For formerly, as we have before observed, when men sacrificed to the Gods fruits and not animals, and did not assume the latter for food, it is said, that a common sacrifice being celebrated at Athens, one Diomus, or Sopater, who was not a native, but cultivated some land in Attica, seizing a sharp axe which was near to him, and being excessively indignant, struck with it an ox, who, coming from his labour, approached to a table, on which were openly placed cakes and other offerings which were to be burnt as a sacrifice to the Gods, and ate some, but trampled on the rest of the offerings. The ox, therefore, being killed, Diomus, whose anger was now appeased, at the same time perceived what kind of deed he had perpetrated. And the ox, indeed, he buried. But embracing a voluntary banishment, as if he had been accused of impiety, he fled to Crete. A great dryness, however, taking place in the Attic land from vehement heat, and a dreadful sterility of fruit, and the Pythian deity being in

consequence of it consulted by the general consent, the God answered, that the Cretan exile must expiate the crime; and that, if the murderer was punished, and the statue of the slain ox was erected in the place in which it fell, this would be beneficial both to those who had and those who had not tasted its flesh. An inquiry therefore being made into the affair, and Sopater, together with the deed, having been discovered, he, thinking that he should be liberated from the difficulty in which he was now involved, through the accusation of impiety, if the same thing was done by all men in common, said to those who came to him, that it was necessary an ox should be slain by the city. But, on their being dubious who should strike the ox, he said that he would undertake to do it, if they would make him a citizen, and would be partakers with him of the slaughter. This, therefore, being granted, they returned to the city, and ordered the deed to be accomplished in such a way as it is performed by them at present, [and which was as follows:]

30. They selected virgins who were drawers of water; but these brought water for the purpose of sharpening an axe and a knife. And these being sharpened, one person gave the axe, another struck with it the ox, and a third person cut the throat of the ox. But after this, having excoriated the animal, all that were present ate of its flesh. These things therefore being performed, they sewed up the hide of the ox, and having stuffed it with straw, raised it upright in the same form which it had when alive, and yoked it to a plough, as if it was about to work with it. Instituting also a judicial process, respecting the slaughter of the ox, they cited all those who were partakers of the deed, to defend their conduct. But as the drawers of water accused those who sharpened the axe and the knife, as more culpable than themselves, and those who sharpened these instruments accused him who gave the axe, and he accused him who cut the throat of the ox, and this last person accused the knife,—hence,

as the knife could not speak, they condemned it as the cause of the slaughter. From that time also, even till now, during the festival sacred to Jupiter, in the Acropolis, at Athens, the sacrifice of an ox is performed after the same manner. For, placing cakes on a brazen table, they drive oxen round it, and the ox that tastes of the cakes that are distributed on the table, is slain. The race likewise of those who perform this, still remains. And all those, indeed, who derive their origin from Sopater are called *boutupoi* [i. e. *slayers of oxen*]; but those who are descended from him that drove the ox round the table, are called *kentriadai*, [*or stimulators.*] And those who originate from him that cut the throat of the ox, are denominated *daitroi*, [*or dividers,*] on account of the banquet which takes place from the distribution of flesh. But when they have filled the hide, and the judicial process is ended, they throw the knife into the sea.

31. Hence, neither did the ancients conceive it to be holy to slay animals that co-operated with us in works beneficial to our life, and we should avoid doing this even now. And as formerly it was not pious for men to injure these animals, so now it should be considered as unholy to slay them for the sake of food. If, however, this is to be done from motives of religious reverence of the Gods, yet every passion or affection which is essentially produced from bodies is to be rejected, in order that we may not procure food from improper substances, and thus have an incentive to violence as the intimate associate of our life. For by such a rejection we shall, at least, all of us derive great benefit in what pertains to our mutual security, if we do not in any thing else. For those whose sense is averse to the destruction of animals of a species different from their own, will evidently abstain from injuring those of their own kind. Hence it would perhaps have been best, if men in after-times had immediately abstained from slaughtering these animals; but since no one is free from error, it remains for posterity to take

away by purifications the crime of their ancestors, respecting nutriment. This, however, will be effected, if, placing before our eyes the dire nature of such conduct, we exclaim with Empedocles:

> Ah me, while yet exempt from such a crime,
> Why was I not destroyed by cruel Time,
> Before these lips began the guilty deed,
> On the dire nutriment of flesh to feed?

For in those only the appropriate sense sympathetically grieves for errors that have been committed, who endeavour to find a remedy for the evils with which they are afflicted; so that every one, by offering pure and holy sacrifices to divinity, may through sanctity obtain the greatest benefits from the Gods.

32. But the benefit derived from fruits is the first and the greatest of all others, and which, as soon as they are matured, should alone be offered to the Gods, and to Earth, by whom they are produced. For she is the common Vesta of Gods and men; and it is requisite that all of us, reclining on her surface, as on the bosom of our mother and nurse, should celebrate her divinity, and love her with a parental affection, as the source of our existence. For thus, when we exchange this life for another, we shall again be thought worthy of a residence in the heavens, and of associating with all the celestial Gods, whom, now beholding[a], we ought to venerate with those fruits of which they are the causes, sacrificing indeed to

---

[a] In the original, ως νυν ορωντας τιμαν τουτως, κ.τ.λ., instead of which, Reisk proposes to read, ως νυν ουχ ορωντας τιμαν δει [vel χρη] τουτως, κ.τ.λ. But the insertion of ουχ is most absurd: for the celestial are called the *visible* Gods. Thus Plato, in the Timæus, in the speech of the Demiurgus to the junior or mundane Gods, who consist of the *celestial* and *sublunary* deities, calls the *celestial Gods* those that *visibly* revolve, and the *sublunary*, those that become apparent when they please: Εστι ουν παντες οσοι τε περιπολουσι φανερως, και οσοι φαινονται καθ' οσον αν εθελωσι θεοι, γενεσιν εσχον, κ.τ.λ. Conformably, therefore, to the above translation, I read, ως νυν ορωντας τιμαν δει τουτως, κ.τ.λ. To which may be added, that our author, in paragraph 37, expressly calls the stars *visible Gods*.

them from all these, when they have arrived at maturity, but not conceiving all of us to be sufficiently worthy to sacrifice to the Gods. For as all things are not to be sacrificed to the Gods, so neither perhaps are the Gods gratified by the sacrifice of every one. This, therefore, is the substance of the arguments adduced by Theophrastus, to show that animals ought not to be sacrificed; exclusive of the interspersed fabulous narrations, and a few things which we have added to what he has said.

33. I, however, shall not attempt to dissolve the legal institutes which the several nations have established. For it is not my design at present to speak about a polity. But as the laws by which we are governed permit us to venerate divinity by things of the most simple, and of an inanimate nature, hence, selecting that which is the least costly, let us sacrifice according to the law of the city, and endeavour to offer an appropriate sacrifice, approaching with consummate purity to the Gods. In short, if the oblation of first-fruits is of any value, and is an acknowledgment of thanks for the benefits which we receive, it will be most irrational to abstain ourselves from animals, and yet offer the first-fruits of these to the Gods. For neither are the Gods worse than we are, so as to be in want of those things of which we are not indigent, nor is it holy to offer the first-fruits of that nutriment from which we ourselves abstain. For we find it is usual with men, that, when they refrain from animal food, they do not make oblations of animals; but that they offer to the Gods the first-fruits of what they themselves eat. Hence also it is now fit, that he who abstains from animals should offer the first-fruits of things which he touches [for the purpose of food].

34. Let us therefore also sacrifice, but let us sacrifice in such a manner as is fit, offering different sacrifices to different powers*; to the God indeed who is above all

---

* In the original, Θυσωμεν τοινυν και ημεις· αλλα Θυσωμεν, ως προσηκει, διαφορους τας θυσιας, ως αν διαφοροις δυναμεσι προσαγοντες. This Valentinus erroneously translates as follows: "Sacrificabimus igitur etiam et nos,

things, as a certain wise man said, neither sacrificing with incense, nor consecrating any thing sensible. For there is nothing material, which is not immediately impure to an immaterial nature. Hence, neither is vocal language, nor internal speech, adapted to the highest God, when it is defiled by any passion of the soul; but we should venerate him in profound silence with a pure soul, and with pure conceptions about him. It is necessary, therefore, that being conjoined with and assimilated to him, we should offer to him, as a sacred sacrifice, the elevation of our intellect, which offering will be both a hymn and our salvation. In an impassive contemplation, therefore, of this divinity by the soul, the sacrifice to him is effected in perfection; but to his progeny, the intelligible Gods, hymns, orally enunciated, are to be offered. For to each of the divinities, a sacrifice is to be made of the first-fruits of the things which he bestows, and through which he nourishes and preserves us. As, therefore, the husbandman offers handfuls of the fruits and berries which the season first produces; thus also we should offer to the divinities the first-fruits of our conceptions of their transcendent excellence, giving them thanks for the contemplation which they impart to us, and for truly nourishing us through the vision of themselves, which they afford us, associating with, appearing to, and shining upon us, for our salvation.

35. Now, however, many of those who apply themselves to philosophy are unwilling to do this; and, pursuing renown rather than honouring divinity, they are busily employed about statues, neither considering whether they are to be reverenced or not, nor endeavouring to learn from those who are divinely wise, to what extent, and to what degree, it is requisite to proceed in this affair. We, however, shall by no means contend with

---

sed prout decet, victimas scilicet *eximias* potestatibus *eximiis* adducentes." For διαφορους and διαφοραις, in this passage, evidently mean *different*, and not *excellent*.

these, nor are we very desirous of being well instructed in a thing of this kind; but imitating holy and ancient men, we offer to the Gods, more than any thing else, the first-fruits of contemplation, which they have imparted to us, and by the use of which we become partakers of true salvation.

36. The Pythagoreans, therefore, diligently applying themselves to the study of numbers and lines, sacrificed for the most part from these to the Gods, denominating, indeed, a certain number Minerva, but another Diana, and another Apollo: and again, they called one number justice, but another temperance [p]. In diagrams also they adopted a similar mode. And thus, by offerings of this kind, they rendered the Gods propitious to them, so as to obtain of them the object of their wishes, by the things which they dedicated to, and the names by which they invoked them. They likewise frequently employed their aid in divination, and if they were in want of a certain thing for the purpose of some investigation. In order, therefore, to effect this, they made use of the Gods within the heavens, both the erratic and non-erratic, of all of whom it is requisite to consider the sun as the leader; but to rank the moon in the second place; and we should conjoin with these fire, in the third place, from its alliance to them, as the theologist [q] says. He also says that no animal is to be sacrificed; but that first-fruits are to be offered from meal and honey, and the vegetable productions of the earth. He adds, that fire is not to be enkindled on a hearth defiled with gore; and asserts other things of the like kind. For what occasion is there to transcribe all that he says? for he who is studious of piety knows, indeed, that to the Gods no

---

[p] Concerning the appellations which the Pythagoreans gave to numbers, see my Theoretic Arithmetic, in which also the occult meaning of these appellations is unfolded.

[q] "Plotinus ni fallor, aut Plato, sed ille potius," says Reisk; but every one who is at all conversant with Platonic writers, will immediately see that by *the theologist*, Porphyry means *Orpheus*.

animal is to be sacrificed, but that a sacrifice of this kind pertains to dæmons, and other powers, whether they are beneficent, or depraved[r]. He likewise knows who those

[r] Though Porphyry excelled in all philosophical knowledge, whence also he was called κατ' εξοχην, *the philosopher*, yet he was inferior to his auditor Iamblichus, in theological information. On this account, Iamblichus was called by all the Platonists posterior to him, *the divine*, and *the great* priest. I shall present the reader, therefore, with an extract from my translation of his treatise on the Mysteries, which appears to me to be an admirable supplement to what Porphyry has said in this book, about sacrificing animals, and a satisfactory answer to the question whether they are to be sacrificed or not.

In Chap. 14, therefore, of Sect. 5, he observes as follows: "We shall begin the elucidation of this subject in the best possible manner, if we demonstrate that the sacred law of sacrifices is connected with the order of the Gods. In the first place, therefore, we say, that of the Gods some are material, but others immaterial. And the material, indeed, are those that comprehend matter in themselves, and adorn it; but the immaterial are those that are perfectly exempt from, and transcend matter: but, according to the sacrific art, it is requisite to begin sacred operations from the material Gods; for the ascent to the immaterial Gods will not otherwise be effected. The material Gods, therefore, have a certain communication with matter, so far as they preside over it. Hence they have dominion over things which happen about matter, such as the division, percussion, repercussion, mutation, generation, and corruption of all material bodies. He, therefore, who wishes to worship these theurgically, in a manner adapted to them, and to the dominion which they are allotted, should, as they are material, employ a material mode of worship. For thus we shall be wholly led to a familiarity with them, and worship them in an allied and appropriate manner. *Dead bodies, therefore, and things deprived of life, the slaying of animals, and the consumption of victims, and, in short, the mutation of the matter which is offered, pertain to these Gods, not by themselves, but on account of the matter over which they preside.* For though they are, in the most eminent degree, separate from it, yet, at the same time, they are present with it; and, though they comprehend matter in an immaterial power, yet they are co-existent with it. Things also that are governed, are not foreign from their governors; and things which are subservient as instruments, are not unadapted to those that use them. Hence it is foreign to the immaterial Gods, to offer matter to them through sacrifices, but this is most adapted to all the material Gods."

In the following chapter, Iamblichus observes, " that as there is a

are that ought to sacrifice to these, and to what extent they ought to proceed in the sacrifices which they make.

time when we become wholly soul, are out of the body, and sublimely revolve on high, in conjunction with all the immaterial Gods; so, likewise, there is a two-fold mode of worship, one of which is simple, incorporeal, and pure from all generation; and this mode pertains to undefiled souls; but the other is replete with every thing of a material nature, and is adapted to souls which are neither pure, nor liberated from all generation." He adds, " we must admit, therefore, that there are two-fold species of sacrifices; one kind, indeed, pertaining to men who are not entirely purified, which, as Heraclitus says, rarely happens to one man, or to a certain easily-to-be-numbered few of mankind; but the other kind being material, and consisting in mutation, is adapted to souls that are still detained by the body. Hence, to cities and people not yet liberated from sublunary fate, and the impending communion of bodies, if such a mode of sacrifice as this latter is not permitted, they will wander both from immaterial and material good. For they will not be able to receive the former, and to the latter they will not offer what is appropriate."

He farther informs us, in Chap. 22, that though the summit of the sacrific art recurs to the most principal one of the whole multitude of Gods [*i. e.* to the ineffable cause of all,] and at one and the same time worships the many essences and principles that are [rooted and concentred] in it; yet this happens at the latest period, and to a very few, and that we must be satisfied, if it takes place, when the sun of life is setting. " But," says he, " our present discussion does not ordain laws for a man of this kind; for he is superior to all law; but it promulgates a law such as that of which we are now speaking, to those who are in want of a certain divine legislation." In the above passage, by " *a man of this kind,*" Iamblichus most probably alludes to Plotinus, as both his works, and the life of him, written by Porphyry, show that he was a man capable of recurring to, and becoming united with the highest God, and thus at the same time worshipping all the divine powers that are rooted in him.

To what Iamblichus has thus excellently observed, may be added what the philosopher Sallust says in his golden treatise On the Gods and the World, viz. " that since life primarily subsists in the Gods, and there is also a certain human life, but the latter desires to be united to the former, a medium is required; for natures much distant from each other cannot be conjoined without a medium; and it is necessary that the medium should be similar to the connected natures. Life, therefore, must necessarily be the medium of life. Hence, men of the present day that are happy, and all the ancients, have sacrificed animals; and this, indeed, not rashly, but in a way accommodated to every God,

Other things, however, will be passed over by me in silence. But what some Platonists have divulged, I shall lay before the reader, in order that the things proposed to be discussed, may become manifest to the intelligent. What they have unfolded, therefore, is as follows:

37. The first God being incorporeal, immoveable, and impartible, and neither subsisting in any thing, nor restrained in his energies, is not, as has been before observed, in want of any thing external to himself, as neither is the soul of the world; but this latter, containing in itself the principle of that which is triply divisible, and being naturally self-motive, is adapted to be moved in a beautiful and orderly manner, and also to move the body of the world according to the most excellent reasons [i. e. productive principles or powers]. It is, however, connected with and comprehends body, though it is itself incorporeal, and liberated from the participation of any passion. To the remaining Gods, therefore, to the world, to the inerratic and erratic stars, who are visible Gods, consisting of soul and body, thanks are to be returned after the above-mentioned manner, through sacrifices from inanimate natures. The multitude, therefore, of those invisible beings remains for us, whom Plato indiscriminately calls dæmons*; but of these, some being denominated by men, obtain from them honours, and other religious observances, similar to those which are paid to the Gods; but others, who for the most part are not explicitly denominated, receive an occult religious reverence and appellation from certain persons in villages and certain cities; and the remaining multitude is called in common by the name of dæmons. The

---

with many other ceremonies respecting the cultivation of divinity." Let the *truly intellectual and pious man*, however, never forget that prayer, as Proclus divinely observes, possesses *of itself* a supernatural perfection and power.

* For a more *theological* account of dæmons, I refer the reader to my translation of the before-mentioned admirable treatise of Iamblichus on the Mysteries.

general persuasion, however, respecting all these invisible beings, is this, that if they become angry through being neglected, and deprived of the religious reverence which is due to them, they are noxious to those by whom they are thus neglected, and that they again become beneficent, if they are appeased by prayers, supplications, and sacrifices, and other similar rites.

38. But the confused notion which is formed of these beings, and which has proceeded to great crimination, necessarily requires that the nature of them should be distinguished according to reason. For perhaps it will be said, that it is requisite to show whence the error concerning them originated among men. The distinction, therefore, must be made after the following manner. Such souls as are the progeny of the whole soul of the universe, and who govern the great parts of the region under the moon, these, being incumbent on a pneumatic substance or spirit, and ruling over it conformably to reason, are to be considered as good dæmons, who are diligently employed in causing every thing to be beneficial to the subjects of their government, whether they preside over certain animals, or fruits, which are arranged under their inspective care, or over things which subsist for the sake of these, such as showers of rain, moderate winds, serene weather, and other things which cooperate with these, such as the good temperament of the seasons of the year. They are also our leaders in the attainment of music, and the whole of erudition, and likewise of medicine and gymnastic, and of every thing else similar to these. For it is impossible that these dæmons should impart utility, and yet become, in the very same things, the causes of what is detrimental. Among these two, those *transporters*, as Plato calls them, [in his Banquet] are to be enumerated, who announce the affairs of men to the Gods, and the will of the Gods to men; carrying our prayers, indeed, to the Gods as judges, but oracularly unfolding to us the exhortations and admonitions of the Gods. But such souls as do not rule over the

pneumatic substance with which they are connected, but for the most part are vanquished by it; these are vehemently agitated and borne along [in a disorderly manner,] when the irascible motions and the desires of the pneumatic substance, receive an impetus. These souls, therefore, are indeed dæmons, but are deservedly called malefic dæmons.

39. All these beings, likewise, and those who possess a contrary power, are invisible, and perfectly imperceptible by human senses; for they are not surrounded with a solid body, nor are all of them of one form, but they are fashioned in numerous figures. The forms, however, which characterize their pneumatic substance, at one time become apparent, but at another are invisible. Sometimes also those that are malefic, change their forms; but the pneumatic substance, so far as it is corporeal, is passive and corruptible: and though, because it is thus bound by the souls [that are incumbent on it,] the form of it remains for a long time, yet it is not eternal. For it is probable that something continually flows from it, and also that it is nourished. The pneumatic substance, therefore, of good dæmons, possesses symmetry, in the same manner as the bodies of the visible Gods; but the spirit of malefic dæmons is deprived of symmetry, and in consequence of its abounding in passivity, they are distributed about the terrestrial region. Hence, there is no evil which they do not attempt to effect; for, in short, being violent and fraudulent in their manners, and being also deprived of the guardian care of more excellent dæmons, they make, for the most part, vehement and sudden attacks; sometimes endeavouring to conceal their incursions, but at other times assaulting openly. Hence the molestations which are produced by them are rapid; but the remedies and corrections which proceed from more excellent dæmons, appear to be more slowly effected: for every thing which is good being tractable and equable, proceeds in an orderly manner, and does not pass beyond what is fit. By forming this

opinion, therefore, you will never fall into that most absurd notion, that evil may be expected from the good, or good from the evil. For this notion is not only attended with absurdity, but the multitude, receiving through it the most erroneous conceptions of the Gods, disseminate them among the rest of mankind.

40. It must be admitted, therefore, that one of the greatest injuries occasioned by malefic dæmons is this, that though they are the causes of the calamities which take place about the earth, such as pestilence, sterility, earthquakes, excessive dryness, and the like, yet they endeavour to persuade us, that they are the causes of things the most contrary to these, viz. of fertility, [salubrity, and elementary peace.] Hence, they exonerate themselves from blame, and, in the first place, endeavour to avoid being detected as the sources of injury; and, in the next place, they convert us to supplications and sacrifices to the beneficent Gods, as if they were angry. But they effect these, and things of a similar nature, in consequence of wishing to turn us from right conceptions of the Gods, and convert us to themselves; for they are delighted with all such as act thus incongruously and discordantly, and, as it were, assuming the persons of other Gods, they enjoy the effects of our imprudence and folly; conciliating to themselves the good opinion of the vulgar, by inflaming the minds of men with the love of riches, power, and pleasure, and filling them with the desire of vain glory, from which sedition, and war, and other things allied to these, are produced. But that which is the most dire of all things, they proceed still farther, and persuade men that similar things are effected by the greatest Gods, and do not stop till they even subject the most excellent of the divinities to these calumnies, through whom they say every thing is in perfect confusion. And not only the vulgar are affected in this manner, but not a few also of those who are conversant with philosophy. The cause of this, however, extends equally to philosophers, and the vulgar; for of

philosophers, those who do not depart from the prevailing notions, fall into the same error with the multitude; and again, the multitude, on hearing assertions from celebrated men conformable to their own opinions, are in a greater degree corroborated in conceiving things of this kind of the Gods.

41. For poetry also inflames the opinions of men, by employing a diction adapted to produce astonishment and enchantment, and not only allures the ears, but is also capable of procuring belief in things that are most impossible. At the same time, however, it is requisite to be firmly persuaded, that what is good can never injure, nor what is evil can ever be beneficial; for, as Plato says, it is not the province of heat to refrigerate, but of that which is contrary to heat; and, in like manner, neither is it the province of that which is just to injure. But divinity is naturally the most just of all things; since otherwise he would not be divinity. Hence this power and portion of good is not to be abscinded from beneficent dæmons; for the power which is naturally adapted, and wishes to injure, is contrary to the power which is beneficent: but contraries can never subsist about the same thing. As malefic dæmons, therefore, injure the mortal race in many respects, and sometimes in things of the greatest consequence, good dæmons not only never cease to act conformably to their office, but also, as much as possible, presignify to us the dangers which are impendent from malefic dæmons, unfolding these through dreams, through a divinely inspired soul, and through many other things; so that he who is capable of explaining what is signified, may know and avoid all the perils with which he is threatened. For they indicate [future events] to all men, but every one cannot understand what they indicate, nor is every one able to read what is written by them; but he alone is able to do this, who has learnt their letters. All enchantment, however, [or witchcraft,] is effected through dæmons of a contrary nature; for those who perpetrate

evil through enchantments, especially venerate these malefic beings, and the power that presides over them.

42. For they are full of every kind of imagination, and are sufficiently qualified to deceive, through effects of a prodigious nature; and through these, unhappy men procure philtres, and amatory allurements. For all intemperance, and hope of possessing wealth and renown, and especially deception, exist through these, since falsehood is allied to these malevolent beings; *for they wish to be considered as Gods, and the power which presides over them is ambitious to appear to be the greatest God.* These are they that rejoice in libations, and the savour of sacrifices, through which their pneumatic vehicle is fattened; for this vehicle lives through vapours and exhalations, and the life of it is various through various exhalations. It is likewise corroborated by the savour of blood and flesh.

43. On this account, a wise and temperate man will be religiously afraid to use sacrifices of this kind, through which he will attract to himself such-like dæmons; but he will endeavour in all possible ways to purify his soul. For these malefic beings do not attack a pure soul, because it is dissimilar to them; but if it is necessary to cities to render them propitious, this is nothing to us. For by these riches, and things external and corporeal, are thought to be good, and their contraries evil; but the smallest attention is paid by them to the good of the soul. We however, to the utmost of our ability, endeavour not to be in want of those things which they impart; but all our endeavour is to become similar to God, and to the [divine] powers with which he is surrounded both from what pertains to the soul, and from externals; and *this is effected through an entire liberation from the dominion of the passions, an evolved perception of truly existing beings, and a vital tendency towards them.* On the other hand, we strive to become dissimilar to depraved men and evil dæmons, and, in short, to every being that rejoices in a mortal and material nature. So

that, conformably to what is said by Theophrastus, we also shall sacrifice from those things which theologists permit us to use for this purpose; as well knowing, that by how much the more we neglect to exempt ourselves from the passions of the soul, by so much the more we connect ourselves with a depraved power, and render it necessary that he should become propitious to us. For, as theologists say, it is necessary that those who are bound* to things external, and have not yet vanquished their passions, should avert the anger of this [malefic] power; since, if they do not, there will be no end to their labours.

44. Thus far what pertains to sacrifices has been elucidated. As we said, however, at first, as it is not entirely necessary, if animals are to be sacrificed, that they are also to be eaten, we shall now show that it is necessary we should not eat them, though it may be sometimes necessary that they should be sacrificed. For all theologists agree in this, that in sacrifices, which are made for the purpose of averting some evil, the immolated animals are not to be tasted, but are to be used as expiations. For, say they, no one should go into the city, nor into his own house, till he has first purified his garments, and his body, in rivers, or some fountain. So that they order those whom they permit to sacrifice, to abstain from the victims, and to purify themselves before they sacrifice by fasting, and especially by abstaining from animals. They add, *that purity is the guardian of piety; and is, as it were, a symbol or divine seal, which secures its possessor from the attacks and allurements of evil dæmons.* For such a one, being contrarily disposed to, and more divine in his

---

* In the original, ως γαρ φασιν οι θεολογοι τοις δεομενοις υπο των εκτος και μηδεπω κρατουσιν των παθων, κ. τ. λ. But for δεομενοις, it is necessary to read δεδεμενοις; and it is evident that both the Latin translators of this work found δεδεμενοις in their manuscripts. For Felicianus has " qui *devincti* externis rebus sunt," and Valentinus, " qui rebus externis *illigantur*." Reisk, however, has taken no notice of this error in the printed text.

operations than those by whom he is attacked, because he is more pure both in his body and in the passions of his soul, remains uninjured, in consequence of being surrounded with purity as with a bulwark.

45. Hence a defence of this kind has appeared to be necessary even to enchanters; though it is not efficacious with them on all occasions. For they invoke evil dæmons for lascivious purposes. So that purity does not belong to enchanters, but to divine men, and such as are divinely wise; since it every where becomes a guard to those that use it, and conciliates them with a divine nature. I wish, therefore, that enchanters would make use of purity continually, for then they would not employ themselves in incantations, because, through this, they would be deprived of the enjoyment of those things, for the sake of which they act impiously. Whence becoming full of passions, and abstaining for a short time from impure food, they are notwithstanding replete with impurity, and suffer the punishment of their illegal conduct towards the whole of things, partly from those whom they irritate, and partly from Justice, who perceives all mortal deeds and conceptions. Both inward, therefore, and external purity pertain to a divine man, who earnestly endeavours to be liberated from the passions of the soul, and who abstains from such food as excites the passions, and is fed with divine wisdom; and by right conceptions of, is assimilated to divinity himself. For such a man, being consecrated by an intellectual sacrifice, approaches to God in a white garment, and with a truly pure *impassivity* of soul, and levity of body, and is not burdened with foreign and external juices, and the passions of the soul.

46. For, indeed, it must not be admitted as necessary in temples, which are consecrated by men to the Gods, that those who enter into them should have their feet pure, and their shoes free from every stain, but that in the temple of the father [of all], which is this world, it is not proper to preserve our ultimate and cutaneous vest-

ment pure, and to dwell in this temple with an undefiled garment. For if the danger consisted only in the defilement of the body, it might, perhaps, be lawful to neglect it. But now, since every sensible body is attended with an efflux of material dæmons, hence, together with the impurity produced from flesh and blood, the power which is friendly to, and familiar with, this impurity, is at the same time present through similitude and alliance.

47. Hence theologists have rightly paid attention to abstinence. And these things were indicated to us by a certain Egyptian[u], who also assigned a most natural cause of them, which was verified by experience. For, since a depraved and irrational soul, when it leaves the body, is still compelled to adhere to it, since the souls also of those men who die by violence, are detained about the body; this circumstance should prevent a man from forcibly expelling his soul from the body. The violent slaughter, therefore, of animals, compels souls to be delighted with the bodies which they have left, but the soul is by no means prevented from being there, where it is attracted by a kindred nature; whence many souls are seen to lament, and some remain about the bodies that are unburied; which souls are improperly used by enchanters, as subservient to their designs, being compelled by them to occupy the body, or a part of the body, which they have left. Since, therefore, these things were well known to theologists, and they also perceived the nature of a depraved soul, and its alliance to the

[u] Reisk, with his usual stupidity, where merely verbal emendations are not concerned, says that this Egyptian is Plotinus, whose country was Lycopolis, in Egypt. But what instance can be adduced, in all antiquity, of the disciple of a philosopher speaking of his preceptor in this indefinite manner? Is it not much more probable that this Egyptian is the priest mentioned by Porphyry in his Life of Plotinus, who, at the request of a certain friend of Plotinus, (which friend was, perhaps, Porphyry himself,) exhibited to Plotinus, in the temple of Isis, at Rome, the familiar dæmon, or, in modern language, the guardian angel of that philosopher?

bodies from which it was divulsed, and the pleasure which it received from a union with them, they very properly avoided animal food, in order that they might not be disturbed by alien souls, violently separated from the body and impure, and which are attracted to things of a kindred nature, and likewise that they might not be impeded by the presence of evil dæmons, in approaching alone [or without being burdened with things of a foreign nature] to the highest God [x].

48. For that the nature of a kindred body is attractive of soul, experience abundantly taught these theologians. Hence those who wish to receive into themselves the souls of prophetic animals, swallow the most principal parts of them, such as the hearts of crows, or of moles, or of hawks. For thus they have soul present with, and predicting to them like a God, and entering into them together with the intromission of the body.

49. Very properly, therefore, will the philosopher, and who is also the priest of the God that is above all things, abstain from all animal food, in consequence of earnestly endeavouring to approach through himself alone to the alone [y] God, without being disturbed by any attendants. Such a one likewise is cautious, as being well acquainted with the necessities of nature. For he who is truly a philosopher, is skilled in, and an observer of many things, understands the works of nature, is sagacious, temperate

---

[x] Conformably to this, the Pythagorean Demophilus beautifully observes, Γυμνος αποσταλεις σοφος, γυμνιτευων καλεσει τον πεμψαντα· μονου γαρ του μη τοις αλλοτριοις πεφορτισμενου επηκοος ο Θεος. *i. e.* " The wise man being sent hither naked, should naked invoke him by whom he was sent. For he alone is heard by divinity, who is not burdened with things of a foreign nature."

[y] This expression of "approaching *alone* to the *alone* God," Porphyry derived from his master, the great Plotinus, who divinely concludes his Enneads as follows: — και ουτω θεων και ανθρωπων θειων και ευδαιμονων βιος, απαλλαγη των αλλων των τηδε, αηδονος των τηδε, φυγη μονου προς μονον— *i. e.* " This, therefore, is the life of the Gods, and of divine and happy men, a liberation from all terrene concerns, a life unaccompanied by human pleasures, and *a flight of the alone to the alone.*"

and modest, and is in every respect the saviour of himself. And as he who is the priest of a certain particular God, is skilled in placing the statues of that divinity, and in his orgies, mysteries, and the like, thus also he who is the priest of the highest God, is skilled in the manner in which his statue ought to be fashioned, and in purifications, and other things through which he is conjoined to this divinity.

50. But if in the sacred rites which are here, those that are priests and diviners order both themselves and others to abstain from sepulchres, from impious men, from menstrual purgations, and from venereal congress, and likewise from base and mournful spectacles, and from those auditions which excite the passions, (because frequently, through those that are present being impure, something appears which disturbs the diviner; on which account it is said, that to sacrifice inopportunely, is attended with greater detriment than gain);—if this, therefore, is the case, will he, who is the priest of the father of all things, suffer himself to become the sepulchre of dead bodies? And will such a one, being full of defilement, endeavour to associate with the transcendent God? It is sufficient, indeed, that in fruits we assume parts of death, for the support of our present life. This, however, is not yet the place for such a discussion. We must, therefore, still farther investigate what pertains to sacrifices.

51. For some one may say that we shall subvert a great part of divination, viz. that which is effected through an inspection of the viscera, if we abstain from destroying animals. He, therefore, who makes this objection, should also destroy men: for it is said that future events are more apparent in the viscera of men than in those of brutes; and many of the Barbarians exercise the art of divination through the entrails of men. As, however, it would be an indication of great injustice, and inexhaustible avidity, to destroy those of our own species for the sake of divination, thus also it is unjust for the sake of this to slay an irrational animal. But it does not

belong to the present discussion to investigate whether Gods, or dæmons, or soul liberated from the animal [with which it had been connected], exhibit signs of future events to those who explore such signs, through the indications which the viscera afford.

52. Nevertheless, we permit those whose life is rolled about externals, having once acted impiously towards themselves, to be borne along to that to which they tend; but we rightly say, that the man whom we designate as a philosopher, and who is separated from externals, will not be disturbed by dæmons, nor be in want of diviners, nor of the viscera of animals. For he earnestly endeavours to be separated from those things for the sake of which divinations are effected. For he does not betake himself to nuptials, in order that he may molest the diviner about wedlock, or merchandise, or inquiries about a servant, or an increase of property, or any other object of vulgar pursuit. For the subjects of his investigation are not clearly indicated by any diviner or viscera of animals. But he, as we have said, approaching through himself to the [supreme] God, who is established in the true inward parts of himself, receives from thence the precepts of eternal life, tending thither by a conflux of the whole of himself, and instead of a diviner praying that he may become a confabulator of the mighty Jupiter.

53. For if such a one is impelled by some necessary circumstance, there are good dæmons, who, to the man living after this manner, and who is a domestic of divinity, will indicate and prevent, through dreams and symbols, and omens, what may come to pass, and what is necessarily to be avoided. For it is only requisite to depart from evil, and to know what is most honourable in the whole of things, and every thing which in the universe is good, friendly, and familiar. But vice, and an ignorance of divine concerns, are dire, through which a man is led to despise and defame things of which he has no knowledge; since nature does not proclaim these particulars with a voice which can be heard by the ears,

but being herself intellectual*, she initiates through intellect those who venerate her. And even though some one should admit the art of divination for the sake of predicting what is future, yet it does not from thence necessarily follow that the flesh of animals is to be eaten; as neither does it follow, that because it is proper to sacrifice to Gods or dæmons, food from animals is therefore to be introduced. For, not only the history which is related by Theophrastus, but also many other narrations inform us, that in ancient times men were sacrificed, yet it must not be inferred that on this account men are to be eaten.

54. And that we do not carelessly assert these things, but that what we have said is abundantly confirmed by history, the following narrations sufficiently testify. For in Rhodes, on the sixth day of June, a man was sacrificed to Saturn; which custom having prevailed for a long time, was afterwards changed [into a more human mode of sacrificing]. For one of those men who, by the public decision, had been sentenced to death, was kept in prison till the Saturnalia commenced; but as soon as this festival began, they brought the man out of the gates of the city, opposite to the temple of Aristobulus, and giving him wine to drink, they cut his throat. But in the island which is now called Salamis, but was formerly denominated Coronis, in the month according to the Cyprians Aphrodisius, a man was sacrificed to Agraule, the daughter of Cecrops, and the nymph Agraulis. And this custom continued till the time of Diomed. After-

---

* Nature, considered as the last of the causes which fabricate this corporeal and sensible world, " bounds (says Proclus in Tim.) the progressions of incorporeal essences, and is full of forms and powers, through which she governs mundane affairs. And she is a Goddess, indeed, considered as deified; but not according to the primary signification of the word. By her summit likewise she comprehends the heavens, but through these rules over the fluctuating empire of generation; and she every where weaves together partial natures in admirable conjunction with wholes." See more on this subject in my translation of that work.

wards it was changed, so that a man was sacrificed to Diomed. But the temples of Minerva, of Agraule, and Diomed, were contained in one and the same enclosure. The man also who was about to be slain, was first led by young men thrice round the altar, afterwards the priest pierced him with a lance in the stomach, and thus being thrown on the pyre, he was entirely consumed.

55. This sacred institute was, however, abolished by Diphilus, the king of Cyprus, who flourished about the time of Seleucus, the theologist. But Dæmon substituted an ox for a man; thus causing the latter sacrifice to be of equal worth with the former. Amosis also abolished the law of sacrificing men in the Egyptian city Heliopolis; the truth of which is testified by Manetho in his treatise on Antiquity and Piety. But the sacrifice was made to Juno, and an investigation took place, as if they were endeavouring to find pure calves, and such as were marked by the impression of a seal. Three men also were sacrificed on the day appointed for this purpose, in the place of whom Amosis ordered them to substitute three waxen images. In Chios likewise, they sacrificed a man to Omadius Bacchus [a], the man being for this purpose torn in pieces; and the same custom, as Euelpis Carystius says, was adopted in Tenedos. To which may be added, that the Lacedæmonians, as Apollodorus says, sacrificed a man to Mars.

56. Moreover the Phœnicians, in great calamities,

---

[a] This epithet is used in two of the Orphic hymns, viz. in Hymn LI. 7., and Hymn XXIX. 5. But the following appears to be the reason why Bacchus is so called. Bacchus is the intellect, and Ippa the soul of the world, according to the Orphic Theology; and the former is said by Orpheus to be carried on the head of the latter. For so we are informed by Proclus, in Tim. p. 124. Jacob de Rhoer, therefore, the editor of this work, was grossly mistaken in saying, " Non dubito, quin ωμαδιος Διονυσος, idem sit qui ωμηστης, crudivorus." Scaliger, in his version of the Hymns, very improperly translates ωμαδιος *bajulus, a porter*. For Bacchus is *carried on*, but does not *carry* Ippa.

either of war, or excessive dryness, or pestilence, sacrificed some one of their dearest friends, who was selected by votes for this purpose. The Phœnician history also is replete with instances of men being sacrificed, which history was written by Sanchoniatho in the Phœnician tongue, and was interpreted into Greek in eight books, by Philo Byblius. But Ister, in his collection of the Cretan sacrifices, says that the Curetes formerly sacrificed children to Saturn. And Pallas, who is the best of those that have collected what pertains to the mysteries of Mithras, says, that under the Emperor Adrian the sacrificing of men was nearly totally abolished. For, prior to his time, in Laodicea, which is in Syria, they anciently sacrificed a virgin to Minerva, but now they sacrifice a stag. The Carthaginians too, who dwell in Libya, formerly sacrificed men; but this custom was abolished by Iphicrates. And the Dumatii, a people of Arabia, annually sacrificed a boy, whom they buried under the altar, which was used by them as a statue. But Phylarchus narrates, that it was the general custom of all the Greeks, before they went to war, to immolate men. I omit to mention the Thracians and Scythians, and also the Athenians, who slew the daughter of Erechtheus and Praxithea. And even at present, who is ignorant that in the great city of Rome, in the festival of Jupiter Latialis, they cut the throat of a man? Human flesh, however, is not on this account to be eaten; though, through a certain necessity, a man should be sacrificed. For, when a famine takes place during a siege, some of the besieged feed on each other, yet at the same time those who do so are deemed execrable, and the deed is thought to be impious.

57. After the first war, likewise, waged by the Romans against the Carthaginians, in order to obtain Sicily, when the mercenary soldiers of the Phœnicians revolted, and, together with them, those of Africa deserted, Amilcar, who was surnamed Barkas, in attacking the Romans, was

reduced to such a scarcity of food, that at first his men ate those that fell in battle; but afterwards, these failing, they ate their captives; in the third place, their servants; and in the last place, they attacked each other, and devoured their fellow-soldiers, who were led to be slaughtered for this purpose by lot. But Amilcar, taking those men that were in his power, caused his elephants to trample on such of the soldiers as had acted in this manner, conceiving that it was not holy to suffer them to be any longer mingled with other men; and neither did he admit that men should be eaten because certain persons had dared to do this; nor his son Hannibal, who, when he was leading his army into Italy, was advised by a certain person to accustom his troops to feed on human flesh, in order that they might never be in want of food. It does not follow, therefore, that because famine and war have been the causes of eating other animals, it is also requisite to feed on them for the sake of pleasure; as neither must we admit, that on this account men are to be eaten. Nor does it follow, that because animals are sacrificed to certain powers, it is also requisite to eat them. For neither do those who sacrifice men, on this account, feed on human flesh. Through what has been said, therefore, it is demonstrated, that it does not entirely follow that animals are to be eaten because they are sacrificed.

58. But that those who had learnt what the nature is of the powers in the universe, offered sacrifices through blood, not to Gods, but to dæmons, is confirmed by theologists themselves. For they also assert, that of dæmons, some are malefic, but others beneficent, who will not molest us, if we offer to them the first-fruits of those things alone which we eat, and by which we nourish either the soul or the body. After, therefore, we have added a few observations more, in order to show that the unperverted conceptions of the multitude accord with a right opinion respecting the Gods, we shall conclude

this book. Those poets, therefore, who are wise, though but in a small degree, say,

> What man so credulous and void of mind,
> What man so ignorant, as to think the Gods
> In fiery bile and fleshless bones rejoice,
> For hungry dogs a nutriment not fit;
> Or that such offerers they will e'er reward?

But another poet says,

> My offerings to the Gods from cakes alone
> And frankincense shall be; for not to friends
> But deities my sacrifice I make.

59. Apollo also, when he orders men to sacrifice according to paternal institutes, appears to refer every thing to ancient custom. But the ancient custom of sacrificing was, as we have before shown, with cakes and fruits. Hence also, sacrifices were called θυσιαι, *thusiai*, and θυηλαι, *thuelai,* and θυμελαι, *thumelai,* and αυτο το θυειν, *auto to thuein,* i. e. *the act of sacrificing,* signified the same thing as του θυμιαν, *tou thumian,* i. e. *to offer incense,* and which is now called by us, επιθυειν, *epithuein,* i. e. *to sacrifice something more.* For what we now call θυειν, *thuein, i. e. to sacrifice,* the ancients denominated ερδειν, *erdein,* i. e. *to perform* or *make.*

> They perfect hecatombs of bulls, or goats,
> *Made* to Apollo.

60. But those who introduced costliness into sacrifices, were ignorant that, in conjunction with this, they also introduced a swarm of evils, viz. superstition, luxury, an opinion that a divine nature may be corrupted by gifts, and that a compensation may be made by sacrifices for injustice. Or whence do some make an oblation of three animals with gilded horns, but others of hecatombs? And whence did Olympias, the mother of Alexander [the Great,] sacrifice a thousand of each species of animals, unless sumptuousness had at length proceeded to

superstition? But when the young man was informed that the Gods rejoiced in magnificent sacrifices, and, as they say, in solemn banquets of oxen and other animals, how, though he was willing to act wisely, was it possible that he could? How also, when he conceived that these sacrifices were acceptable to the Gods, was it possible he should not fancy that he was permitted to act unjustly, when he might exonerate himself from erroneous conduct through sacrifices? But if he had been persuaded that the Gods have no need of these things, and that they look to the manners of those who approach to them, *and conceive that a right opinion of them, and of things themselves, is the greatest sacrifice,* how is it possible that he should not have been temperate, holy, and just?

61. To the Gods, indeed, the most excellent offering is a pure intellect and an impassive soul, and also a moderate oblation of our own property and of other things, and this not negligently, but with the greatest alacrity. For the honours which we pay to the Gods should be accompanied by the same promptitude as that with which we give the first seat to worthy men, and with which we rise to, and salute them, and not by the promptitude with which we pay a tribute. For man must not use such language as the following to God:

> If, O Philinus, you recal to mind,
> And love me for, the benefits which I
> On you conferr'd, 'tis well, since for the sake
> Of these alone my bounty was bestow'd.

For divinity is not satisfied with such assertions as these. And hence Plato says [in his Laws], that it pertains to a good man to sacrifice, and to be always conversant with the Gods by prayers, votive offerings, sacrifices, and every kind of religious worship; but that to the bad man, much labour about the Gods is inefficacious and vain. For the good man knows what ought to be sacrificed, and from what it is requisite to abstain;

what things are to be offered to divinity, and of what the first-fruits are to be sacrificed; but the bad man exhibiting honours to the Gods from his own disposition and his own pursuits, acts in so doing more impiously than piously. Hence Plato thought, that a philosopher ought not to be conversant with men of depraved habits; for this is neither pleasing to the Gods, nor useful to men; but the philosopher should endeavour to change such men to a better condition, and if he cannot effect this, he should be careful that he does not himself become changed into their depravity. He adds, that having entered into the right path, he should proceed in it, neither fearing danger from the multitude, nor any other blasphemy which may happen to take place. For it would be a thing of a dire nature, that the Syrians indeed will not taste fish, nor the Hebrews swine, nor most of the Phœnicians and Egyptians cows; and though many kings have endeavoured to change these customs, yet those that adopt them would rather suffer death, than a transgression of the law [which forbids them to eat these animals]; and yet that we should choose to transgress the laws of nature and divine precepts through the fear of men, or of a certain denunciation of evil from them. For the divine choir of Gods, and divine men, may justly be greatly indignant with us, if it perceives us directing our attention to the opinions of depraved men, and idly looking to the terror with which they are attended, though we daily meditate how we may become [philosophically] dead to other things in the present life.

ON ABSTINENCE FROM ANIMAL FOOD.

BOOK THE THIRD.

1. In the two preceding books, O Firmus Castricius, we have demonstrated, that animal food does not contribute either to temperance and frugality, or to the piety which especially gives completion to the theoretic life, but is rather hostile to it. Since, however, the most beautiful part of justice consists in piety to the Gods, and this is principally acquired through abstinence, there is no occasion to fear that we shall violate justice towards men, while we preserve piety towards the Gods. Socrates therefore says, in opposition to those who contend that pleasure is the supreme good, that though all swine and goats should accord in this opinion, yet he should never be persuaded that our felicity was placed in the enjoyment of corporeal delight, as long as intellect has dominion over all things. And we also say, that though all wolves and vultures should praise the eating of flesh, we should not admit that they spoke justly, as long as man is by nature innoxious, and ought to abstain from procuring pleasure for himself by injuring others. We shall pass on, therefore, to the discussion of justice; and since our opponents say that this ought only to be extended to those of a similar species, and on this account deny that irrational animals can be injured by men, let us exhibit the true, and at the same time Pythagoric opinion, and demonstrate that every soul which participates of

sense and memory is rational. For this being demonstrated, we may extend, as our opponents will also admit, justice to every animal. But we shall epitomize what has been said by the ancients on this subject.

2. Since, however, with respect to reason, one kind, according to the doctrine of the Stoics, is internal, but the other external[a]; and again, one kind being right, but the other erroneous, it is requisite to explain of which of these two, animals, according to them, are deprived. Are they therefore deprived of right reason alone? or are they entirely destitute both of internal and externally proceeding reason? They appear, indeed, to ascribe to brutes an entire privation of reason, and not a privation of right reason alone. For if they merely denied that brutes possess right reason, animals would not be irrational, but rational beings, in the same manner as nearly all men are according to them. For, according to their opinion, one or two wise men may be found in whom alone right reason prevails, but all the rest of mankind are depraved; though some of these make a certain proficiency, but others are profoundly depraved, and yet, at the same time, all of them are similarly rational. Through the influence, therefore, of self-love, they say, that all other animals are irrational; wishing to indicate by irrationality, an entire privation of reason. If, however, it be requisite to speak the truth, not only reason may plainly be perceived in all animals, but in many of them it is so great as to approximate to perfection.

3. Since, therefore, reason is two-fold, one kind consisting in external speech, but the other in the disposition of the soul, we shall begin from that which is external, and which is arranged according to the voice. But if external reason is voice, which through the tongue is significant of the internal passions of the soul (for this is the most common definition of it, and is not adopted by one sect [of philosophers] only, and if it is alone indicative of

---

[a] This *external reason* (λογος προφορικος) is speech.

the conception of [internal] reason)—if this be the case, in what pertaining to this are such animals as have a voice deficient? Do they not discursively perceive the manner in which they are inwardly affected, before it is vocally enunciated by them? By a discursive perception, however, I mean the perception produced by the silent discourse which takes place in the soul. Since, therefore, that which is vocally expressed by the tongue is reason, in whatever manner it may be expressed, whether in a barbarous or a Grecian, a canine or a bovine mode, other animals also participate of it that are vocal; men, indeed, speaking conformably to the human laws [of speech], but other animals conformably to the laws which they received from the Gods and nature. But if we do not understand what they say, what is this to the purpose? For the Greeks do not understand what is said by the Indians, nor those who are educated in Attica the language of the Scythians, or Thracians, or Syrians; but the sound of the one falls on the ears of the other like the clangor of cranes, though by others their vocal sounds can be written and articulated, in the same manner as ours can by us. Nevertheless, the vocal sounds of the Syrians, for instance, or the Persians, are to us inarticulate, and cannot be expressed by writing, just as the speech of animals is unintelligible to all men. For as we, when we hear the Scythians speak, apprehend, by the auditory sense, a noise only and a sound, but are ignorant of the meaning of what they say, because their language appears to us to be nothing but a clangor, to have no articulation, and to employ only one sound either longer or shorter, the variety of which is not at all significant to us, but to them the vocal sounds are intelligible, and have a great difference, in the same manner as our language has to us; the like also takes place in the vocal sounds of other animals. For the several species of these understand the language which is adapted to them, but we only hear a sound, of the signification of which we are ignorant, because no one who has learnt our language, is able to teach us through ours the meaning of what is said by brutes. If, however, it is requisite to believe in the ancients, and also in those who have lived in our times, and the times of our fathers, there are some among these who are said to have heard and to have understood the speech of animals. Thus, for instance, this is narrated of Melampus and Tiresias, and others of the like kind; and the same thing, not much prior to our time, is related of Apollonius Tyanæus. For it is narrated of him, that once, when he was with his associates, a swallow happening to be present, and twittering, he said, that the swallow indicated to other birds, that an ass laden with corn had fallen down before the city, and that in consequence of the fall of the ass, the corn was spread on the ground[b]. An associate, also, of mine informed me, that he once had a boy for a servant, who understood the meaning of all the sounds of birds, and who said, that all of them were prophetic, and declarative of what would shortly happen. He added, that he was deprived of this knowledge through his mother, who, fearing that he would be sent to the Emperor as a gift, poured urine into his ear when he was asleep.

4. Omitting, however, these things, through the passion of incredulity, which is connascent with us, I think there is no one who is ignorant, that there are some nations even now who understand the sounds of certain animals, through an alliance to those animals. Thus, the Arabians understand the language of crows, and the Tyrrhenians of eagles. And, perhaps, all men would understand the language of all animals, if a dragon were to lick their ears. Indeed, the variety and difference in the vocal sounds of animals, indicate that they are significant. Hence, we hear one sound when they are terrified, but another, of a different kind, when they call their associates, another when they summon their

[b] Philostratus relates this of Apollonius, in his Life of him.

young to food, another when they lovingly embrace each other, and another when they incite to battle. And so great is the difference in their vocal sounds, that, even by those who have spent their whole life in the observation of them, it is found to be extremely difficult to ascertain their meaning, on account of their multitude. Diviners, therefore, who predict from ravens and crows, when they have noted the difference of the sounds, as far as to a certain multitude, omit the rest, as not easily to be apprehended by man. But when animals speak to each other, these sounds are manifest and significant to them, though they are not known to all of us. If, however, it appears that they imitate us, that they learn the Greek tongue, and understand their keepers, what man is so impudent as not to grant that they are rational, because he does not understand what they say? Crows, therefore, and magpies, the robin redbreast, and the parrot, imitate men, recollect what they have heard, are obedient to their preceptor while he is teaching them; and many of them, through what they have learnt, point out those that have acted wrong in the house. But the Indian hyæna, which the natives call crocotta, speaks in a manner so human, and this without a teacher, as to go to houses, and call that person whom he knows he can easily vanquish. He also imitates the voice of him who is most dear, and would most readily attend to the person whom he calls; so that, though the Indians know this, yet being deceived through the similitude, and obeying the call, they come forth, and are destroyed. If, however, all animals do not imitate, and all of them are not adapted to learn our language, what is this to the purpose? For neither is every man docile or imitative, I will not say of the vocal sounds of animals, but of the five dialects of the Greek tongue. To which may be added, that some animals, perhaps, do not speak, because they have not been taught, or because they are impeded by the ill conformation of the instruments of speech. We, therefore, when we were at Carthage, nurtured a tame partridge, which we caught flying, and which, in process of time, and by associating with us, became so exceedingly mild, that it was not only sedulously attentive to us, caressed and sported with us, but uttered a sound corresponding to the sound of our voice, and, as far as it was capable, answered us; and this in a manner different from that by which partridges are accustomed to call each other. For it did not utter a corresponding sound when we were silent, but when we spoke to it.

5. It is also narrated, that some dumb animals obey their masters with more readiness than any domestic servants. Hence, a lamprey was so accustomed to the Roman Crassus, as to come to him when he called it by its name; on which account Crassus was so affectionately disposed towards it, that he exceedingly lamented its death, though, prior to this, he had borne the loss of three of his children with moderation. Many likewise relate that the eels in Arethusa, and the shell-fish denominated saperdæ, about Mæander, are obedient to those that call them. Is not the imagination, therefore, of an animal that speaks, the same, whether it proceeds as far as to the tongue, or does not? And if this be the case, is it not absurd to call the voice of man alone [external] reason, but refuse thus to denominate the voice of other animals? For this is just as if crows should think that their voice alone is external reason, but that we are irrational animals, because the meaning of the sounds which we utter is not obvious to them; or as if the inhabitants of Attica should thus denominate their speech alone, and should think that those are irrational who are ignorant of the Attic tongue, though the inhabitants of Attica would sooner understand the croaking of a crow, than the language of a Syrian or a Persian. But is it not absurd to judge of rationality and irrationality from apprehending or not apprehending the meaning of vocal sounds, or from silence and speech? For thus some one might say, that the God who is above all things, and likewise the other

Gods, are not rational, because they do not speak. The Gods, however, silently indicate their will, and birds apprehend their will more rapidly than men, and when they have apprehended it, they narrate it to men as much as they are able, and different birds are the messengers to men of different Gods. Thus, the eagle is the messenger of Jupiter, the hawk and the crow of Apollo, the stork of Juno, the crex and the bird of night of Minerva, the crane of Ceres, and some other bird is the messenger of some other deity. Moreover, those among us that observe animals, and are nurtured together with them, know the meaning of their vocal sounds. The hunter, therefore, from the barking of his dog, perceives at one time, indeed, that the dog explores a hare, but at another, that the dog has found it; at one time, that he pursues the game, at another that he has caught it, and at another that he is in the wrong track, through having lost the scent of it. Thus, too, the cowherd knows, at one time, indeed, that a cow is hungry, or thirsty, or weary, and at another, that she is incited to venery, or seeks her calf, [from her different lowings]^c. A lion also manifests by his roaring that he threatens, a wolf by his howling that he is in a bad condition, and shepherds, from the bleating of sheep, know what the sheep want.

6. Neither, therefore, are animals ignorant of the meaning of the voice of men, when they are angry, or speak kindly to, or call them, or pursue them, or ask them to do something, or give something to them; nor, in short, are they ignorant of any thing that is usually said to them, but are aptly obedient to it; which it would be impossible for them to do, unless that which is similar to intellection energized, in consequence of being excited by its similar. The immoderation of their passions, also, is suppressed by certain modulations, and stags, bulls, and

---

^c The words within the brackets are added from the version of Felicianus. Hence it appears, that the words εκ των διαφορων μυκηματων are wanting in the original, after the word ζητει. But this defect is not noticed by any of the editors.

other animals, from being wild become tame. Those, too, who are decidedly of opinion that brutes are deprived of reason, yet admit that dogs have a knowledge of dialectic, and make use of the syllogism which consists of many disjunctive propositions, when, in searching for their game, they happen to come to a place where there are three roads. For they thus reason, the beast has either fled through this road, or through that, or through the remaining road; but it has not fled either through this, or through that, and therefore it must have fled through the remaining third of these roads[d]. After which syllogistic process, they resume their pursuit in that road. It may, however, be readily said, that animals do these things naturally, because they were not taught by any one to do them; as if we also were not allotted reason by nature, though we likewise give names to things, because we are naturally adapted to do so. Besides, if it be requisite to believe in Aristotle, animals are seen to teach their offspring, not only something pertaining to other things, but also to utter vocal sounds; as the nightingale, for instance, teaches her young to sing. And as he likewise says, animals learn many things from each other, and many from men; and the truth of what he asserts is testified by all the tamers of colts, by every jockey, horseman, and charioteer, and by all hunters, herdsmen, keepers of elephants, and masters of wild beasts and birds. He, therefore, who estimates things rightly, will be led, from these instances, to ascribe intelligence to brutes; but he who is inconsiderate, and is ignorant of these things, will be induced to act rashly, through his inexhaustible avidity co-operating with him against them. For how is it possible that he should not defame and calumniate animals, who has determined to cut them in pieces, as if they were stones? Aristotle, however, Plato, Empedocles, Pythagoras, Democritus, and all such as

---

[d] Porphyry derived this from the treatise of Plutarch, in which it is investigated whether *land* are more sagacious than *aquatic* animals.

endeavoured to discover the truth concerning animals, have acknowledged that they participate of reason.

7. But it is now requisite to show that brutes have internal reason. The difference, indeed, between our reason and theirs, appears to consist, as Aristotle somewhere says, not in essence, but in the more and the less; just as many are of opinion, that the difference between the Gods and us is not essential, but consists in this, that in them there is a greater, and in us a less accuracy, of the reasoning power[e]. And, indeed, so far as pertains to sense and the remaining organization, according to the sensoria and the flesh, every one nearly will grant that these are similarly disposed in us, as they are in brutes. For they not only similarly participate with us of natural passions, and the motions produced through these, but we may also survey in them such affections as are preternatural and morbid. No one, however, of a sound mind, will say that brutes are unreceptive of the reasoning power, on account of the difference between their habit of body and ours, when he sees that there is a great variety of habit in men, according to their race, and the nations to which they belong, and yet, at the same time, it is granted that all of them are rational. An ass, therefore, is afflicted with a catarrh, and if the disease flows to his lungs, he dies in the same manner as a man. A horse, too, is subject to purulence, and wastes away through it, like a man. He is likewise attacked with rigour, the gout, fever, and fury, in which case he is also said to have a depressed countenance. A mare, when pregnant, if she happens to smell a lamp when it is just extinguished, becomes abortive, in the same manner as a woman. An ox, and likewise a camel, are subject to

---

[e] This was the opinion of the Stoics; but is most erroneous. For the supreme divinity, being superessential, transcends even intellect itself, and much more reason, which is an evolved perception of things; and this is also the case with every other deity, according to the Platonic theology, when considered according to his hyparxis, or summit. See my translation of Proclus on the Theology of Plato.

fever and insanity; a raven becomes scabby, and has the leprosy; and also a dog, who, besides this, is afflicted with the gout, and madness: but a hog is subject to hoarseness, and in a still greater degree a dog; whence this disease in a man is denominated from the dog, *cynanche*. And these things are known to us, because we are familiar with these animals; but of the diseases of other animals we are ignorant, because we do not associate with them. Castrated animals also become more effeminate. Hence cocks, when they are castrated, no longer crow; but their voice becomes effeminate, like that of men who lose their testicles. It is not possible, likewise, to distinguish the bellowing and horns of a bull, when he is castrated, from those of a cow. But stags, when they are castrated, no longer cast off their horns, but retain them in the same manner as eunuchs do their hairs; and if, when they are castrated, they are without horns, they do not afterwards produce them, just as it happens to those who, before they have a beard, are made eunuchs. So that nearly the bodies of all animals are similarly affected with ours, with respect to the bodily calamities to which they are subject.

8. See, however, whether all the passions of the soul in brutes, are not similar to ours; for it is not the province of man alone to apprehend juices by the taste, colours by the sight, odours by the smell, sounds by the hearing, cold or heat, or other tangible objects, by the touch; but the senses of brutes are capable of the same perceptions. Nor are brutes deprived of sense because they are not men, as neither are we to be deprived of reason, because the Gods, if they possess it, are rational beings. With respect to the senses, however, other animals appear greatly to surpass us; for what man can see so acutely as a dragon? (for this is not the fabulous Lynceus). And hence the poets denominate *to see* δρακειν, *drakein:* but an eagle, from a great height, sees a hare. What man hears more acutely than cranes, who

are able to hear from an interval so great, as to be beyond the reach of human sight? And as to smell, almost all animals so much surpass us in this sense, that things which fall on it, and are obvious to them, are concealed from us; so that they know and smell the several kinds of animals by their footsteps. Hence, men employ dogs as their leaders, for the purpose of discovering the retreat of a boar, or a stag. And we, indeed, are slowly sensible of the constitution of the air; but this is immediately perceived by other animals, so that from them we derive indications of the future state of the weather. With respect to juices also, they so accurately know the distinction between them, that their knowledge of what are morbific, salubrious, and deleterious among these, surpasses that of physicians. But Aristotle says, that animals whose sensitive powers are more exquisite, are more prudent. And the diversities, indeed, of bodies are capable of producing a facility or difficulty of being passively affected, and of having reason, more or less prompt in its energies; but they are not capable of changing the essence of the soul, since neither are they able to change the senses, nor to alter the passions, nor to make them entirely abandon their proper nature. It must be granted, therefore, that animals participate more or less of reason, but not that they are perfectly deprived of it; as neither must it be admitted that one animal has reason, but another not. As, however, in one and the same species of animals, one body is more, but another less healthy; and, in a similar manner, in diseases, in a naturally good, and a naturally bad, disposition, there is a great difference; thus also in souls, one is naturally good, but another depraved: and of souls that are depraved, one has more, but another less, of depravity. In good men, likewise, there is not the same equality; for Socrates, Aristotle, and Plato, are not similarly good. Nor is there sameness in a concordance of opinions. Hence it does not follow, if we have more intelligence than other animals, that on this account they are to be deprived of intelligence; as neither must it be said, that partridges do not fly, because hawks fly higher; nor that other hawks do not fly, because the bird called phassophonos[f] flies higher than these, and than all other birds. Some one, therefore, may admit that the soul is co-passive with the body, and that the former suffers something from the latter, when the latter is well or ill affected; but in this case it by no means changes its nature: but if the soul is only co-passive to, and uses the body as an instrument, she may be able to effect many things through it, which we cannot, even when it is organized differently from ours, and when it is affected in a certain manner, may sympathize with it, and yet may not change its proper nature.

9. It must be demonstrated, therefore, that there is a rational power in animals, and that they are not deprived of prudence. And in the first place, indeed, each of them knows whether it is imbecile or strong, and, in consequence of this, it defends some parts of itself, but attacks with others. Thus the panther uses its teeth, the lion its nails and teeth, the horse its hoofs, the ox its horns, the cock its spurs, and the scorpion its sting; but the serpents in Egypt use their spittle, (whence also they are called πτυαδες, *ptuades*, i. e. *spitters*,) and with this they blind the eyes of those that approach them: and thus a different animal uses a different part of itself for attack, in order to save itself. Again, some animals, viz. such as are robust, feed [and live] remote from men; but others, who are of an ignoble nature, live remote from stronger animals, and, on the contrary, dwell nearer men. And of these, some dwell at a greater distance from more robust animals, as sparrows and swallows, who build their nests in the roofs of houses; but others associate with men, as, for instance, dogs. They likewise change their places of abode at certain

---

[f] A musket, or male hawk of a small kind. This bird is mentioned by Homer, Iliad, XIV. v. 238.

times, and know every thing which contributes to their advantage. In a similar manner, in fishes and in birds, a reasoning energy of this kind may be perceived; all which particulars are abundantly collected by the ancients, in their writings concerning the prudence of animals; and they are copiously discussed by Aristotle, who says, that by all animals an habitation subservient to their subsistence and their safety, is most exquisitely contrived.

10. But he who says that these things are naturally present with animals, is ignorant in asserting this, that they are by nature rational; or if this is not admitted, neither does reason subsist in us naturally, nor with the perfection of it receive an increase, so far as we are naturally adapted to receive it. A divine nature, indeed, does not become rational[g] through learning, for there never was a time in which he was irrational; but rationality is consubsistent with his existence, and he is not prevented from being rational, because he did not receive reason through discipline: though, with respect to other animals, in the same manner as with respect to men, many things are taught them by nature, and some things are imparted by discipline. Brutes, however, learn some things from each other, but are taught others, as we have said, by men. They also have memory, which is a most principal thing in the resumption of reasoning and prudence. They likewise have vices, and are envious; though their bad qualities are not so widely extended as in men: for their vices are of a lighter nature than those of men. This, indeed, is evident; for the builder of a house will never be able to lay the foundation of it, unless he is sober; nor can a shipwright properly place

---

[g] Reason in a divine intellect subsists causally, or in a way better than reason, and therefore is not a discursive energy (διεξοδικη ενεργεια), but an evolved cause of things. And though, in a divine soul, it is discursive, or transitive, yet it differs from our reason in this, that it perceives the whole of one form at once, and not by degrees, as we do when we reason.

the keel of a ship, unless he is in health; nor a husbandman plant a vine, unless he applies his mind to it; yet nearly all men, when they are intoxicated, can beget children. This, however, is not the case with other animals; for they propagate for the sake of offspring, and for the most part, when the males have made the female pregnant, they no longer attempt to be connected with her; nor, if they should attempt it, would the female permit them. But the magnitude of the lascivious insolence and intemperance of men in these things, is evident. In other animals, however, the male is conscious of the parturient throes of the female, and, for the most part, partakes of the same pains; as is evident in cocks. But others incubate together with the females; as the males of doves. They likewise provide a proper place for the delivery of their offspring; and after they have brought forth their offspring, they both purify them and themselves. And he who properly observes, will see that every thing proceeds with them in an orderly manner; that they fawn on him who nourishes them, and that they know their master, and give indications of him who acts insidiously.

11. Who likewise is ignorant how much gregarious animals preserve justice towards each other? for this is preserved by ants, by bees, and by other animals of the like kind. And who is ignorant of the chastity of female ring-doves towards the males with whom they associate? for they destroy those who are found by them to have committed adultery. Or who has not heard of the justice of storks towards their parents? For in the several species of animals, a peculiar virtue is eminent, to which each species is naturally adapted; nor because this virtue is natural and stable, is it fit to deny that they are rational? For it might be requisite to deprive them of rationality, if their works were not the proper effects of virtue and rational sagacity; but if we do not understand how these works are effected, because we are unable to penetrate into the reasoning which they use,

we are not on this account to accuse them of irrationality; for neither is any one able to penetrate into the intellect of that divinity the sun, but from his works we assent to those who demonstrate him to be an intellectual and rational essence.

12. But some one may very properly wonder at those who admit that justice derives its subsistence from the rational part, and who call those animals that have no association with men, savage and unjust, and yet do not extend justice as far as to those that do associate with us; and which, in the same manner as men, would be deprived of life, if they were deprived of human society. Birds, therefore, and dogs, and many quadrupeds, such as goats, horses, sheep, asses, and mules, would perish, if deprived of an association with mankind. Nature also, the fabricator of their frame, constituted them so as to be in want of men, and fashioned men so as to require their assistance; thus producing an innate justice in them towards us, and in us towards them. But it is not at all wonderful, if some of them are savage towards men; for what Aristotle says is true, that if all animals had an abundance of nutriment, they would not act ferociously, either towards each other, or towards men. For on account of food, though necessary and slender, enmities and friendships are produced among animals, and also on account of the places which they occupy; but if men were reduced to such straits as brutes are [with respect to food,] how much more savage would they become than those animals that appear to be wild? War and famine are indications of the truth of this; for then men do not abstain from eating each other; and even without war and famine, they eat animals that are nurtured with them, and are perfectly tame.

13. Some one, however, may say, that brutes are indeed rational animals, but have not a certain habitude, proximity, or alliance to us; but he who asserts this will, in the first place, make them to be irrational animals, in

consequence of depriving them of an alliance to our nature. And, in the next place, he will make their association with us to depend on the utility which we derive from them, and not on the participation of reason. The thing proposed by us, however, is to show that brutes are rational animals, and not to inquire whether there is any compact between them and us. For, with respect to men, all of them do not league with us, and yet no one would say, that he who does not enter into a league with us is irrational. But many brutes are slaves to men, and, as some one rightly says, though they are in a state of servitude themselves, through the improbity of men, yet, at the same time, by wisdom and justice, they cause their masters to be their servants and curators. Moreover, the vices of brutes are manifest, from which especially their rationality is demonstrated. For they are envious, and the males are rivals of each other with respect to the favour of the females, and the females with respect to the regard of the males. There is one vice, however, which is not inherent in them, viz. acting insidiously towards their benefactors, but they are perfectly benevolent to those who are kind to them, and place so much confidence in them, as to follow wherever they may lead them, though it should even be to slaughter and manifest danger. And though some one should nourish them, not for their sake, but for his own, yet they will be benevolently disposed towards their possessor. But men [on the contrary] do not act with such hostility towards any one, as towards him who has nourished them; nor do they so much pray for the death of any one, as for his death.

14. Indeed, the operations of brutes are attended with so much consideration[h], that they frequently perceive, that the food which is placed for them is nothing else

---

[h] In the original, Ουτω δ' εστι λογιστικα αν δρα, κ.τ.λ. But for λογιστικα, Lipsius proposes to read, λογικα, and Meerman λογικη. There is, however, no occasion whatever to substitute any other word for λογιστικα, as, with Platonic writers, το λογιστικον is equivalent to το λογιζομενον.

than a snare, though, either through intemperance or hunger, they approach to it. And some of them, indeed, do not approach to it immediately, but others slowly accede to it. They also try whether it is possible to take the food without falling into danger, and frequently in consequence of rationality vanquishing passion, they depart without being injured. Some of them too revile at, and discharge their urine on the stratagem of men; but others, through voracity, though they know that they shall be captured, yet no less than the associates of Ulysses, suffer themselves to die rather than not eat. Some persons, likewise, have not badly endeavoured to show from the places which animals are allotted, that they are far more prudent than we are. For as those beings that dwell in æther are rational, so also, say they, are the animals which occupy the region proximate to æther, viz. the air; afterwards aquatic animals differ from these, and in the last place, the terrestrial differ from the aquatic [in degrees of rationality]. And we belong to the class of terrene animals dwelling in the sediment of the universe. For in the Gods, we must not infer that they possess a greater degree of excellence from the places [which they illuminate], though in mortal natures this may be admitted.

15. Since, also, brutes acquire a knowledge of the arts, and these such as are human, and learn to dance, to drive a chariot, to fight a duel, to walk on ropes, to write and read, to play on the pipe and the harp, to discharge arrows, and to ride,—this being the case, can you any longer doubt whether they possess that power which is receptive of art, since the recipient of these arts may be seen to exist in them? For where will they receive them, unless reason is inherent in them in which the arts subsist? For they do not hear our voice as if it was a mere sound only, but they also perceive the difference in the meaning of the words, which is the effect of rational intelligence. But our opponents say, that animals perform badly what is done by men. To this we reply, that

neither do men perform all things well. For if this be not admitted, some men would be in vain victors in a contest, and others vanquished. They add, that brutes do not consult, nor form assemblies, nor act in a judicial capacity. But tell me whether all men do this? Do not actions in the multitude precede consultation? And whence can any one demonstrate that brutes do not consult? For no one can adduce an argument sufficient to prove that they do not. But those show the contrary to this, who have written minutely about animals. As to other objections, which are adduced by our adversaries in a declamatory way, they are perfectly frivolous; such, for instance, as that brutes have no cities of their own. For neither have the Scythians, who live in carts, nor the Gods. Our opponents add, that neither have brutes any written laws. To this we reply, that neither had men while they were happy. For Apis is said to have been the first that promulgated laws for the Greeks, when they were in want of them.

16. To men, therefore, on account of their voracity, brutes do not appear to possess reason; but by the Gods and divine men, they are honoured equally with sacred suppliants. Hence, the God[i] said to Aristodicus, the Cumean, that sparrows were his suppliants. Socrates also, and prior to him, Rhadamanthus, swore by animals. But the Egyptians conceive them to be Gods, whether they, in reality, thought them to be so, or whether they intentionally represented the Gods in the forms of oxen, birds, and other animals, in order that these animals might be no less abstained from than from men, or whether they did this through other more mystical causes[k]. Thus also the Greeks united a ram to the

---

[i] See the first book of Herodotus, chap. 159.

[k] The more mystical cause why the Egyptians worshipped animals, appears to me to be this, that they conceived a *living* to be preferable to an *inanimate* image of divinity. Hence, they reverenced animals as visible and living resemblances of certain invisible powers of the Gods. — See Plutarch's Treatise on Isis and Osiris.

statue of Jupiter, but the horns of a bull to that of Bacchus. They likewise fashioned the statue of Pan from the form of a man and a goat; but they represented the Muses and the Sirens winged, and also Victory, Iris, Love, and Hermes. Pindar too, in his hymns, represents the Gods, when they were expelled by Typhon, not resembling men, but other animals. And Jupiter, when in love with Pasiphae, is said to have become a bull; but at another time, he is said to have been changed into an eagle and a swan; through all which the ancients indicated the honour which they paid to animals, and this in a still greater degree when they assert that Jupiter was nursed by a goat. The Cretans, from a law established by Rhadamanthus, swore by all animals. Nor was Socrates in jest when he swore by the dog and the goose; but in so doing, he swore conformably to the just son of Jupiter [Rhadamanthus]; nor did he sportfully say that swans were his fellow-servants. But fables obscurely signify, that animals have souls similar to ours, when they say that the Gods in their anger changed men into brutes, and that, when they were so changed, they afterwards pitied and loved them. For things of this kind are asserted of dolphins and halcyons, of nightingales and swallows.

17. Each of the ancients, likewise, who had been prosperously nursed by animals, boasted more of this than of their parents and educators. Thus, one boasted of having been nursed by a she-wolf, another by a hind, another by a she-goat, and another by a bee. But Semiramis gloried in having been brought up by doves, Cyrus in being nursed by a dog, and a Thracian in having a swan for his nurse, who likewise bore the name of his nurse. Hence also, the Gods obtained their surnames, as Bacchus that of *Hinnuleus*, Apollo that of *Lyceus*, and, likewise *Delphinius*, Neptune and Minerva that of *Equestris*. But Hecate, when invoked by the names of a bull, a dog, and a lioness, is more propitious. If, however, those who sacrifice animals and eat them, assert that they are irra-

tional, in order that they may mitigate the crime of so doing, the Scythians also, who eat their parents, may in like manner say that their parents are destitute of reason.

18. Through these arguments, therefore, and others which we shall afterwards mention, in narrating the opinions of the ancients, it is demonstrated that brutes are rational animals, reason in most of them being indeed imperfect, of which, nevertheless, they are not entirely deprived. Since, however, justice pertains to rational beings, as our opponents say, how is it possible not to admit, that we should also act justly towards brutes? For we do not extend justice to plants, because there appears to be much in them which is unconnected with reason; though of these, we are accustomed to use the fruits, but not together with the fruits to cut off the trunks. We collect, however, corn and leguminous substances, when, being efflorescent, they have fallen on the earth, and are dead. But no one uses for food the flesh of dead animals, that of fish being excepted, unless they have been destroyed by violence. So that in these things there is much injustice. As Plutarch also says[1], it does not follow that, because our nature is indigent of certain things, and we use these, we should therefore act unjustly towards all things. For we are allowed to injure other things to a certain extent, in order to procure the necessary means of subsistence (if to take any thing from plants, even while they are living, is an injury to them); but to destroy other things through luxury, and for the enjoyment of pleasure, is perfectly savage and unjust. And the abstinence from these neither diminishes our life nor our living happily. For if, indeed, the destruction of animals and the eating of flesh were as requisite as air and water, plants and fruits, without which it is impossible to live, this injustice would be necessarily connected with our nature. But if many priests of the

---

[1] See the Symposiacs of Plutarch, lib. ix. 8.

Gods, and many kings of the barbarians, being attentive to purity, and if, likewise, infinite species of animals never taste food of this kind, yet live, and obtain their proper end according to nature, is not he absurd who orders us, because we are compelled to wage war with certain animals, not to live peaceably with those with whom it is possible to do so, but thinks, either that we ought to live without exercising justice towards any thing, or that, by exercising it towards all things, we should not continue in existence? As, therefore, among men, he who, for the sake of his own safety, or that of his children or country, either seizes the wealth of certain persons, or oppresses some region or city, has necessity for the pretext of his injustice; but he who acts in this manner through the acquisition of wealth, or through satiety or luxurious pleasure, and for the purpose of satisfying desires which are not necessary, appears to be inhospitable, intemperate, and depraved;—thus too, divinity pardons the injuries which are done to plants, the consumption of fire and water, the shearing of sheep, the milking of cows, and the taming of oxen, and subjugating them to the yoke, for the safety and continuance in life of those that use them. But to deliver animals to be slaughtered and cooked, and thus be filled with murder, not for the sake of nutriment and satisfying the wants of nature, but making pleasure and gluttony the end of such conduct, is transcendently iniquitous and dire. For it is sufficient that we use, for laborious purposes, though they have no occasion to labour themselves, the progeny of horses, and asses, and bulls, as Æschylus says, as our substitutes, who, by being tamed and subjugated to the yoke, alleviate our toil.

19. But with respect to him who thinks that we should not use an ox for food, nor destroying and corrupting spirit and life, place things on the table which are only the allurements and elegancies of satiety, of what does he deprive our life, which is either necessary to our safety, or subservient to virtue? To compare

plants, however, with animals, is doing violence to the order of things. For the latter are naturally sensitive, and adapted to feel pain, to be terrified and hurt; on which account also they may be injured. But the former are entirely destitute of sensation, and in consequence of this, nothing foreign, or evil, or hurtful, or injurious, can befall them. For sensation is the principle of all alliance, and of every thing of a foreign nature. But Zeno and his followers assert, that alliance is the principle of justice. And is it not absurd, since we see that many of our own species live from sense alone, but do not possess intellect and reason, and since we also see, that many of them surpass the most terrible of wild beasts in cruelty, anger, and rapine, being murderous of their children and their parents, and also being tyrants, and the tools of kings [is it not, I say, absurd,] to fancy that we ought to act justly towards these, but that no justice is due from us to the ox that ploughs, the dog that is fed with us, and the animals that nourish us with their milk, and adorn our bodies with their wool? Is not such an opinion most irrational and absurd?

20. But, by Jupiter, the assertion of Chrysippus is considered by our opponents to be very probable, that the Gods made us for the sake of themselves, and for the sake of each other, and that they made animals for the sake of us; horses, indeed, in order that they might assist us in battle, dogs, that they might hunt with us, and leopards, bears, and lions, for the sake of exercising our fortitude. But the hog (for here the pleasantry of Chrysippus is most delightful) was not made for any other purpose than to be sacrificed; and God mingled soul, as if it were salt, with the flesh of this animal, that he might procure for us excellent food. In order, likewise, that we might have an abundance of broth, and luxurious suppers, divinity provided for us all-various kinds of shell-fish, the fishes called purples, sea-nettles, and the various kinds of winged animals; and this not from a certain other cause, but only that he might supply

man with an exuberance of pleasure; in so doing, surpassing all nurses [in kindness], and thickly filling with pleasures and enjoyments the terrestrial place. Let him, however, to whom these assertions appear to possess a certain probability, and to participate of something worthy of deity, consider what he will reply to the saying of Carneades, that every thing which is produced by nature, is *benefited* when it obtains the end to which it is adapted, and for which it was generated. But *benefit* is to be understood in a more general way, as signifying what the Stoics call *useful*. The hog, however, [says he] was produced by nature for the purpose of being slaughtered and used for food; and when it suffers this, it obtains the end for which it is adapted, and is benefited. But if God fashioned animals for the use of men, in what do we use flies, lice, bats, beetles, scorpions, and vipers? of which some are odious to the sight, defile the touch, are intolerable to the smell, and in their voice dire and unpleasant; and others, on the contrary, are destructive to those that meet with them. And with respect to the *balænæ, pistrices,* and other species of whales, an infinite number of which, as Homer says[m], the loud-sounding Amphitrite nourishes, does not the Demiurgus teach us, that they were generated for the utility of the nature of things[n]? And if our opponents should admit that all things were not generated for us, and with a view to our advantage, in addition to the distinction which they make being very confused and obscure, we shall not avoid acting unjustly, in attacking and noxiously using those animals which were not produced for our sake, but according to nature [*i.e.* for the sake of the universe], as we were. I omit to mention, that if we define, by utility,

---

[m] Odyss. XII. v. 96.

[n] The latter part of this sentence, which in the original is τι ουκ εδιδαξεν ημας ο δημιουργος οπη χρησιμα τη φυσει γεγονε; Valentinius most erroneously translates, " quare nos rerum opifex non edocuit, quomodo à natura in nostros usus facta fuerint?"

things which pertain to us, we shall not be prevented from admitting, that we were generated for the sake of the most destructive animals, such as crocodiles, balænæ, and dragons. For we are not in the least benefited by them; but they seize and destroy men that fall in their way, and use them for food; in so doing acting not at all more cruelly than we do, excepting that they commit this injustice through want and hunger, but we through insolent wantonness, and for the sake of luxury, frequently sporting in theatres, and in hunting slaughter the greater part of animals. And by thus acting, indeed, a murderous disposition and a brutal nature become strengthened in us, and render us insensible to pity: to which we may add, that those who first dared to do this, blunted the greatest part of lenity, and rendered it inefficacious. The Pythagoreans, however, made lenity towards beasts to be an exercise of philanthropy and commiseration. So that, how is it possible they should not in a greater degree excite us to justice, than those who assert that, by not slaughtering animals, the justice which is usually exercised towards men will be corrupted? For custom is most powerful in increasing those passions in man which were gradually introduced into his nature.

21. It is so, say our antagonists; but as the immortal is opposed to the mortal, the incorruptible to the corruptible, and the incorporeal to the corporeal, so to the rational essence which has an existence in the nature of things, the irrational essence must be opposed, which has a subsistence contrary to it; nor in so many conjugations of things, is this alone to be left imperfect and mutilated. [Our opponents, however, thus speak], as if we did not grant this, or as if we had not shown that there is much of the irrational among beings. For there is an abundance of it in all the natures that are destitute of soul, nor do we require any other opposition to that which is rational; but immediately every thing which is deprived of soul,

being irrational and without intellect, is opposed to that which possesses reason and *dianoia*°. If, however, some one should think fit to assert that not nature in common, but the animated nature, is divided into that which possesses and that which is without imagination, and into that which is sensitive, and that which is deprived of sensation, in order that these oppositions of habits and privations may subsist about the same genus, as being equiponderant;—he who says this speaks absurdly. For it would be absurd to investigate in the animated nature that which is sensitive, and that which is without sensation, that which employs, and that which is without, imagination, because every thing animated is immediately adapted to be sensitive and imaginative. So that neither thus will he justly require, that one part of the animated nature should be rational, but another irrational, when he is speaking to men, who think that nothing participates of sense which does not also participate of intelligence, and that nothing is an animal in which opinion and reasoning are not inherent, in the same manner as with animals every sense and impulse are naturally present. For nature, which they rightly assert produced all things for the sake of a certain thing, and with reference to a certain end, did not make an animal sensitive merely that it might be passively affected, and possess sensible perception; but as there are many things which are allied and appropriate, and many which are foreign to it, it would not be able to exist for the shortest space of time, unless it learnt how to avoid some things, and to pursue others. The knowledge, therefore, of both these, sense similarly imparts to every animal; but the apprehension and pursuit of what is useful, and the depulsion and avoidance of what is destructive and painful, can by no possible contrivance be present with those animals that are incapable of reasoning, judging, and remembering, and that do not naturally possess an animadversive power.

° *i. e.* The discursive energy of reason.

For to those animals from whom you entirely take away expectation, memory, design, preparation, hope, fear, desire, and indignation, neither the eyes when present, nor the ears, nor sense, nor phantasy, will be beneficial, since they will be of no use; and it will be better to be deprived of them than to labour, be in pain, and be afflicted, without possessing the power of repelling these molestations. There is, however, a treatise of Strato, the physiologist, in which it is demonstrated, that it is not possible to have a sensible perception of any thing without the energy of intellection. For frequently the letters of a book, which we cursorily consider by the sight, and words which fall on the auditory sense, are concealed from and escape us, when our intellect is attentive to other things; but afterwards, when it returns to the thing to which it was before inattentive, then, by recollection, it runs through and pursues each of the before-mentioned particulars. Hence also it is said [by Epicharmus],—

> 'Tis mind alone that sees and hears,
> And all besides is deaf and blind.

For the objects which fall on the eyes and the ears do not produce a sensible perception of themselves, unless that which is intellective is present. On which account, also, king Cleomenes, when something that was recited was applauded, being asked, if it did not also appear to him to be excellent, left this to the decision of those that asked him the question; for he said, that his intellect was at the time in Peloponnesus. Hence it is necessary that intellect should be present with all those with whom sensible perception is present.

22. Let us, however, admit that sense does not require intellect for the accomplishment of its proper work, yet, when energizing about what is appropriate and what is foreign, it discerns the difference between the two, it must then exercise the power of memory, and must dread that which will produce pain, desire that which will be beneficial, and contrive, if it is absent, how it may be

present, and will procure methods of pursuing and investigating what is advantageous, and of avoiding and flying from hostile occurrences. Indeed, our opponents, in their Introductions, [as they call them], every where inculcate these things with a tedious prolixity, defining design to be an indication of perfection; the tendency of intellect to the object of its perception, an impulse prior to impulse; preparation, an action prior to action; and memory, the comprehension of some past thing [p], the perception of which, when present, was obtained through sense. For there is not any one of these which is not rational, and all of them are present with all animals. Thus, too, with respect to intellections, those which are reposited in the mind, are called by them εννοιαι, *notions;* but when they are in motion [through a discursive energy] they denominate them διανοησεις, or *perceptions obtained by a reasoning process.* But with respect to all the passions, as they are in common acknowledged to be depraved natures and opinions, it is wonderful that our opponents should overlook the operations and motions of brutes, many of which are the effects of anger, many of fear, and, by Jupiter, of envy also and emulation. Our opponents, too, themselves punish dogs and horses when they do wrong; and this not in vain, but in order to make them better, producing in them, through the pain, a sorrow which we denominate repentance. But the name of the pleasure which is received through the ears is κηλησις, *i. e. an ear-alluring sweetness;* and the delight which is received through the eyes is denominated γοητεια, *i. e. enchantment.* Each of these, however, is used towards brutes. Hence stags and horses are *allured* by the harmony produced from reeds and flutes; and the

---

[p] In the original, μνημην δε καταληψιν αξιωματος παρεληλυθος, ὡ το παρον εξ αισθησεως κατειληφθη; but for αξιωματος, I read πραγματος. Felicianus also appears to have found this reading in his manuscript copy of this work; for his version of the passage is, " vel memoriam *rei* præteritæ comprehensionem, quam præsentem sensus perciperat."

crabs, called παγουροι, *paguri*, are evocated from their caverns by the melody of reeds. The fish *thrissa*, likewise, is said through harmony to come forth from its retreats. Those, however, who speak stupidly about these things, assert that animals are neither delighted, nor enraged, nor terrified, nor make any provision for what is necessary, nor remember; but they say that the bee *as it were* remembers, that the swallow *as it were* provides what is requisite, that the lion is *as it were* angry, and that the stag is *as it were* afraid. And I know not what answer to give to those who say that animals neither see nor hear, but see *as it were*, and *as it were* hear; that they do not utter vocal sounds, but *as it were* utter them; and that, in short, they do not live, but *as it were* live. For he who is truly intelligent, will readily admit that these assertions are no more sane than the former, and are similarly destitute of evidence. When, however, on comparing with human manners and lives, actions, and modes of living, those of animals, I see much depravity in the latter, and no manifest tendency to virtue as to the principal end, nor any proficiency, or appetition of proficiency, I am dubious why nature gave the beginning of perfection to those that are never able to arrive at the end of it[q]. But this to our opponents does not appear to be at all absurd. For as they admit that the love of parents towards their offspring is the principle in us of association and justice; yet, though they perceive that this affection is abundant and strong in animals, they nevertheless deny that they participate of justice; which assertion is similarly defective with the nature of mules, who, though they are not in want of any generative member, since they have a penis and vulva,

[q] This doubt may, perhaps, be solved, by admitting that brutes have an imperfect rationality, or the very dregs of the rational faculty, by which they form a link between men and zoophytes, just as zoophytes are a link between brutes and merely vegetable substances. Brutes, therefore, having an imperfect reason, possess only the beginning of perfection.

and receive pleasure from employing these parts, yet they are not able to accomplish the end of generation. Consider the thing, too, in another way: Is it not ridiculous to say that such men as Socrates, Plato, and Zeno, were not less vicious than any slave, but resembled slaves in stupidity, intemperance, and injustice, and afterwards blame the nature of brutes, as neither pure, nor formed with sufficient accuracy for the attainment of virtue; thus attributing to them a privation, and not a depravity and imbecility of reason? Especially since they acknowledge that there is a vice of the rational part of the soul, with which every brute is replete. For we may perceive that timidity, intemperance, injustice, and malevolence, are inherent in many brutes.

23. But he who thinks that the nature which is not adapted to receive rectitude of reason, does not at all receive reason, he, in the first place, does not differ from one who fancies that an ape does not naturally participate of deformity, nor a tortoise of tardity; because the former is not receptive of beauty, nor the latter of celerity. And, in the next place, this is the opinion of one who does not perceive the obvious difference of things. For reason, indeed, is ingenerated by nature; but right and perfect reason is acquired by study and discipline. Hence all animated beings participate of reason, but our opponents cannot mention any man who possesses rectitude of reason and wisdom [naturally], though the multitude of men is innumerable. But as the sight of one animal differs from that of another, and the flying of one bird from that of another, (for hawks and grasshoppers do not similarly see, nor eagles and partridges); thus, also, neither does every thing which participates of reason possess genius and acuteness in the highest perfection. Indeed there are many indications in brutes of association, fortitude, and craft, in procuring what is necessary, and in economical conduct; as, on the contrary, there are also indications in them of injustice, timidity, and fatuity. Hence it is a question with some, which

are the more excellent, terrestrial or aquatic animals'? And that there are these indications, is evident from comparing storks with river horses: for the former nourish, but the latter destroy their fathers, in order that they may have connexion with their mothers. This is likewise seen on comparing doves with partridges: for the latter conceal and destroy their eggs, if the female, during her incubation, refuses to be connected with the male. But doves successively relieve each other in incubation, alternately cherishing the eggs; and first, indeed, they feed the young, and afterwards the male strikes the female with his beak, and drives her to the eggs and her young, if she has for a long time wandered from them. Antipater, however, when he blames asses and sheep for the neglect of purity, overlooks, I know not how, lynxes and swallows; of which, the former remove and entirely conceal and bury their excrement, but the latter teach their young to throw it out of their nest. Moreover, we do not say that one tree is more ignorant than another, as we say that a sheep is more stupid than a dog. Nor do we say that one herb is more timid than another, as we do that a stag is more timid than a lion. For, as in things which are immoveable, one is not slower than another, and in things which are not vocal, one is not less vocal than another: thus, too, in all things in which the power of intellection is wanting, one thing cannot be said to be more timid, more dull, or more intemperate than another. For, as these qualities are present differently in their different participants, they produce in animals the diversities which we perceive. Nor is it wonderful that man should so much excel other animals in docility, sagacity, justice, and association. For many brutes surpass all men in magnitude of body, and celerity of foot, and likewise in strength of sight, and accuracy of hearing; yet man is not on this account either deaf, or blind, or powerless. But we run, though slower than

---

' Plutarch has written a most ingenious treatise on this subject.

stags, and we see, though not so accurately as hawks; and nature has not deprived us of strength and magnitude, though our possession of these is nothing, when compared with the strength and bulk of the elephant and the camel. *Hence, in a similar manner, we must not say that brutes, because their intellection is more dull than ours, and because they reason worse than we do, neither energize discursively, nor, in short, possess intellection and reason; but it must be admitted that they possess these, though in an imbecile and turbid manner, just as a dull and disordered eye participates of sight.*

24. Innumerable instances, however, might be adduced in proof of the natural sagacity of animals, if many things of this kind had not by many persons been collected and narrated. But this subject must be still further considered. For it appears that it belongs to the same thing, whether it be a part or a power, which is naturally adapted to receive a certain thing, to be also disposed to fall into a preternatural mode of subsistence, when it becomes mutilated or diseased. Thus, the eye is adapted to fall into blindness, the leg into lameness, and the tongue into stammering; but nothing else is subject to such defects. For blindness does not befall that which is not naturally adapted to see, nor lameness that which is not adapted to walk; nor is that which is deprived of a tongue fitted to stammer, or lisp, or be dumb. Hence, neither can that animal be delirious, or stupid, or insane, in which intellection, and the discursive energy of reason, are not naturally inherent. For it is not possible for any thing to be passively affected which does not possess a power, the passion of which is either privation, or mutilation, or some other deprivation. Moreover, I have met with mad dogs, and also rabid horses; and some persons assert that oxen and foxes become mad. The example of dogs, however, is sufficient for our purpose: for it is a thing indubitable, and testifies that the animal possesses no despicable portion of reason and discursive energy, the passion of which, when disturbed and con-

founded, is fury and madness. For, when they are thus affected, we do not see that there is any change in the quality of their sight or hearing. But as he is absurd who denies that a man is beside himself, and that his intellectual, reasoning, and recollective powers, are corrupted, when he is afflicted with melancholy or delirium, (for it is usually said of those that are insane, that they are not themselves, but have fallen off from reason): thus, also, he who thinks that mad dogs suffer any thing else than that of having the power, which is naturally intellective, and is adapted to reason and recollect, full of tumult and distortion, so as to cause them to be ignorant of persons most dear to them, and abandon their accustomed mode of living;—he who thus thinks, appears either to overlook what is obvious; or, if he really perceives what takes place, voluntarily contends against the truth. And such are the arguments adduced by Plutarch in many of his treatises against the Stoics and Peripatetics.

25. But Theophrastus employs the following reasoning:—Those that are generated from the same sources, I mean from the same father and mother, are said by us to be naturally allied to each other. And moreover, we likewise conceive that those who derive their origin from the same ancestors that we do, are allied to us, and also that this is the case with our fellow-citizens, because they participate with us of the same land, and are united to us by the bonds of association. For we do not think that the latter are allied to each other, and to us, through deriving their origin from the same ancestors, unless it should so happen that the first progenitors of these were the sources of our race, or were derived from the same ancestors. Hence I think we should say, that Greek is allied and has an affinity to Greek, and Barbarian to Barbarian, and all men to each other; for one of these two reasons, either because they originate from the same ancestors, or because they participate of the same food, manners, and genus. Thus also we must admit that all

men have an affinity, and are allied to each other. And, moreover, the principles of the bodies of all animals are naturally the same. I do not say this with reference to the first elements of their bodies; for plants also consist of these; but I mean the seed, the flesh, and the connascent genus of humours which is inherent in animals. But animals are much more allied to each other, through naturally possessing souls, which are not different from each other, I mean in desire and anger; and besides these, in the reasoning faculty, and, above all, in the senses. But as with respect to bodies, so likewise with respect to souls, some animals have them more, but others less perfect, yet all of them have naturally the same principles. And this is evident from the affinity of their passions. If, however, what we have said is true, viz. that such is the generation of the manners of animals, all the tribes of them are indeed intellective, but they differ in their modes of living, and in the temperature of the first elements of which they consist. And if this be admitted, the genus of other animals has an affinity, and is allied to us. For, as Euripides says, they have all of them the same food and the same spirit, the same purple streams; and they likewise demonstrate that the common parents of all of them are Heaven and Earth.

26. Hence, since animals are allied to us, if it should appear, according to Pythagoras, that they are allotted the same soul that we are, he may justly be considered as impious who does not abstain from acting unjustly towards his kindred. Nor because some animals are savage, is their alliance to us to be on this account abscinded. For some men may be found who are no less, and even more malefic than savage animals to their neighbours, and who are impelled to injure any one they may meet with, as if they were driven by a certain blast of their own nature and depravity. Hence also, we destroy such men; yet we do not cut them off from an alliance to animals of a mild nature. Thus, therefore, if likewise some animals are savage, these, as such, are to

be destroyed, in the same manner as men that are savage; but our habitude or alliance to other and wilder animals is not on this account to be abandoned. But neither tame nor savage animals are to be eaten; as neither are unjust men. Now, however, we act most unjustly, destroying, indeed, tame animals, because some brutes are savage and unjust, and feeding on such as are tame. With respect to tame animals, however, we act with a twofold injustice, because, though they are tame, we slay them, and also, because we eat them. And, in short, the death of these has a reference to the assumption of them for food.

To these, also, such arguments as the following may be added. For he who says that the man who extends the just as far as to brutes, corrupts the just, is ignorant that he does not himself preserve justice, but increases pleasure, which is hostile to justice. By admitting, therefore, that pleasure is the end [of our actions], justice is evidently destroyed. For to whom is it not manifest that justice is increased through abstinence? For he who abstains from every thing animated, though he may abstain from such animals as do not contribute to the benefit of society, will be much more careful not to injure those of his own species. For he who loves the genus, will not hate any species of animals; and by how much the greater his love of the genus is[a], by so much the more will he preserve justice towards a part of the genus, and that to which he is allied. He, therefore, who admits that he is allied to all animals, will not injure any animal. But he who confines justice to man alone, is prepared, like one enclosed in a narrow space, to hurl from him the prohibition of injustice. So that the Pythagorean is more pleasing than the Socratic banquet. For Socrates

---

[a] In the original, οσω μειζον το γενος το των ζωων, τοσουτω και προς το μερος και το οικειον ταυτην διασωσει. On this passage, Reisk observes, " Forte οσω μειζων η οικειωσις προς το γενος το των ζωων, τοσουτω (scilicet μαλλον) και προς το μερος, κ.τ.λ." But, instead of η οικειωσις, it appears to me that η φιλια should be substituted.

said, that hunger is the sauce of food; but Pythagoras said, that to injure no one, and to be exhilarated with justice, is the sweetest sauce; as the avoidance of animal food, will also be the avoidance of unjust conduct with respect to food. For God has not so constituted things, that we cannot preserve ourselves without injuring others; since, if this were the case, he would have connected us with a nature which is the principle of injustice. Do not they, however, appear to be ignorant of the peculiarity of justice, who think that it was introduced from the alliance of men to each other? For this will be nothing more than a certain philanthropy; but justice consists in abstaining from injuring any thing which is not noxious. And our conception of the just man must be formed according to the latter, and not according to the former mode. Hence, therefore, since justice consists in not injuring any thing, it must be extended as far as to every animated nature. On this account, also, the essence of justice consists in the rational ruling over the irrational, and in the irrational being obedient to the rational part. For when reason governs, and the irrational part is obedient to its mandates, it follows, by the greatest necessity, that man will be innoxious towards every thing. For the passions being restrained, and desire and anger wasting away, but reason possessing its proper empire, a similitude to a more excellent nature [and to deity] immediately follows. But the more excellent nature in the universe is entirely innoxious, and, through possessing a power which preserves and benefits all things, is itself not in want of any thing. We, however, through justice [when we exercise it], are innoxious towards all things, but, through being connected with mortality, are indigent of things of a necessary nature. But the assumption of what is necessary, does not injure even plants, when we take what they cast off; nor fruits, when we use such of them as are dead; nor sheep, when through shearing we rather benefit than injure them, and by partaking of their milk, we in return afford them every proper attention. Hence, the just man appears to be one who deprives himself of things pertaining to the body; yet he does not [in reality] injure himself. For, by this management of his body, and continence, he increases his inward good, *i.e.* his similitude to God.

27. By making pleasure, therefore, the end of life, that which is truly justice cannot be preserved; since neither such things as are primarily useful according to nature, nor all such as are easily attainable, give completion to felicity. For in many instances, the motions of the irrational nature, and utility and indigence, have been, and still are the sources of injustice. For men became indigent [as they pretended] of animal food, in order that they might preserve, as they said, the corporeal frame free from molestation, and without being in want of those things after which the animal nature aspires. But if an assimilation to divinity is the end of life, an innoxious conduct towards all things will be in the most eminent degree preserved. As, therefore, he who is led by his passions is innoxious only towards his children and his wife, but despises and acts fraudulently towards other persons, since, in consequence of the irrational part predominating in him, he is excited to, and astonished about mortal concerns; but he who is led by reason, preserves an innoxious conduct towards his fellow-citizens, and still more so towards strangers, and towards all men, through having the irrational part in subjection, and is therefore more rational and divine than the former character;—thus also, he who does not confine harmless conduct to men alone, but extends it to other animals, is more similar to divinity; and if it was possible to extend it even to plants, he would preserve this image in a still greater degree. As, however, this is not possible, we may in this respect lament, with the ancients[t], the defect of our nature, that we consist of such adverse and discordant principles, so that we are unable to preserve our

---

[t] Porphyry here particularly alludes to Empedocles.

divine part incorruptible, and in all respects innoxious. For we are not unindigent in all things; the cause of which is generation, and our becoming needy through the abundant corporeal efflux which we sustain. But want procures safety and ornament from things of a foreign nature, which are necessary to the existence of our mortal part.' He, therefore, who is indigent of a greater number of externals, is in a greater degree agglutinated to penury; and by how much his wants increase, by so much is he destitute of divinity, and an associate of penury. For that which is similar to deity, through this assimilation immediately possesses true wealth. But no one who is [truly] rich and perfectly unindigent injures any thing. For as long as any one injures another, though he should possess the greatest wealth, and all the acres of land which the earth contains, he is still poor, and has want for his intimate associate. On this account, also, he is unjust, without God, and impious, and enslaved to every kind of depravity, which is produced by the lapse of the soul into matter, through the privation of good. Every thing, therefore, is nugatory to any one, as long as he wanders from the principle of the universe; and he is indigent of all things, while he does not direct his attention to Porus [or the source of true abundance]. He likewise yields to the mortal part of his nature, while he remains ignorant of his real self. But Injustice is powerful in persuading and corrupting those that belong to her empire, because she associates with her votaries in conjunction with Pleasure. As, however, in the choice of lives, he is the more accurate judge who has obtained an experience of both [the better and the worse kind of life], than he is who has only experienced one of them; thus also, in the choice and avoidance of what is proper, he is a safer judge who, from that which is more, judges of that which is less excellent, than he who from the less, judges of the more excellent. Hence, he who lives according to intellect, will more accurately define what is eligible and what is not, than he who lives under the dominion of irrationality. For the former has passed through the irrational life, as having from the first associated with it; but the latter, having had no experience of an intellectual life, persuades those that resemble himself, and acts with nugacity, like a child among children. If, however, say our opponents, all men were persuaded by these arguments, what would become of us? Is it not evident that we should be happy, injustice, indeed, being exterminated from men, and justice being conversant with us, in the same manner as it is in the heavens? But now this question is just the same as if men should be dubious what the life of the Danaids would be, if they were liberated from the employment of drawing water in a sieve, and attempting to fill a perforated vessel. For they are dubious what would be the consequence if we should cease to replenish our passions and desires, the whole of which replenishing continually flows away through the want of real good; since this fills up the ruinous clefts of the soul more than the greatest of external necessaries. Do you therefore ask, O man, what we should do? We should imitate those that lived in the golden age, we should imitate those of that period who were [truly] free. For with them modesty, Nemesis, and Justice associated, because they were satisfied with the fruits of the earth.

> The fertile earth for them spontaneous yields
> Abundantly her fruits ª.

But those who are liberated from slavery, obtain for themselves what they before procured for their masters. In like manner, also, do you, when liberated from the servitude of the body, and a slavish attention to the passions produced through the body, as, prior to this, you nourished them in an all-various manner with externals, so now nourish yourself all-variously with internal good, justly assuming things which are [properly] your own, and no longer by violence taking away things which are foreign [to your true nature and real good].

ª Hesiod. Oper. v. 117.

ON

ABSTINENCE FROM ANIMAL FOOD.

BOOK THE FOURTH.

1. In the preceding books, O Castricius, we have nearly answered all the arguments which in reality defend the feeding on flesh, for the sake of incontinence and intemperance, and which adduce impudent apologies for so doing by ascribing a greater indigence to our nature than is fit. Two particular inquiries, however, still remain; in one of which the promise of advantage especially deceives those who are corrupted by pleasure. And, moreover, we shall confute the assertion of our opponents, that no wise man, nor any nation, has rejected animal food, as it leads those that hear it to great injustice, through the ignorance of true history; and we shall also endeavour to give the solutions of the question concerning advantage, and to reply to other inquiries.

2. But we shall begin from the abstinence of certain nations, in the narration of which, what is asserted of the Greeks will first claim our attention, as being the most allied to us, and the most appropriate of all the witnesses that can be adduced. Among those, therefore, that have concisely, and at the same time accurately collected an account of the affairs of the Greeks, is the Peripatetic Dicæarchus[a], who, in narrating the pristine life of the Greeks, says, the

---

[a] There were many celebrated men of this name among the ancients, concerning which vid. Fabric. Biblioth. Græc. L. III. c. 11.

ancients, being generated with an alliance to the Gods, were naturally most excellent, and led the best life; so that, when compared to us of the present day, who consist of an adulterated and most vile matter, they were thought to be a golden race; and they slew no animal whatever. The truth of this, he also says, is testified by the poets, who denominate these ancients the golden race, and assert that every good was present with them.

> The fertile earth for them spontaneous bore
> Of fruits a copious and unenvy'd store;
> In blissful quiet then, unknown to strife,
> The worthy with the worthy passed their life[b].

Which assertions, indeed, Dicæarchus explaining, says, that a life of this kind was under Saturn; if it is proper to consider it as a thing that once existed, and that it is a life which has not been celebrated in vain, and if, laying aside what is extremely fabulous, we may refer it to a physical narration. All things, therefore, are very properly said to have been then spontaneously produced; for

---

[b] These lines are from Hesiod. Oper. 116. The different ages, however, of mankind, which are celebrated by Hesiod in his Works and Days, signify the different lives which the individuals of the human species pass through; and as Proclus on Hesiod beautifully observes, they may be comprehended in this triad, the *golden*, the *silver*, and the *brazen* age. But by the *golden* age an intellectual life is implied. For such a life is pure, impassive, and free from sorrow; and of this impassivity and purity, gold is an image, through never being subject to rust or putrefaction. Such a life, too, is very properly said to be under Saturn, because Saturn is an *intellectual* God, or a God characterised by intellect. By the *silver* age, a rustic and natural life is implied, in which the attention of the rational soul is entirely directed to the care of the body, but without proceeding to extreme depravity. And by the *brazen* age, a dire, tyrannic, and cruel life is implied, which is entirely passive, and proceeds to the very extremity of vice. The order, also, of these metals, harmonizes, as Proclus observes, with that of the lives. "For," says he, "*gold* is *solar-form*, because the sun is solely immaterial light. But *silver* is *lunar-form*, because the moon partakes of shadow, just as silver partakes of rust. And *brass* is *earthly*, so far as not having a nature similar to a lucid body; it is replete with abundance of corruption."

men did not procure any thing by labour, because they were unacquainted with the agricultural art, and, in short, had no knowledge of any other art. This very thing, likewise, was the cause of their leading a life of leisure, free from labours and care; and if it is proper to assent to the decision of the most skilful and elegant of physicians, it was also the cause of their being liberated from disease. *For there is not any precept of physicians which more contributes to health, than that which exhorts us not to make an abundance of excrement,* from which those pristine Greeks always preserved their bodies pure. For they neither assumed such food as was stronger than the nature of the body could bear, but such as could be vanquished by the corporeal nature, nor more than was moderate, on account of the facility of procuring it, but for the most part less than was sufficient, on account of its paucity. Moreover, there were neither any wars among them, nor seditions with each other. For no reward of contention worth mentioning was proposed as an incentive, for the sake of which some one might be induced to engage in such dissensions. So that the principal thing in that life was leisure and rest from necessary occupations, together with health, peace, and friendship. But to those in after times, who, through aspiring after things which greatly exceeded mediocrity, fell into many evils, this pristine life became, as it was reasonable to suppose it would, desirable. The slender and extemporaneous food, however, of these first men, is manifested by the saying which was afterwards proverbially used, *enough of the oak;* this adage being probably introduced by him who first changed the ancient mode of living. A pastoral life succeeded to this, in which men procured for themselves superfluous possessions, and meddled with animals. For, perceiving that some of them were innoxious, but others malefic and savage, they tamed the former, but attacked the latter. At the same time, together with this life, war was introduced. And these things, says Dicæarchus, are not asserted by us, but by those who have historically discussed a multitude of particulars. For, as possessions were now of such a magnitude as to merit attention, some ambitiously endeavoured to obtain them, by collecting them [for their own use], and calling on others to do the same, but others directed their attention to the preservation of them when collected. Time, therefore, thus gradually proceeding, and men always directing their attention to what appeared to be useful, they at length became conversant with the third, and agricultural form of life. And this is what is said by Dicæarchus, in his narration of the manners of the ancient Greeks, and the blessed life which they then led, to which abstinence from animal food contributed, no less than other things. Hence, at that period there was no war, because injustice was exterminated. But afterwards, together with injustice towards animals, war was introduced among men, and the endeavour to surpass each other in amplitude of possessions. On which account also, the audacity of those is wonderful, who say that abstinence from animals is the mother of injustice, since both history and experience testify, that together with the slaughter of animals, war and injustice were introduced.

3. Hence, this being afterwards perceived by the Lacedemonian Lycurgus, though the eating of animals then prevailed, yet he so arranged his polity, as to render food of this kind requisite in the smallest degree. For the allotted property of each individual did not consist in herds of oxen, flocks of sheep, or an abundance of goats, horses, and money, but in the possession of land, which might produce for a man seventy medimni[c] of barley, and for a woman twelve, and the quantity of liquid fruits in the same proportion. For he thought that this quantity of nutriment was sufficient to procure a good habit of body and health, nothing else to obtain these being requisite. Whence also it is said, that on returning to his country,

---

[c] The medimnus was a measure containing six bushels.

after he had been for some time absent from it, and perceiving, as he passed through the fields, that the corn had just been reaped, and that the threshing-floors and the heaps were parallel and equable, he laughed, and said to those that were present, that all Laconia seemed to belong to many brothers, who had just divided the land among themselves. He added, that as he had therefore expelled luxury from Sparta, it would be requisite also to annul the use of money, both golden and silver, and to introduce iron alone, as its substitute, and this of a great bulk and weight, and of little value; so that as much of it as should be worth ten minæ, should require a large receptacle to hold it, and a cart drawn by two oxen to carry it. But this being ordained, many species of injustice were exterminated from Lacedæmon. For who would attempt to thieve, or suffer himself to be corrupted by gifts, or defraud or plunder another, when it was not possible for him to conceal what he had taken, nor possess it so as to be envied by others, nor derive any advantage from coining it? Together with money also, the useless arts were expelled, the works of the Lacedæmonians not being saleable. For iron money could not be exported to the other Greeks, nor was it esteemed by them, but ridiculed. Hence, neither was it lawful to buy any thing foreign, and which was intrinsically of no worth, nor did ships laden with merchandise sail into their ports, nor was any verbal sophist, or futile diviner, or bawd, or artificer of golden and silver ornaments, permitted to come to Laconia, because there money was of no use. And thus luxury, being gradually deprived of its incitements and nourishment, wasted away of itself. Those likewise who possessed much derived no greater advantage from it, than those who did not, as no egress was afforded to abundance, since it was so obstructed by impediments, that it was forced to remain in indolent rest. Hence such household furniture as was in constant use, and was necessary, such as beds, chairs, and tables, these were made by them in the best manner; and the

Laconic cup, which was called *cothon*, was, as Critias says, especially celebrated in military expeditions. For in these expeditions, the water which they drank, and which was unpleasant to the sight, was concealed by the colour of the cup; and the turbid part of the water falling against the lips, through their prominency, that part of it which was drank, was received in a purer condition by the mouth. As we are informed, however, by Plutarch, the legislator was the cause of these things. For the artificers being liberated from useless works, exhibited the beauty of art in things of a necessary nature.

4. That he might also in a still greater degree oppose luxury, and take away the ardent endeavour to obtain wealth, he introduced a third, and most beautiful political institution, viz. that of the citizens eating and drinking together publicly; so that they might partake of the same prescribed food in common, and might not be fed at home, reclining on sumptuous couches, and placed before elegant tables, through the hands of artificers and cooks, being fattened in darkness, like voracious animals, and corrupting their bodies, together with their morals, by falling into every kind of luxury and repletion; as such a mode of living would require much sleep, hot baths, and abundant quiet, and such attentions as are paid to the diseased. This indeed was a great thing; but still greater than this, that, as Theophrastus says, he caused wealth to be neglected, and to be of no value, through the citizens eating at common tables, and the frugality of their food. For there was no use, nor enjoyment of riches; nor, in short, was there any thing to gratify the sight, or any ostentatious display in the whole apparatus, because both the poor and the rich sat at the same table. Hence it was universally said, that in Sparta alone, Plutus was seen to be blind, and lying like an inanimate and immoveable picture. For it was not possible for the citizens, having previously feasted at home, to go to the common tables with appetites already satiated with food. For the rest care-

fully observed him who did not eat and drink with them, and reviled him, as an intemperate person, and as one who conducted himself effeminately with respect to the common food. Hence these common tables were called *phiditia*; either as being the causes of friendship and benevolence, as if they were *philitia*, assuming δ for λ; or as accustoming men [προς ευτελειαν και φειδω] to frugality, and a slender diet. But the number of those that assembled at the common table was fifteen, more or less. And each person brought every month, for the purpose of furnishing the table, a medimnus of flour, eight choas.[d] of wine, five pounds of cheese, two pounds and a half of figs, and, besides all these, a very little quantity of money.

5. Hence the children of those who ate thus sparingly and temperately, came to these common tables, as to schools of temperance, where they also heard political discourses, and were spectators of liberal sports. Here, likewise, they learnt to jest acrimoniously, without scurrility, and to receive, without being indignant, the biting jests of others. For this appeared to be extremely Laconic, to be able to endure acrimonious jests; though he who could not endure was permitted to refuse hearing them, and the scoffer was immediately silent. Such, therefore, was the frugality of the Lacedæmonians, with respect to diet, though it was legally instituted for the sake of the multitude. Hence those who came from this polity are said to have been more brave and temperate, and paid more attention to rectitude, than those who came from other communities, which are corrupted both in souls and bodies. And it is evident that perfect abstinence is adapted to such a polity as this, but to corrupt communities luxurious food[e]. If, likewise, we

---

[d] An Attic measure, containing six Attic pints.

[e] In the original, και δηλον ως τοιαυτη πολιτεια οικειον, το της αποχης της παντελους, ταις δε διεφθαρμεναις, το της βρωσεως. But the latter part of this sentence is evidently defective, though the defect is not noticed either by Valentinus, or Reiske, or Rhoer. It appears therefore to me, that

direct our attention to such other nations as regarded equity, mildness, and piety to the Gods, it will be evident that abstinence was ordained by them, with a view to the safety and advantage, if not of all, yet at least of some of the citizens, who, sacrificing to, and worshipping the Gods, on account of the city, might expiate the sins of the multitude. For, in the mysteries, what the boy who attends the altar accomplishes, by performing accurately what he is commanded to do, in order to render the Gods propitious to all those who have been initiated, as far as to *muesis*[f] [αντι παντων των μυουμενων], that, in nations and cities, priests are able to effect, by sacrificing for all the people, and through piety inducing the Gods to be attentive to the welfare of those that belong to them. With respect to priests, therefore, the eating of all animals is prohibited to some, but of certain animals to others, whether you consider the customs of the Greeks or of the barbarians, which are different in different nations. So that all of them, collectively considered, or existing as one, being assumed, it will be found that they abstain from all animals. If, therefore, those who preside over the safety of cities, and to whose care piety to the Gods is committed, abstain from animals, how can any one dare to accuse this abstinence as disadvantageous to cities?

6. Chæremon the Stoic, therefore, in his narration of the Egyptian priests, who, he says, were considered by the Egyptians as philosophers, informs us, that they chose temples, as the places in which they might philoso-

---

της τρυφης is wanting; so that for το της βρωσεως, we should read το της τρυφης της βρωσεως. And my conjecture is justified by the version of Felicianus, which is, " Huic autem abstinentiam, cæteris *luxuriam* victus fuisse peculiarem perspicuum est."

[f] Those who, in being initiated, *closed the eyes*, which *muesis* signifies, no longer (says Hermias in Phædrum) received by sense those divine mysteries, but with the pure soul itself. See my Dissertation on the Eleusinian and Bacchic Mysteries.

phize. For to dwell with the statues of the Gods is a thing allied to the whole desire, by which the soul tends to the contemplation of their divinities. And from the divine veneration indeed, which was paid to them through dwelling in temples, they obtained security, all men honouring these philosophers, as if they were certain sacred animals. They also led a solitary life, as they only mingled with other men in solemn sacrifices and festivals. But at other times the priests were almost inaccessible to any one who wished to converse with them. For it was requisite that he who approached to them should be first purified, and abstain from many things; and this is as it were a common sacred law respecting the Egyptian priests. But these [philosophic priests], having relinquished every other employment, and human labours[g], gave up the whole of their life to the contemplation and worship of divine natures and to divine inspiration; through the latter, indeed, procuring for themselves honour, security, and piety; but through contemplation science; and through both, a certain occult exercise of manners, worthy of antiquity[h]. For to be always conversant with divine knowledge and inspiration, removes those who are so from all avarice, suppresses the passions, and excites to an intellectual life. But they were studious of frugality in their diet and apparel, and also of continence and endurance, and in all things were attentive to justice and equity. They likewise were rendered venerable, through rarely mingling with other men. For during the time of what are called purifications, they scarcely mingled with their nearest kindred, and those of their own order; nor were they to be seen by any one, unless it was requisite

[g] In the original, και πορους ανθρωπινους; but for πορους I read πονους, and Felicianus appears to have found the same reading in his MS.; for his version is, "laboribusque humanis." Neither Reisk, however, nor Rhoer, have at all noticed the word πορους as improper in this place.

[h] Much is related about the Egyptian priests by Herodotus, lib. ii. 37. With respect to Chæremon, the decisions of the ancients concerning him are very discordant.

for the necessary purposes of purification. For the sanctuary was inaccessible to those who were not purified, and they dwelt in holy places for the purpose of performing divine works; but at all other times they associated more freely with those who lived like themselves. They did not, however, associate with any one who was not a religious character. But they were always seen near to the Gods, or to the statues of the Gods, the latter of which they were beheld either carrying, or preceding in a sacred procession, or disposing in an orderly manner, with modesty and gravity; each of which operations was not the effect of pride, but an indication of some physical reason. Their venerable gravity also was apparent from their manners. For their walking was orderly, and their aspect sedate; and they were so studious of preserving this gravity of countenance, that they did not even wink, when at any time they were unwilling to do so; and they seldom laughed, and when they did, their laughter proceeded no farther than to a smile. But they always kept their hands within their garments. Each likewise bore about him a symbol, indicative of the order which he was allotted in sacred concerns; for there were many orders of priests. Their diet also was slender and simple. For, with respect to wine, some of them did not at all drink it, but others drank very little of it, on account of its being injurious to the nerves, oppressive to the head, an impediment to invention, and an incentive to venereal desires. In many other things also they conducted themselves with caution; neither using bread at all in purifications, and at those times in which they were not employed in purifying themselves, they were accustomed to eat bread with hyssop, cut into small pieces. For it is said, that hyssop very much purifies the power of bread. But they, for the most part, abstained from oil, the greater number of them entirely; and if at any time they used it with pot-herbs, they took very little of it, and only as much as was sufficient to mitigate the taste of the herbs.

7. It was not lawful for them therefore to meddle with the esculent and potable substances, which were produced out of Egypt, and this contributed much to the exclusion of luxury from these priests. But they abstained from all the fish that was caught in Egypt, and from such quadrupeds as had solid, or many-fissured hoofs, and from such as were not horned; and likewise from all such birds as were carnivorous. Many of them, however, entirely abstained from all animals; and in purifications this abstinence was adopted by all of them, for then they did not even eat an egg. Moreover, they also rejected other things, without being calumniated for so doing. Thus, for instance, of oxen, they rejected the females, and also such of the males as were twins, or were speckled, or of a different colour, or alternately varied in their form, or which were now tamed, as having been already consecrated to labours, and resembled animals that are honoured, or which were the images of any thing [that is divine], or those that had but one eye, or those that verged to a similitude of the human form. There are also innumerable other observations pertaining to the art of those who are called μοσχοϕραγισται, or who stamp calves with a seal, and of which books have been composed. But these observations are still more curious respecting birds; as, for instance, that a turtle should not be eaten; for it is said that a hawk frequently dismisses this bird after he has seized it, and preserves its life, as a reward for having had connexion with it. The Egyptian priests, therefore, that they might not ignorantly meddle with a turtle of this kind, avoided the whole species of those birds. And these indeed were certain common religious ceremonies; but there were different ceremonies, which varied according to the class of the priests that used them, and were adapted to the several divinities. But chastity and purifications were common to all the priests. When also the time arrived in which they were to perform something pertaining to the sacred rites of religion, they spent some days in preparatory ceremonies,

some indeed forty-two, but others a greater, and others a less number of days; yet never less than seven days; and during this time they abstained from all animals, and likewise from all pot-herbs and leguminous substances, and, above all, from a venereal connexion with women; for they never at any time had connexion with males. They likewise washed themselves with cold water thrice every day; viz. when they rose from their bed, before dinner, and when they betook themselves to sleep. But if they happened to be polluted in their sleep by the emission of the seed, they immediately purified their body in a bath. They also used cold bathing at other times, but not so frequently as on the above occasion. Their bed was woven from the branches of the palm tree, which they call *bais;* and their bolster was a smooth semi-cylindric piece of wood. But they exercised themselves in the endurance of hunger and thirst, and were accustomed to paucity of food through the whole of their life.

8. This also is a testimony of their continence, that, though they neither exercised themselves in walking or riding, yet they lived free from disease, and were sufficiently strong for the endurance of moderate labours. They bore therefore many burdens in the performance of sacred operations, and accomplished many ministrant works, which required more than common strength. But they divided the night into the observation of the celestial bodies, and sometimes devoted a part of it to offices of purification; and they distributed the day into the worship of the Gods, according to which they celebrated them with hymns thrice or four times, viz. in the morning and evening, when the sun is at his meridian altitude, and when he is declining to the west. The rest of their time they devoted to arithmetical and geometrical speculations, always labouring to effect something, and to make some new discovery, and, in short, continually exercising their skill. In winter nights also they were occupied in the same employments, being vigilantly engaged in literary

pursuits, as paying no attention to the acquisition of externals, and being liberated from the servitude of that bad master, excessive expense. Hence their unwearied and incessant labour testifies their endurance, but their continence is manifested by their liberation from the desire of external good. To sail from Egypt likewise, [i. e., to quit Egypt,] was considered by them to be one of the most unholy things, in consequence of their being careful to avoid foreign luxury and pursuits; for this appeared to them to be alone lawful to those who were compelled to do so by regal necessities. Indeed, they were very anxious to continue in the observance of the institutes of their country, and those who were found to have violated them, though but in a small degree, were expelled [from the college of the priests]. The true method of philosophizing, likewise, was preserved by the prophets, by the *hierostolistæ*[i], and the sacred scribes, and also by the *horologi*, or calculators of nativities. But the rest of the priests, and of the pastophori[k], curators of temples, and ministers of the Gods, were similarly studious of purity, yet not so accurately, and with such great continence, as the priests of whom we have been speaking. And such are the particulars which are narrated of the Egyptians, by a man who was a lover of truth, and an accurate writer, and who among the Stoics strenuously and solidly philosophized.

9. But the Egyptian priests, through the proficiency which they made by this exercise, and similitude to divinity, knew that divinity does not pervade through man alone, and that soul is not enshrined in man alone on the earth, but that it nearly passes through all animals. On this account, in fashioning the images of the Gods, they assumed every animal, and for this purpose mixed together the human form and the forms of wild beasts, and again the bodies of birds with the body of a

---

[i] *i. e.* Those to whose care the sacred vestments were committed.

[k] These were so denominated from carrying the little receptacles in which the images of the Gods were contained.

man. For a certain deity was represented by them in a human shape as far as to the neck, but the face was that of a bird, or a lion, or of some other animal. And again, another divine resemblance had a human head, but the other parts were those of certain other animals, some of which had an inferior, but others a superior position; through which they manifested, that these [*i. e.* brutes and men], through the decision of the Gods, communicated with each other, and that tame and savage animals are nurtured together with us, not without the concurrence of a certain divine will. Hence also, a lion is worshipped as a God, and a certain part of Egypt, which is called Nomos, has the surname of Leontopolis [or the city of the lion], and another is denominated Busiris [from an ox], and another Lycopolis [or the city of the wolf]. For they venerated the power of God which extends to all things through animals which are nurtured together, and which each of the Gods imparts. They also reverenced water and fire the most of all the elements, as being the principal causes of our safety. And these things are exhibited by them in temples; for even now, on opening the sanctuary of Serapis, the worship is performed through fire and water; he who sings the hymns making a libation with water, and exhibiting fire, when, standing on the threshold of the temple, he invokes the God in the language of the Egyptians. Venerating, therefore, these elements, they especially reverence those things which largely participate of them, as partaking more abundantly of what is sacred. But after these, they venerate all animals, and in the village Anubis they worship a man, in which place also they sacrifice to him, and victims are there burnt in honour of him on an altar; but he shortly after only eats that which was procured for him as a man. Hence, as it is requisite to abstain from man, so, likewise, from other animals. And farther still, the Egyptian priests, from their transcendent wisdom and association with divinity, discovered what animals are more acceptable to the Gods [when dedicated to them] than man. Thus they found that a hawk is dear to the sun, since the whole of its nature consists of blood and spirit. It also commiserates man, and laments over his dead body, and scatters earth on his eyes, in which these priests believe a solar light is resident. They likewise discovered that a hawk lives many years, and that, after it leaves the present life, it possesses a divining power, is most rational and prescient when liberated from the body, and gives perfection to statues, and moves temples. A beetle will be detested by one who is ignorant of and unskilled in divine concerns, but the Egyptians venerate it, as an animated image of the sun. For every beetle is a male, and emitting its genital seed in a muddy place, and having made it spherical, it turns round the seminal sphere in a way similar to that of the sun in the heavens. It likewise receives a period of twenty-eight days, which is a lunar period. In a similar manner, the Egyptians philosophize about the ram, the crocodile, the vulture, and the ibis, and, in short, about every animal; so that, from their wisdom and transcendent knowledge of divine concerns, they came at length to venerate all animals[1]. An unlearned man, however, does not even suspect that they, not being borne along with the stream of the vulgar who know nothing, and not walking in the path of ignorance, but passing beyond the illiterate multitude, and that want of knowledge which befals every one at first, were led to reverence things which are thought by the vulgar to be of no worth.

10. This also, no less than the above-mentioned particulars, induced them to believe, that animals should be reverenced [as images of the Gods], viz. that the soul of every animal, when liberated from the body, was discovered by them to be rational, to be prescient of futurity, to possess an oracular power, and to be effective of every thing which man is capable of accomplishing when separated from the body. Hence they very properly

---

[1] See on this subject Plutarch's excellent treatise of Isis and Osiris.

honoured them, and abstained from them as much as possible. Since, however, the cause through which the Egyptians venerated the Gods through animals requires a copious discussion, and which would exceed the limits of the present treatise, what has been unfolded respecting this particular is sufficient for our purpose. Nevertheless, this is not to be omitted, that the Egyptians, when they buried those that were of noble birth, privately took away the belly and placed it in a chest, and together with other things which they performed for the sake of the dead body, they elevated the chest towards the sun, whom they invoked as a witness; an oration for the deceased being at the same time made by one of those to whose care the funeral was committed. But the oration which Euphantus[m] has interpreted from the Egyptian tongue was as follows: " O sovereign Sun, and all ye Gods who impart life to men, receive me, and deliver me to the eternal Gods as a cohabitant. For I have always piously worshipped those divinities which were pointed out to me by my parents as long as I lived in this age, and have likewise always honoured those who procreated my body. And, with respect to other men, I have never slain any one, nor defrauded any one of what he deposited with me, nor have I committed any other atrocious deed. If, therefore, during my life I have acted erroneously, by eating or drinking things which it is unlawful to eat or drink, I have not erred through myself, but through these," pointing to the chest in which the belly was contained. And having thus spoken, he threw the chest into the river [Nile]; but buried the rest of the body as being pure. After this manner, they thought an apology ought to be made to divinity for what they had eaten and drank, and for the insolent conduct which they had been led to through the belly.

---

[m] Fabricius is of opinion, that this *Euphantus* is the same with the *Ecphantus* mentioned by Iamblichus (in Vit. Pyth.) as one of the Pythagoreans. Vid. Fabric. Bibl. Græc. lib. ii. c. 13.

11. But among those who are known by us, the Jews, before they first suffered the subversion of their legal institutes under Antiochus, and afterwards under the Romans, when also the temple in Jerusalem was captured, and became accessible to all men to whom, prior to this event, it was inaccessible, and the city itself was destroyed;—before this took place, the Jews always abstained from many animals, but peculiarly, which they even now do, from swine. At that period, therefore, there were three kinds of philosophers among them. And of one kind, indeed, the Pharisees were the leaders, but of another, the Sadducees, and of the third, which appears to have been the most venerable, the Essæans. The mode of life, therefore, of these third was as follows, as Josephus frequently testifies in many of his writings. For in the second book of his Judaic History, which he has completed in seven books, and in the eighteenth of his Antiquities, which consists of twenty books, and likewise in the second of the two books which he wrote against the Greeks, he speaks of these Essæans, and says, that they are of the race of the Jews, and are in a greater degree than others friendly to one another. They are averse to pleasures, conceiving them to be vicious, but they are of opinion that continence, and the not yielding to the passions, constitute virtue. And they despise, indeed, wedlock, but receiving the children of other persons, and instructing them in disciplines while they are yet of a tender age, they consider them as their kindred, and form them to their own manners. And they act in this manner, not for the purpose of subverting marriage, and the succession arising from it, but in order to avoid the lasciviousness of women. They are, likewise, despisers of wealth, and the participation of external possessions among them in common is wonderful; nor is any one to be found among them who is richer than the rest. For it is a law with them, that those who wish to belong to their sect, must give up their property to it in common; so that among all of them, there is not to be seen either the abjectness of poverty, or the insolence of wealth; but the posses-

sions of each being mingled with those of the rest, there was one property with all of them, as if they had been brothers. They likewise conceived oil to be a stain to the body, and that if any one, though unwillingly, was anointed, he should [immediately] wipe his body. For it was considered by them as beautiful to be squalid[n], and to be always clothed in white garments. But curators of the common property were elected by votes, indistinctly for the use of all. They have not, however, one city, but in each city many of them dwell together, and those who come among them from other places, if they are of their sect, equally partake with them of their possessions, as if they were their own. Those, likewise, who first perceive these strangers, behave to them as if they were their intimate acquaintance. Hence, when they travel, they take nothing with them for the sake of expenditure. But they neither change their garments nor their shoes, till they are entirely torn, or destroyed by time. They neither buy nor sell any thing, but each of them giving what he possesses to him that is in want, receives in return for it what will be useful to him. Nevertheless, each of them freely imparts to others of their sect what they may be in want of, without any remuneration.

12. Moreover, they are peculiarly pious to divinity. For before the sun rises they speak nothing profane, but they pour forth certain prayers to him which they had received from their ancestors, as if beseeching him to rise. Afterwards, they are sent by their curators to the exercise of the several arts in which they are skilled, and having till the fifth hour strenuously laboured in these arts, they are afterwards collected together in one place; and there, being begirt with linen teguments, they wash their bodies with cold water. After this purification, they enter into their own

---

[n] This is not wonderful; for the Jews appear to have been always negligent of cleanliness. The intelligent reader will easily perceive that there is some similitude between these Essæans and the ancient Pythagoreans, but that the latter were infinitely superior to the former. See my translation of Iamblichus' Life of Pythagoras.

proper habitation, into which no heterodox person is permitted to enter. But they being pure, betake themselves to the dining room, as into a certain sacred fane. In this place, when all of them are seated in silence, the baker places the bread in order, and the cook distributes to each of them one vessel containing one kind of eatables. Prior, however, to their taking the food which is pure and sacred, a priest prays, and it is unlawful for any one prior to the prayer to taste of the food. After dinner, likewise, the priest again prays; so that both when they begin, and when they cease to eat, they venerate divinity. Afterwards, divesting themselves of these garments as sacred, they again betake themselves to their work till the evening; and, returning from thence, they eat and drink in the same manner as before, strangers sitting with them, if they should happen at that time to be present. No clamour or tumult ever defiles the house in which they dwell; but their conversation with each other is performed in an orderly manner; and to those that are out of the house, the silence of those within it appears as if it was some terrific mystery. The cause, however, of this quietness is their constant sobriety, and that with them their meat and drink is measured by what is sufficient [to the wants of nature]. But those who are very desirous of belonging to their sect, are not immediately admitted into it, but they must remain out of it for a year, adopting the same diet, the Essæans giving them a rake; a girdle, and a white garment. And if, during that time, they have given a sufficient proof of their continence, they proceed to a still greater conformity to the institutes of the sect, and use purer water for the purposes of sanctity; though they are not yet permitted to live with the Essæans. For after this exhibition of endurance, their manners are tried for two years more, and he who after this period appears to deserve to associate with them, is admitted into their society.

13. Before, however, he who is admitted touches his common food, he takes a terrible oath, in the first place,

that he will piously worship divinity; in the next place, that he will preserve justice towards men, and that he will neither designedly, nor when commanded, injure any one; in the third place, that he will always hate the unjust, but strenuously assist the just; and in the fourth place, that he will act faithfully towards all men, but especially towards the rulers of the land, since no one becomes a ruler without the permission of God; in the fifth place, that if he should be a ruler, he will never employ his power to insolently iniquitous purposes, nor will surpass those that are in subjection to him in his dress, or any other more splendid ornament; in the sixth place, that he will always love the truth, and be hostile to liars; in the seventh place, that he will preserve his hands from theft, and his soul pure from unholy gain°; and, in the eighth place, that he will conceal nothing from those of his sect, nor divulge any thing to others pertaining to the sect, though some one, in order to compel him, should threaten him with death. In addition to these things, also, they swear, that they will not impart the dogmas of the sect to any one in any other way than that in which they received them; that they will likewise abstain from robbery^p, and preserve the books of their sect with the same care as the names of the angels. Such, therefore, are their oaths. But those among them that act criminally, and are ejected, perish by an evil destiny. For, being bound by their oaths and their customs, they are not capable of receiving food from others; but feeding on herbs, and having their body emaciated by hunger, they perish. Hence the Essæans, commiserating many of these unfortunate men, receive them in their last extremities into their society, thinking that they have suffered sufficiently for their offences in having

---

° This was a very necessary oath for these Essæans to take; as the Jews in general, if we may believe Tacitus and other ancient historians, were always a people immoderately addicted to gain.

ᵖ As the Essæans appear to have been an exception to the rest of the Jews, the reason is obvious why they took this oath.

been punished for them till they were on the brink of the grave. But they give a rake to those who intend to belong to their sect, in order that, when they sit for the purpose of exonerating the belly, they may make a trench a foot in depth, and completely cover themselves by their garment, in order that they may not act contumeliously towards the sun by polluting the rays of the God. And so great, indeed, is their simplicity and frugality with respect to diet, that they do not require evacuation till the seventh day after the assumption of food, which day they spend in singing hymns to God, and in resting from labour. But from this exercise they acquire the power of such great endurance, that even when tortured and burnt, and suffering every kind of excruciating pain, they cannot be induced either to blaspheme their legislator, or to eat what they have not been accustomed to. And the truth of this was demonstrated in their war with the Romans. For then they neither flattered their tormentors, nor shed any tears, but smiled in the midst of their torments, and derided those that inflicted them, and cheerfully emitted their souls, as knowing that they should possess them again. For this opinion was firmly established among them, that their bodies were indeed corruptible, and that the matter of which they consisted was not stable, but that their souls were immortal, and would endure for ever, and that, proceeding from the most subtle ether, they were drawn down by a natural flux, and complicated with bodies; but that, when they are no longer detained by the bonds of the flesh, then, as if liberated from a long slavery, they will rejoice, and ascend to the celestial regions. But from this mode of living, and from being thus exercised in truth and piety, there were many among them, as it is reasonable to suppose there would be, who had a foreknowledge of future events, as being conversant from their youth with sacred books, different purifications, and the declarations of the prophets. And such is the order [or sect] of the Essæans among the Jews.

14. All of them, however, were forbidden to eat the flesh of swine, or fish without scales, which the Greeks call σελαχια, *i. e. cartilaginous;* or to eat any animal that has solid hoofs. They were likewise forbidden not only to refrain from eating, but also from killing animals that fled to their houses as supplicants. Nor did the legislator permit them to slay such animals as were parents together with their young; but ordered them to spare, even in a hostile land, and not put to death brutes that assist us in our labours. Nor was the legislator afraid that the race of animals which are not sacrificed, would, through being spared from slaughter, be so increased in multitude as to produce famine among men; for he knew, in the first place, that multiparous animals live but for a short time; and in the next place, that many of them perish, unless attention is paid to them by men. Moreover, he likewise knew that other animals would attack those that increased excessively; of which this is an indication, that we abstain from many animals, such as lizards, worms, flies, serpents, and dogs, and yet, at the same time, we are not afraid of perishing through hunger by abstaining from them, though their increase is abundant. And in the next place, it is not the same thing to eat and to slay an animal. For we destroy many of the above-mentioned animals, but we do not eat any of them.

15. Farther still, it is likewise related that the Syrians formerly abstained from animals, and, on this account, did not sacrifice them to the Gods; but that afterwards they sacrificed them, for the purpose of averting certain evils; yet they did not at all admit of a fleshly diet. In process of time, however, as Neanthes the Cyzicenean and Asclepiades the Cyprian say, about the era of Pygmalion, who was by birth a Phœnician, but reigned over the Cyprians, the eating of flesh was admitted, from an illegality of the following kind, which Asclepiades, in his treatise concerning Cyprus and Phœnicia, relates as follows:—In the first place, they did not sacrifice any thing animated to the Gods; but neither was there any

law pertaining to a thing of this kind, because it was prohibited by natural law. They are said, however, on a certain occasion, in which one soul was required for another, to have, for the first time, sacrificed a victim; and this taking place, the whole of the victim was then consumed by fire. But afterwards, when the victim was burnt, a portion of the flesh fell on the earth, which was taken by the priest, who, in so doing, having burnt his fingers, involuntarily moved them to his mouth, as a remedy for the pain which the burning produced. Having, therefore, thus tasted of the roasted flesh, he also desired to eat abundantly of it, and could not refrain from giving some of it to his wife. Pygmalion, however, becoming acquainted with this circumstance, ordered both the priest and his wife to be hurled headlong from a steep rock, and gave the priesthood to another person, who not long after performing the same sacrifice, and eating the flesh of the victim, fell into the same calamities as his predecessor. The thing, however, proceeding still farther, and men using the same kind of sacrifice, and through yielding to desire, not abstaining from, but feeding on flesh, the deed was no longer punished. Nevertheless abstinence from fish continued among the Syrians till the time of Menander: for he says,

> The Syrians for example take, since these
> When by intemperance led of fish they eat,
> Swoln in their belly and their feet become.
> With sack then cover'd, in the public way
> They on a dunghill sit, that by their lowly state,
> The Goddess may, appeas'd, the crime forgive.

16. Among the Persians, indeed, those who are wise in divine concerns, and worship divinity, are called Magi; for this is the signification of *Magus*, in the Persian tongue. But so great and so venerable are these men thought to be by the Persians, that Darius, the son of Hystaspes, had among other things this engraved on his tomb, that he had been the master of the Magi. They

are likewise divided into three genera, as we are informed by Eubulus, who wrote the history of Mithra, in a treatise consisting of many books. In this work he says, that the first and most learned class of the Magi neither eat nor slay any thing animated, but adhere to the ancient abstinence from animals. The second class use some animals indeed [for food], but do not slay any that are tame. Nor do those of the third class, similarly with other men, lay their hands on all animals. For the dogma with all of them which ranks as the first is this, that there is a transmigration of souls; and this they also appear to indicate in the mysteries of Mithra. For in these mysteries, obscurely signifying our having something in common with brutes, they are accustomed to call us by the names of different animals. Thus they denominate the males who participate in the same mysteries lions, but the females lionesses, and those who are ministrant to these rites crows. With respect to their fathers also, they adopt the same mode. For these are denominated by them eagles and hawks. And he who is initiated in the Leontic mysteries, is invested with all-various forms of animals[q]; of which particulars, Pallas, in his treatise concerning Mithra, assigning the cause, says, that it is the common opinion that these things are to be referred to the circle of the zodiac, but that truly and accurately speaking, they obscurely signify something pertaining to human souls, which, according to the Per-

---

[q] Similar to this was the garment with which Apuleius was invested after his initiation into the mysteries of Isis, and which he describes as follows:—" There [*i. e.* on a wooden throne] I sat conspicuous, in a garment which was indeed linen, but was elegantly painted. A precious cloak also depended from my shoulders behind my back, as far as to my heels. Nevertheless, to whatever part of me you directed your view, you might see that I was remarkable by the animals which were painted round my vestment, in various colours. Here were Indian dragons, there Hyperborean griffins, which the other hemisphere generates in the form of a winged animal. Men devoted to the service of divinity, call this cloak the Olympic garment."— See Book II. of my translation of the Metamorphosis of Apuleius.

sians, are invested with bodies of all-various forms. For the Latins also, says Eubulus, call some men, in their tongue, boars and scorpions, lizards, and blackbirds. After the same manner likewise the Persians denominate the Gods the demiurgic causes of these: for they call Diana a she-wolf; but the sun, a bull, a lion, a dragon, and a hawk; and Hecate, a horse, a bull, a lioness, and a dog. But most theologists say that the name of Proserpine [της φερεφατης] is derived from nourishing a ringdove, [παρα το φερβειν την φατ7αν]: for the ringdove is sacred to this Goddess[r]. Hence, also, the priests of Maia dedicate

---

[r] Proclus, however, in his Scholia on the Cratylus of Plato, gives a much more theological account of the derivation of the name of Proserpine, as follows:—" Socrates now delivers these three vivific monads in a consequent order, viz. Ceres, Juno, Proserpine; calling the first the mother, the second the sister, and the third the daughter of the Demiurgus [Jupiter]. All of them, however, are partakers of the whole of fabrication; the first in an exempt manner, and intellectually; the second in a fontal manner, and, at the same time, in a way adapted to a principle [αρχικως]; and the third in a manner adapted to a principle and a leader [αρχικως και ηγεμονικως].

Of these Goddesses the last is allotted triple powers, and impartibly and uniformly comprehends three monads of Gods. But she is called Core [κορη] through the purity of her essence, and her undefiled transcendency in her generations. She also possesses a first, middle, and last empire; and according to her summit, indeed, she is called Diana by Orpheus; but, according to her middle, Proserpine; and according to the extremity of the order, Minerva. Likewise, according to an essence transcending the other powers of this triple vivific order, the dominion of Hecate is established; but according to a middle power, and which is generative of wholes, that of soul; and, according to intellectual conversion, that of Virtue[*]. Ceres, therefore, subsisting on high, and among the supermundane Gods, uniformly extends this triple order of divinities; and, together with Jupiter, generates Bacchus, who impartibly presides over partible fabrication. But beneath, in conjunction with Pluto, she is particularly beheld according to the middle characteristic: for it is this which, proceeding every where, imparts vivification to the last of

---

[*] Proclus says this conformably to the theology of the Chaldeans; for, according to that theology, the first monad of the vivific triad is *Hecate*, the second *Soul*, and the third *Virtue*.

to her a ringdove. And Maia is the same with Proserpine, as being obstetric, and a nurse*. For this God-

things. Hence she is called Proserpine, because she especially associates with Pluto, and, together with him, distributes in an orderly manner the extremities of the universe. And, according to her extremities, indeed, she is said to be a virgin, and to remain undefiled; but, according to her middle, to be conjoined with Hades, and to beget the Furies in the subterranean regions. She, therefore, is also called Ceres, but after another manner than the supermundane and ruling Ceres. For the one is the connective unity of the three vivific principles; but the other is the middle of them, in herself possessing the peculiarities of the extremes. Hence, in the Proserpine conjoined with Pluto, you will find the peculiarities of Hecate and Minerva; but these extremes subsist in her occultly, while the peculiarity of the middle shines forth, and that which is characteristic of ruling soul, which in the supermundane Ceres was of a *ruling*° nature, but here subsists according to a mundane peculiarity."

Proclus farther observes, " that Proserpine is denominated either through judging of forms, and separating them from each other, thus obscurely signifying the subversion of slaughter†, (δια το κρινειν τα ειδη, και χωριζειν αλληλων ως του φονου την αναιρεσιν αινιττομενον,) or through separating souls perfectly from bodies, through a conversion to things on high, which is the most fortunate slaughter and death to such as are worthy of it. (ἡ δια το χωριζειν τας ψυχας τελεως εκ των σωματων δια της προς τα ανω επιστροφης, οπερ εστιν ευτυχεσιατος φονος και θανατος τοις αξιουμενοις ταυτου.) But the name Φερεφαττα, *Pherephatta*, is adapted to Proserpine, according to a contact with generation; but according to wisdom and counsel, to Minerva. At the same time, however, all the appellations by which she is distinguished, are adapted to the perfection of soul. On this account, also, she is called Proserpine, and not by the names of the extremes; since that which was ravished by Pluto, is this middle deity; the extremes at the same time being firmly established in themselves; according to which Ceres is said to remain a virgin.

---

* The first subsistence of Maia, who, according to the Orphic theology, is the same with the Goddess Night, is at the summit of *the intelligible,*

° That is, of a supermundane nature; for the *ruling* are the *supermundane* Gods.

† Proclus here alludes to the war which subsists among forms through their union with matter, and which Proserpine subverts by separating them from each other.

dess is terrestrial, and so likewise is Ceres. To this Goddess, also, a cock is consecrated; and on this account those that are initiated in her mysteries abstain from domestic birds. In the Eleusinian mysteries, likewise, the initiated are ordered to abstain from domestic birds, from fishes and beans, pomegranates and apples; which fruits are as equally defiling to the touch, as a woman recently delivered, and a dead body. But whoever is acquainted with the nature of divinely-luminous appearances [φασματα,] knows also on what account it is requisite to abstain from all birds, and especially for him who hastens to be liberated from terrestrial concerns, and to be established with the celestial Gods. Vice, however, as we have frequently said, is sufficiently able to patronize itself, and especially when it pleads its cause among the ignorant. Hence, among those that are moderately vicious, some think that a dehortation of this kind is vain babbling, and, according to the proverb, the nugacity of old women; and others are of opinion that it is superstition. But those who have made greater advances in improbity, are prepared, not only to blaspheme those who exhort to, and demonstrate the propriety of this abstinence, but calumniate purity itself as enchantment and pride. They, however, suffering the punishment of their sins, both from Gods and men, are, in the first place, sufficiently punished by a disposition [*i. e.* by a depravity] of this kind. We shall, therefore, still farther make mention of another foreign nation, renowned and

---

and at the same time intellectual order, and is wholly absorbed in the intelligible. As we are also informed by Proclus (in Cratylum), " She is the paradigm of Ceres. For immortal Night is the nurse of the Gods [according to Orpheus]. Night, however, is the cause of aliment intelligibly: for the intelligible is, as the Chaldean Oracle says, the aliment of the intellectual orders of Gods. But Ceres, first of all, separates the two kinds of aliment [nectar and ambrosia] in the Gods." He adds, " Hence our sovereign mistress [δεσποινα], Ceres, not only generates life, but that which gives perfection to life; and this from supernal natures, to such as are last. For *virtue is the perfection of souls.*"

just, and believed to be pious in divine concerns, and then pass on to other particulars.

17. For the polity of the Indians being distributed into many parts, there is one tribe among them of men divinely wise, whom the Greeks are accustomed to call Gymnosophists[t]. But of these there are two sects, over one of which the Bramins preside, but over the other the Samanæans. The race of the Bramins, however, receive divine wisdom of this kind by succession, in the same manner as the priesthood. But the Samanæans are elected, and consist of those who wish to possess divine knowledge. And the particulars respecting them are the following, as the Babylonian Bardesanes[u] narrates, who lived in the times of our fathers, and was familiar with those Indians who, together with Damadamis, were sent to Cæsar. All the Bramins originate from one stock; for all of them are derived from one father and one mother. But the Samanæans are not the offspring of one family, being, as we have said, collected from every nation of Indians. A Bramin, however, is not a subject of any government, nor does he contribute any thing together with others to government. And with respect to those that are philosophers, among these some dwell on mountains, and others about the river Ganges. And those that live on mountains feed on autumnal fruits, and on cows' milk coagulated with herbs. But those that reside near the Ganges, live also on autumnal fruits, which are produced in abundance about that river. The land likewise nearly always bears new fruit, together with much rice, which grows spontaneously, and which they use when there is a deficiency of autumnal fruits. But to taste of any other nutriment, or, in short, to touch animal food, is considered by them as equivalent to extreme

---

[t] Concerning the Indian philosophers, see the second book of Diodorus Siculus.

[u] This is the Bardesanes who lived in the time of Marcus Antoninus, and who wrote a treatise on the Lake of Probation in India, which is mentioned by Porphyry in his fragment De Styge, preserved by Stobæus.

impurity and impiety. And this is one of their dogmas. They also worship divinity with piety and purity. They spend the day, and the greater part of the night, in hymns and prayers to the Gods; each of them having a cottage to himself, and living, as much as possible, alone. For the Bramins cannot endure to remain with others, nor to speak much; but when this happens to take place, they afterwards withdraw themselves, and do not speak for many days. They likewise frequently fast. But the Samanæans are, as we have said, elected. When, however, any one is desirous of being enrolled in their order, he proceeds to the rulers of the city; but abandons the city or village that he inhabited, and the wealth and all the other property that he possessed. Having likewise the superfluities of his body cut off, he receives a garment, and departs to the Samanæans, but does not return either to his wife or children, if he happens to have any, nor does he pay any attention to them, or think that they at all pertain to him. And, with respect to his children indeed, the king provides what is necessary for them, and the relatives provide for the wife. And such is the life of the Samanæans. But they live out of the city, and spend the whole day in conversation pertaining to divinity. They have also houses and temples, built by the king, in which there are stewards, who receive a certain emolument from the king, for the purpose of supplying those that dwell in them with nutriment. But their food consists of rice, bread, autumnal fruits, and pot-herbs. And when they enter into their house, the sound of a bell being the signal of their entrance, those that are not Samanæans depart from it, and the Samanæans begin immediately to pray. But having prayed, again, on the bell sounding as a signal, the servants give to each Samanæan a platter, (for two of them do not eat out of the same dish,) and feed them with rice. And to him who is in want of a variety of food, a pot-herb is added, or some autumnal fruit. But having eaten as much as is requisite, without any delay they proceed to their accustomed employments. All of them likewise are unmarried, and have no possessions: and so much are both these and the Bramins venerated by the other Indians, that the king also visits them, and requests them to pray to and supplicate the Gods, when any calamity befals the country, or to advise him how to act.

18. But they are so disposed with respect to death, that they unwillingly endure the whole time of the present life, as a certain servitude to nature, and therefore they hasten to liberate their souls from the bodies [with which they are connected]. Hence frequently, when they are seen to be well, and are neither oppressed, nor driven to desperation by any evil, they depart from life. And though they previously announce to others that it is their intention to commit suicide, yet no one impedes them; but, proclaiming all those to be happy who thus quit the present life, they enjoin certain things to the domestics and kindred of the dead: so stable and true do they, and also the multitude, believe the assertion to be, that souls [in another life] associate with each other. But as soon as those to whom they have proclaimed that this is their intention, have heard the mandates given to them, they deliver the body to fire, in order that they may separate the soul from the body in the purest manner, and thus they die celebrated by all the Samanæans. For these men dismiss their dearest friends to death more easily than others part with their fellow-citizens when going the longest journeys. And they lament themselves, indeed, as still continuing in life; but they proclaim those that are dead to be blessed, in consequence of having now obtained an immortal allotment. Nor is there any sophist, such as there is now amongst the Greeks, either among these Samanæans, or the above-mentioned Bramins, who would be seen to doubt and to say, if all men should imitate you [*i. e.* should imitate those Samanæans who commit suicide], what would become of us? Nor through these are human affairs confused. For neither do all men imitate them, and those

who have, may be said to have been rather the causes of equitable legislation, than of confusion to the different nations of men. Moreover, the law did not compel the Samanæans and Bramins to eat animal food, but, permitting others to feed on flesh, it suffered these to be a law to themselves, and venerated them as being superior to law. Nor did the law subject these men to the punishment which it inflicts, as if they were the primary perpetrators of injustice, but it reserved this for others. Hence, to those who ask, what would be the consequence if all men imitated such characters as these, the saying of Pythagoras must be the answer; that if all men were kings, the passage through life would be difficult, yet regal government is not on this account to be avoided. And [we likewise say] that if all men were worthy, no administration of a polity would be found in which the dignity that probity merits would be preserved. Nevertheless, no one would be so insane as not to think that all men should earnestly endeavour to become worthy characters. Indeed, the law grants to the vulgar many other things [besides a fleshly diet], which, nevertheless, it does not grant to a philosopher, nor even to one who conducts the affairs of government in a proper manner. For it does not receive every artist into the administration, though it does not forbid the exercise of any art, nor yet men of every pursuit. But it excludes those who are occupied in vile and illiberal arts[x], and, in short, all those who are destitute of justice and the other virtues, from having any thing to do with the management of public affairs. Thus, likewise, the law does not forbid the vulgar from associating with harlots, on whom at the same time it imposes a fine; but thinks that it is disgraceful and base for men that are moderately good to have any connexion with them. Moreover, the law does not prohibit a man from spending the whole of his life in a tavern, yet at the same time this

---

[x] Βαναυσοι, *i. e.* dirty mechanics and bellows-blowers, an appellation by which Plato in his Rivals designates the *experimentalists*.

is most disgraceful even to a man of moderate worth. It appears, therefore, that the same thing must also be said with respect to diet. For that which is permitted to the multitude, must not likewise be granted to the best of men. For the man who is a philosopher, should especially ordain for himself those sacred laws which the Gods, and men who are followers of the Gods, have instituted. But the sacred laws of nations and cities appear to have ordained for sacred men purity, and to have interdicted them animal food. They have also forbidden the multitude to eat certain animals, either from motives of piety, or on account of some injury which would be produced by the food. So that it is requisite either to imitate priests, or to be obedient to the mandates of all legislators; but, in either way, he who is perfectly legal and pious ought to abstain from all animals. For if some who are only partially pious abstain from certain animals, he who is in every respect pious will abstain from all animals.

19. I had almost, however, forgotten to adduce what is said by Euripides, who asserts, that the prophets of Jupiter in Crete abstained from animals. But what is said by the chorus to Minos on this subject, is as follows:

> Sprung from Phœnicia's royal line,
> Son of Europa, nymph divine,
> And mighty Jove, thy envy'd reign
> O'er Crete extending, whose domain
> Is with a hundred cities crown'd —
> I leave yon consecrated ground,
> Yon fane, whose beams the artist's toil
> With cypress, rooted from the soil,
> Hath fashion'd. In the mystic rites
> Initiated, life's best delights
> I place in chastity alone,
> Midst Night's dread orgies wont to rove,
> The priest of Zagreus[y] and of Jove;

[y] Zagreus is an epithet of Bacchus. Wodhull, however, from whose translation of Euripides the above lines are taken, is greatly mistaken in

Feasts of crude flesh I now decline,
And wave aloof the blazing pine
To Cybele, nor fear to claim
Her own Curete's hallow'd name;
Clad in a snowy vest I fly
Far from the throes of pregnancy,
Never amidst the tombs intrude,
And slay no animal for food.

20. For holy men were of opinion that purity consisted in a thing not being mingled with its contrary, and that mixture is defilement. Hence, they thought that nutriment should be assumed from fruits, and not from dead bodies, and that we should not, by introducing that which is animated to our nature, defile what is administered by nature. But they conceived, that the slaughter of animals, as they are sensitive, and the depriving them of their souls, is a defilement to the living; and that the pollution is much greater, to mingle a body which was once sensitive, but is now deprived of sense, with a sensitive and living being. Hence universally, the purity pertaining to piety consists in rejecting and abstaining from many things, and in an abandonment of such as are of a contrary nature, and the assumption of such as are appropriate and concordant. On this account, venereal connexions are attended with defilement. For in these, a conjunction takes place of the female with the male; and the seed, when retained by the woman, and causing her to be pregnant, defiles the soul, through its association with the body; but when it does not produce conception, it pollutes, in consequence of becoming a lifeless mass. The connexion also of males with males defiles, because it is an emission of seed as it were into a dead body, and because it is contrary to nature. And, in short, all venery, and emissions of the seed in sleep,

---

saying, that "it is evident from the hymns of Orpheus that Zagreus was a name given to Bacchus at his sacred rites." For the word Ζαγρευς (Zagreus) is not to be found either in the hymns of Orpheus, or in any other of the Orphic writings that are extant.

pollute, because the soul becomes mingled with the body, and is drawn down to pleasure. The passions of the soul likewise defile, through the complication of the irrational and effeminate part with reason, the internal masculine part. For, in a certain respect, defilement and pollution manifest the mixture of things of an heterogeneous nature, and especially when the abstersion of this mixture is attended with difficulty. Whence, also, in tinctures which are produced through mixture, one species being complicated with another, this mixture is denominated a defilement.

> As when some woman with a lively red
> Stains the pure iv'ry ————

says Homer[z]. And again, painters call the mixtures of colours, corruptions. It is usual, likewise, to denominate that which is unmingled and pure, incorruptible, and to call that which is genuine, unpolluted. For water, when mingled with earth, is corrupted, and is not genuine. But water which is diffluent, and runs with tumultuous rapidity, leaves behind in its course the earth which it carries in its stream.

> When from a limpid and perennial fount
> It defluous runs ————

as Hesiod says[a]. For such water is salubrious, because it is uncorrupted and unmixed. The female, likewise, that does not receive into herself the exhalation of seed, is said to be uncorrupted. So that the mixture of contraries is corruption and defilement. For the mixture of dead with living bodies, and the insertion of beings that were once living and sentient into animals, and of dead into living flesh, may be reasonably supposed to introduce defilement and stains to our nature; just, again, as the soul is polluted when it is invested with the body. Hence, he who is born, is polluted by the mixture of

---

[z] Iliad, IV. v. 141.   [a] Oper. et Dies, 595.

his soul with body; and he who dies, defiles his body, through leaving it a corpse, different and foreign from that which possesses life. The soul, likewise, is polluted by anger and desire, and the multitude of passions of which in a certain respect diet is a co-operating cause. But as water which flows through a rock is more uncorrupted than that which runs through marshes, because it does not bring with it much mud; thus, also, the soul which administers its own affairs in a body that is dry, and is not moistened by the juices of foreign flesh, is in a more excellent condition, is more uncorrupted, and is more prompt for intellectual energy. Thus too, it is said, that the thyme which is the driest and the sharpest to the taste, affords the best honey to bees. The dianoëtic, therefore, or discursive power of the soul, is polluted; or rather, he who energizes dianoëtically, when this energy is mingled with the energies of either the imaginative or doxastic power. But purification consists in a separation from all these, and the wisdom which is adapted to divine concerns, is a desertion of every thing of this kind. The proper nutriment, likewise, of each thing, is that which essentially preserves it. Thus you may say, that the nutriment of a stone is the cause of its continuing to be a stone, and of firmly remaining in a lapideous form; but the nutriment of a plant is that which preserves it in increase and fructification; and of an animated body, that which preserves its composition. It is one thing, however, to nourish, and another to fatten; and one thing to impart what is necessary, and another to procure what is luxurious. Various, therefore, are the kinds of nutriment, and various also is the nature of the things that are nourished. And it is necessary, indeed, that all things should be nourished, but we should earnestly endeavour to fatten our most principal parts. Hence, the nutriment of the rational soul is that which preserves it in a rational state. But this is intellect; so that it is to be nourished by intellect; and we should earnestly endeavour that it may be fattened through this, rather than that the flesh may become pinguid, through esculent substances. For intellect preserves for us eternal life, but the body when fattened causes the soul to be famished, through its hunger after a blessed life not being satisfied, increases our mortal part, since it is of itself insane, and impedes our attainment of an immortal condition of being. It likewise defiles by corporifying the soul, and drawing her down to that which is foreign to her nature. And the magnet, indeed, imparts, as it were, a soul to the iron which is placed near it; and the iron, though most heavy, is elevated, and runs to the spirit of the stone. Should he, therefore, who is suspended from incorporeal and intellectual deity, be anxiously busied in procuring food which fattens the body, that is an impediment to intellectual perception? Ought he not rather, by contracting what is necessary to the flesh into that which is little and easily procured, be *himself* nourished, by adhering to God more closely than the iron to the magnet? I wish, indeed, that our nature was not so corruptible, and that it were possible we could live free from molestation, even without the nutriment derived from fruits. O that, as Homer[b] says, we were not in want either of meat or drink, that we might be truly immortal! — the poet in thus speaking beautifully signifying, that food is the auxiliary not only, of life, but also of death. If, therefore, we were not in want even of vegetable aliment, we should be by so much the more blessed, in proportion as we should be more immortal. But now, being in a mortal condition, we render ourselves, if it be proper so to speak, still more mortal, through becoming ignorant that, by the addition of this mortality, the soul, as Theophrastus says, does not only confer a great benefit on the body by being its inhabitant, but gives herself wholly to it[c]. Hence, it is

[b] Iliad, V. v. 341.

[c] In the original, ου πολυ το ενοικιον, ως φησι που Θεοφραστος, τῳ σωματι διδουσης της ψυχης, κ.τ.λ. But for ου πολυ το ενοικιον, it appears to me to be necessary to read, ου μονον πολυ το ενοικιον, κ.τ.λ.

much to be wished that we could easily obtain the life celebrated in fables, in which hunger and thirst are unknown; so that, by stopping the every-way-flowing river of the body, we might in a very little time be present with the most excellent natures, to which he who accedes, since deity is there, is himself a God. But how is it possible not to lament the condition of the generality of mankind, who are so involved in darkness as to cherish their own evil, and who, in the first place, hate themselves, and him who truly begot them, and afterwards, those who admonish them, and call on them to return from ebriety to a sober condition of being? Hence, dismissing things of this kind, will it not be requisite to pass on to what remains to be discussed?

21. Those then who oppose the Nomades, or Troglodytæ[d], or Ichthyophagi, to the legal institutes of the nations which we have adduced, are ignorant that these people were brought to the necessity of eating animals through the infecundity of the region they inhabit, which is so barren, that it does not even produce herbs, but only shores and sands. And this necessity is indicated by their not being able to make use of fire, through the want of combustible materials; but they dry their fish on rocks, or on the shore. And these indeed live after this manner from necessity. There are, however, certain nations whose manners are rustic, and who are naturally savage; but it is not fit that those who are equitable judges should, from such instances as these, calumniate human nature. For thus we should not only be dubious whether it is proper to eat animals, but also, whether we may not eat men, and adopt all other savage manners. It is related, therefore, that the Massagetæ and the Derbices consider those of their kindred to be most miserable who die spontaneously. Hence, preventing their dearest friends from dying naturally, they slay them when they are old, and eat them. The Tibareni hurl from rocks their nearest relatives, even while

---

[d] Vid. Diod. Sic. lib. iii. 32.

living, when they are old. And with respect to the Hyrcani and Caspii, the one exposed the living, but the other the dead, to be devoured by birds and dogs. But the Scythians bury the living with the dead, and cut their throats on the pyres of the dead by whom they were especially beloved. The Bactrii likewise cast those among them that are old, even while living, to the dogs. And Stasanor, who was one of Alexander's prefects, nearly lost his government through endeavouring to destroy this custom. As, however, we do not on account of these examples subvert mildness of conduct towards men, so neither should we imitate those nations that feed on flesh through necessity, but we should rather imitate the pious, and those who consecrate themselves to the Gods. For Democrates[e] says, that to live badly, and not prudently, temperately, and piously, is not to live in reality[f], but to die for a long time.

22. It now remains that we should adduce a few examples of certain individuals, as testimonies in favour of abstinence from animal food. For the want of these was one of the accusations which were urged against us. We learn, therefore, that Triptolemus was the most ancient of the Athenian legislators; of whom Hermippus[g], in the second book of his treatise on Legislators, writes as follows: "It is said, that Triptolemus established laws for the Athenians. And the philosopher Xenocrates asserts, that three of his laws still remain in Eleusis, which are these, Honour your parents; Sacrifice to the Gods from the fruits of the earth; Injure not animals." Two of these, therefore, he says, are

---

[e] Reisk says, that he does not know who this Democrates is; but there can, I think, be no doubt of its being the Pythagorean of that name, whose Golden Sentences are extant in the Opuscula Mythologica of Gale, of which see Mr. Bridgman's translation.

[f] In the original, ου κακως ζην ειναι. But for ου κακως, I read, ουκ οντως. For without this emendation, Democrates will contradict himself.

[g] This Hermippus is also cited by Diogenes Laertius in Pyth.

properly instituted. For it is necessary that we should as much as possible recompense our parents for the benefits which they have conferred on us; and that we should offer to the Gods the first-fruits of the things useful to our life, which they have imparted to us. But with respect to the third law, he is dubious as to the intention of Triptolemus, in ordering the Athenians to abstain from animals. Was it, says he, because he thought it was a dire thing to slay kindred natures, or because he perceived it would happen, that the most useful animals would be destroyed by men for food? Wishing, therefore, to make our life as mild as possible, he endeavoured to preserve those animals that associate with men, and which are especially tame. Unless, indeed, because having ordained that men should honour the Gods by offering to them first-fruits, he therefore added this third law, conceiving that this mode of worship would continue for a longer time, if sacrifices through animals were not made to the Gods. But as many other causes, though not very accurate, of the promulgation of these laws, are assigned by Xenocrates, thus much from what has been said is sufficient for our purpose, that abstinence from animals was one of the legal institutes of Triptolemus. Hence, those who afterwards violated this law, being compelled by great necessity, and involuntary errors, fell, as we have shown, into this custom of slaughtering and eating animals. The following, also, is mentioned as a law of Draco: " Let this be an eternal *sacred law*[h] to the inhabitants of Attica, and let its authority be predominant for ever; viz. that the Gods, and indigenous Heroes, be worshipped publicly, conformably to the laws of the country, delivered by our ancestors; and also, that they be worshipped privately, according to the ability of each individual, in conjunction with auspicious words, the

---

[h] In the original, θεσμος, which, as we are informed by Proclus, signifies *divine order, and a uniform boundary.*

firstlings of fruits, and annual cakes. So that this law ordains, that divinity should be venerated by the first offerings of fruits which are used by men, and cakes made of the fine flour of wheat[1].

[1] This book is evidently imperfect, because there are wanting at the end examples of illustrious Greeks and Romans, who, from the most remote antiquity, abstained from animal food. And this was also obvious to Reisk.

ON

THE CAVE OF THE NYMPHS,

IN THE

THIRTEENTH BOOK OF THE ODYSSEY.

---

1. WHAT does Homer obscurely signify by the cave in Ithaca, which he describes in the following verses?

> " High at the head a branching olive grows,
> And crowns the pointed cliffs with shady boughs.
> A cavern pleasant, though involv'd in night,
> Beneath it lies, the Naiades' delight:
> Where bowls and urns of workmanship divine
> And massy beams in native marble shine;
> On which the Nymphs amazing webs display,
> Of purple hue, and exquisite array.
> The busy bees within the urns secure
> Honey delicious, and like nectar pure.
> Perpetual waters through the grotto glide,
> A lofty gate unfolds on either side;
> That to the north is pervious to mankind;
> The sacred south t' immortals is consign'd."

That the poet, indeed, does not narrate these particulars from historical information, is evident from this, that those who have given us a description of the island, have, as Cronius[*] says, made no mention of such a cave being found in it. This likewise, says he, is manifest, that it would be absurd for Homer to expect, that in

---

[*] This Cronius, the Pythagorean, is also mentioned by Porphyry, in his Life of Plotinus.

describing a cave fabricated merely by poetical license, and thus artificially opening a path to Gods and men in the region of Ithaca, he should gain the belief of mankind. And it is equally absurd to suppose, that nature herself should point out, in this place, one path for the descent of all mankind, and again another path for all the Gods. For, indeed, the whole world is full of Gods and men: but it is impossible to be persuaded, that in the Ithacensian cave men descend, and Gods ascend. Cronius, therefore, having premised thus much, says, that it is evident, not only to the wise but also to the vulgar, that the poet, under the veil of allegory, conceals some mysterious signification; thus compelling others to explore what the gate of men is, and also what is the gate of the Gods: what he means by asserting that this cave of the Nymphs has two gates; and why it is both pleasant and obscure, since darkness is by no means delightful, but is rather productive of aversion and horror. Likewise, what is the reason why it is not simply said to be the cave of the Nymphs, but it is accurately added, of the Nymphs which are called Naiades? Why, also, is the cave represented as containing bowls and amphoræ, when no mention is made of their receiving any liquor, but bees are said to deposit their honey in these vessels as in hives? Then, again, why are oblong beams adapted to weaving placed here for the Nymphs; and these not formed from wood, or any other pliable matter, but from stone, as well as the amphoræ and bowls? Which last circumstance is, indeed, less obscure; but that, on these stony beams, the Nymphs should weave purple garments, is not only wonderful to the sight, but also to the auditory sense. For who would believe that Goddesses weave garments in a cave involved in darkness, and on stony beams; especially while he hears the poet asserting, that the purple webs of the Goddesses were visible. In addition to these things likewise, this is admirable, that the cave should have a twofold entrance; one made for the descent of men, but the other for the ascent of Gods.

And again, that the gate, which is pervious by men, should be said to be turned towards the north wind, but the portal of the Gods to the south; and why the poet did not rather make use of the west and the east for this purpose; since nearly all temples have their statues and entrances turned towards the east; but those who enter them look towards the west, when standing with their faces turned towards the statues, they honour and worship the Gods. Hence, since this narration is full of such obscurities, it can neither be a fiction casually devised for the purpose of procuring delight, nor an exposition of a topical history; but something allegorical must be indicated in it by the poet, who likewise mystically places an olive near the cave. All which particulars the ancients thought very laborious to investigate and unfold; and we, with their assistance, shall now endeavour to develope the secret meaning of the allegory. Those persons, therefore, appear to have written very negligently about the situation of the place, who think that the cave, and what is narrated concerning it, are nothing more than a fiction of the poet. But the best and most accurate writers of geography, and among these Artemidorus the Ephesian, in the fifth book of his work, which consists of eleven books, thus writes: " The island of Ithaca, containing an extent of eighty-five stadia [b], is distant from Panormus, a port of Cephalenia, about twelve stadia. It has a port named Phorcys, in which there is a shore, and on that shore a cave, in which the Phæacians are reported to have placed Ulysses." This cave, therefore, will not be entirely an Homeric fiction. But whether the poet describes it as it really is, or whether he has added something to it of his own invention, nevertheless the same inquiries remain; whether the intention of the poet is investigated, or of those who founded the cave. For, neither did the ancients establish temples without fabulous symbols, nor

---

[b] *i. e.* Rather more than ten Italian miles and a half, eight stadia making an Italian mile.

does Homer rashly narrate the particulars pertaining to things of this kind. But how much the more any one endeavours to show that this description of the cave is not an Homeric fiction, but prior to Homer was consecrated to the Gods, by so much the more will this consecrated cave be found to be full of ancient wisdom. And on this account it deserves to be investigated, and it is requisite that its symbolical consecration should be amply unfolded into light.

2. The ancients, indeed, very properly consecrated a cave to the world, whether assumed collectively, according to the whole of itself, or separately, according to its parts. Hence they considered earth as a symbol of that matter of which the world consists; on which account some thought that matter and earth are the same; through the cave indicating the world, which was generated from matter. For caves are, for the most part, spontaneous productions, and connascent with the earth, being comprehended by one uniform mass of stone; the interior parts of which are concave, but the exterior parts are extended over an indefinite portion of land. And the world being spontaneously produced, [*i. e.* being produced by no external, but from an internal cause,] and being also self-adherent, is allied to matter; which, according to a secret signification, is denominated a stone and a rock, on account of its sluggish and repercussive nature with respect to form: the ancients, at the same time, asserting that matter is infinite through its privation of form. Since, however, it is continually flowing, and is of itself destitute of the supervening investments of form; through which it participates of *morphe*[c], and becomes visible, the flowing waters, darkness, or, as the poet says, obscurity of the cavern, were considered by the ancients as apt symbols of what the world contains, on account of the matter with which it is connected. Through matter,

---

[c] In the original, δι ου μορφουται. But *morphe*, as we are informed by Simplicius, pertains to the colour, figure, and magnitude of superficies.

therefore, the world is obscure and dark; but through the connecting power, and orderly distribution of form, from which also it is called *world*, it is beautiful and delightful. Hence it may very properly be denominated a cave; as being lovely, indeed, to him who first enters into it, through its participation of forms, but obscure to him who surveys its foundation, and examines it with an intellectual eye. So that its exterior and superficial parts, indeed, are pleasant, but its interior and profound parts are obscure, [and its very bottom is darkness itself]. Thus also the Persians, mystically signifying the descent of the soul into the sublunary regions, and its regression from it, initiate the mystic [or him who is admitted to the arcane sacred rites] in a place which they denominate a cavern. For, as Eubulus says, Zoroaster was the first who consecrated, in the neighbouring mountains of Persia, a spontaneously produced cave, florid, and having fountains, in honour of Mithra, the maker and father of all things; a cave, according to Zoroaster, bearing a resemblance of the world, which was fabricated by Mithra. But the things contained in the cavern being arranged according to commensurate intervals, were symbols of the mundane elements and climates.

3. After this Zoroaster likewise, it was usual with others to perform the rites pertaining to the mysteries in caverns and dens, whether spontaneously produced, or made by the hands. For, as they established temples, groves, and altars, to the celestial Gods, but to the terrestrial Gods, and to heroes, altars alone, and to the subterranean divinities pits and cells; so to the world they dedicated caves and dens; as likewise to Nymphs[d]; on account of the water which trickles, or is diffused in caverns, over which the Naiades, as we shall shortly observe,

---

[d] "Nymphs," says Hermias, in his Scholia on the Phædrus of Plato, " are Goddesses who preside over regeneration, and are ministrant to Bacchus, the offspring of Semele. Hence they dwell near water, that is, they are conversant with generation. But this Bacchus supplies the regeneration of the whole sensible world."

preside. Not only, however, did the ancients make a cavern, as we have said, to be a symbol of the world, or of a generated and sensible nature; but they also assumed it as a symbol of all invisible powers; because, as caverns are obscure and dark, so the essence of these powers is occult. Hence Saturn fabricated a cavern in the ocean itself, and concealed in it his children. Thus, too, Ceres educated Proserpine, with her Nymphs, in a cave; and many other particulars of this kind may be found in the writings of theologists. But that the ancients dedicated caverns to Nymphs, and especially to the Naiades, who dwell near fountains, and who are called Naiades from the streams over which they preside, is manifest from the hymn to Apollo, in which it is said: " The Nymphs residing in caves shall deduce fountains of intellectual waters to thee, (according to the divine voice of the Muses,) which are the progeny of a terrene spirit. Hence waters, bursting through every river, shall exhibit to mankind perpetual effusions of sweet streams*."—From hence, as it appears to me, the Pythagoreans, and after them Plato, showed that the world is a cavern and a den. For the powers which are the leaders of souls, thus speak in a verse of Empedocles:

> Now at this secret cavern we're arrived.

And by Plato, in the 7th book of his Republic, it is said, " Behold men as if dwelling in a subterraneous cavern, and in a den-like habitation, whose entrance is widely expanded to the admission of the light through the whole cave." But when the other person in the Dialogue says, " You adduce an unusual and wonderful similitude," he replies, " The whole of this image, friend Glauco, must be adapted to what has been before said, assimilating this receptacle, which is visible through the sight, to the habitation of a prison; but the light of the fire which is in it to the power of the sun."

* These lines are not to be found in any of the hymns now extant, ascribed to Homer.

4. That theologists therefore considered caverns as symbols of the world, and of mundane powers, is, through this, manifest. And it has been already observed by us, that they also considered a cave as a symbol of the intelligible essence; being impelled to do so by different and not the same conceptions. For they were of opinion, that a cave is a symbol of the sensible world, because caverns are dark, stony, and humid; and they asserted, that the world is a thing of this kind, through the matter of which it consists, and through its repercussive and flowing nature. But they thought it to be a symbol of the intelligible world, because that world is invisible to sensible perception, and possesses a firm and stable essence. Thus, also, partial powers are unapparent, and especially those which are inherent in matter. For they formed these symbols, from surveying the spontaneous production of caves, and their nocturnal, dark, and stony nature; and not entirely, as some suspect, from directing their attention to the figure of a cavern. For every cave is not spherical, as is evident from this Homeric cave with a twofold entrance. But since a cavern has a twofold similitude, the present cave must not be assumed as an image of the intelligible, but of the sensible essence. For in consequence of containing perpetually-flowing streams of water, it will not be a symbol of an intelligible hypostasis, but of a material essence. On this account also, it is sacred to Nymphs, not the mountain, *or rural[f] Nymphs,* or others of the like kind, but to the Naiades, who are thus denominated from streams of water. For we peculiarly call the Naiades, and the powers that preside over waters, Nymphs; and this term, also, is commonly applied to all souls descending into generation. For the ancients thought that these souls are incumbent on water which is inspired by divinity, as Numenius, says, who adds, that on this account, a prophet asserts, that the Spirit of God moved on the waters. The

---

[f] In the original, ουλε αγραιων; but for αγραιων, I read, αγραυων.

Egyptians likewise, on this account, represent all dæmons, and also the sun, and, in short, all the planets [g], not standing on any thing solid, but on a sailing vessel; for souls descending into generation fly to moisture. Hence, also, Heraclitus says, "that moisture appears delightful and not deadly to souls;" but the lapse into generation is delightful to them. And in another place [speaking of unembodied souls], he says, "We live their death, and we die their life." Hence the poet calls those that are in generation *humid*, because they have souls which are *profoundly* steeped in moisture. On this account, such souls delight in blood and humid seed; but water is the nutriment of the souls of plants. Some likewise are of opinion, that the bodies in the air, and in the heavens, are nourished by vapours from fountains and rivers, and other exhalations. But the Stoics assert, that the sun is nourished by the exhalation from the sea; the moon from the vapours of fountains and rivers; and the stars from the exhalation of the earth. Hence, according to them, the sun is an intellectual composition formed from the sea; the moon from river waters; and the stars from terrene exhalations.

5. It is necessary, therefore, that souls, whether they are corporeal or incorporeal, while they attract to themselves body, and especially such as are about to be bound to blood and moist bodies, should verge to humidity, and be corporalized, in consequence of being drenched in moisture. Hence the souls of the dead are evocated by the effusion of bile and blood; and souls

---

[g] In the original, τους τε Αιγυπτιους δια τουτο τους δαιμονας απαντας ουχ ιςταναι επι στερεου, αλλα παντας επι πλοιου, και τον ηλιον, και απλως παντας, ους τινας ειδεναι χρη τας ψυχας επιποτωμενας τῳ υγρῳ, τας εις γενεσιν κατιουσας. But after the words και απλως παντας, it appears to me to be requisite to insert τους πλανητας. For Martianus Capella, in lib. ii. De Nuptiis Philologiæ, speaking of the sun, says: "Ibi quandam navim, totius naturæ cursibus diversa cupiditate moderantem, cunctaque flammarum congestione plenissimam, beatis circumactam mercibus conspicatur. Cui *nautæ septem germani*, tamen suique consimiles præsidebant," &c. For in this passage the seven sailors are evidently the seven planets.

that are lovers of body, by attracting a moist spirit, condense this humid vehicle like a cloud. For moisture condensed in the air constitutes a cloud. But the pneumatic vehicle being condensed in these souls, becomes visible through an excess of moisture. And among the number of these we must reckon those apparitions of images, which, from a spirit coloured by the influence of imagination, present themselves to mankind. But pure souls are averse from generation; so that, as Heraclitus says, "*a dry soul is the wisest.*" Hence, here also, the spirit becomes moist and more aqueous through the desire of coition, the soul thus attracting a humid vapour from verging to generation. Souls, therefore, proceeding into generation, are the Nymphs called Naiades. Hence it is usual to call those that are married Nymphs, as being conjoined to generation, and to pour water into baths from fountains, or rivers, or perpetual rills.

6. This world, then, is sacred and pleasant to souls who have now proceeded into nature, and to natal dæmons, though it is essentially dark and *obscure;* [ηεροειδης;] from which some have suspected that souls also are of an *obscure* nature, [αερωδας,] and essentially consist of air. Hence a cavern, which is both pleasant and dark, will be appropriately consecrated to souls on the earth, conformably to its similitude to the world; in which, as in the greatest of all temples, souls reside. To the Nymphs likewise, who preside over waters, a cavern, in which there are perpetually flowing streams, is adapted. Let, therefore, this present cavern be consecrated to souls; and, among the more partial powers, to nymphs, that preside over streams and fountains, and who, on this account, are called *fontal* and *Naiades.* What, therefore, are the different symbols, some of which are adapted to souls, but others to the aquatic powers, in order that we may apprehend that this cavern is consecrated in common to both? Let the stony bowls, then, and the amphoræ, be symbols of the aquatic Nymphs. For these are, indeed, the symbols of Bacchus, but their composition is

fictile, *i. e.* consists of baked earth; and these are friendly to the vine, the gift of the God; since the fruit of the vine is brought to a proper maturity by the celestial fire of the sun. But the stony bowls and amphoræ, are in the most eminent degree adapted to the Nymphs who preside over the water that flows from rocks. And to souls that descend into generation, and are occupied in corporeal energies, what symbol can be more appropriate than those instruments pertaining to weaving? Hence, also, the poet ventures to say, " that on these the Nymphs weave purple webs, admirable to the view." For the formation of the flesh is on and about the bones, which in the bodies of animals resemble stones. Hence these instruments of weaving consist of stone, and not of any other matter. But the purple webs will evidently be the flesh which is woven from the blood. For purple woollen garments are tinged from blood; and wool is dyed from animal juice. The generation of flesh, also, is through and from blood. Add, too, that the body is a garment with which the soul is invested, a thing wonderful to the sight, whether this refers to the composition of the soul, or contributes to the colligation of the soul [to the whole of a visible essence]. Thus, also, Proserpine, who is the inspective guardian of every thing produced from seed, is represented by Orpheus as weaving a web[h]; and the heavens are called by the ancients.

---

[h] The theological meaning of this Orphic fiction is beautifully unfolded by Proclus, as follows:—" Orpheus says that the vivific cause of partible natures [*i. e.* Proserpine], while she remained on high, weaving the order of celestials, was a nymph, as being undefiled; and in consequence of this connected with Jupiter, and abiding in her appropriate manners; but that, proceeding from her proper habitation, she left her webs unfinished, was ravished; having been ravished, was married; and that being married she generated, in order that she might animate things which have an adventitious life. For the unfinished state of her webs indicates, I think, that the universe is imperfect or unfinished, as far as to perpetual animals [*i. e.* The universe would be imperfect if nothing inferior to the celestial Gods was produced]. Hence Plato says, that the one Demiurgus calls on the many Demiurgi to weave together the

a veil, in consequence of being, as it were, the vestment of the celestial Gods.

7. Why, therefore, are the amphoræ said not to be filled with water, but with honey-combs? For in these Homer says the bees deposit their honey. But this is evident from the word τιθαιβωσσειν, which signifies τιθεναι την βοσιν; *i. e.* to deposit aliment. And honey is the nutriment of bees. Theologists, also, have made honey subservient to many and different symbols, because it consists of many powers; since it is both cathartic and preservative. Hence, through honey, bodies are preserved from putrefaction, and inveterate ulcers are purified. Farther still, it is also sweet to the taste, and is collected by bees, who are ox-begotten, from flowers. When, therefore, those who are initiated in the Leontic sacred rites, pour honey instead of water on their hands; they are ordered [by the initiator] to have their hands pure from every thing productive of molestation, and from every thing noxious and detestable. Other initiators [into the same mysteries] employ fire, which is of a cathartic nature, as an appropriate purification. And they likewise purify the tongue from all the defilement of evil with honey. But the Persians, when they offer honey to the guardian of fruits, consider it as the symbol of a preserving and defending power. Hence some per-

---

mortal and immortal natures; after a manner reminding us, that the addition of the mortal genera is the perfection of the textorial life of the universe, and also exciting our recollection of the divine Orphic fable, and affordin us interpretative causes of the unfinished webs of Proserpine." — See vol. ii. p. 356, of my translation of Proclus on the Timæus.

The *unfinished webs* of Proserpine are also alluded to by Claudian, in his poem De Raptu Proserpinæ, in the following verse:

> Sensit adesse Deas, *imperfectumque laborem Deserit.*

I only add, that, by ancient theologists, the shuttle was considered as a signature of *separating*, a cup of *vivific*, a sceptre of *ruling*, and a key of *guardian* power.

sons have thought that the nectar and ambrosia[1], which the poet pours into the nostrils of the dead, for the purpose of preventing putrefaction, is honey; since honey is the food of the Gods. On this account, also, the same poet somewhere calls nectar ἐρυθρον; for such is the colour of honey, [viz. it is a deep yellow]. But whether or not honey is to be taken for nectar, we shall elsewhere more accurately examine. In Orpheus, likewise, Saturn is ensnared by Jupiter through honey. For Saturn, being filled with honey, is intoxicated, his senses are darkened, as if from the effects of wine, and he sleeps; just as Porus, in the Banquet of Plato, is filled with nectar; for wine was not (says he) yet known. The Goddess Night,

---

[1] The theological meaning of nectar and ambrosia, is beautifully unfolded by Hermias, in his Scholia on the Phædrus of Plato, published by Ast, Lips. 1810, p. 145, where he informs us, " that *ambrosia* is analogous to dry nutriment, and that, on this account, it signifies an establishment in causes; but that *nectar* is analogous to moist food, and that it signifies the providential attention of the Gods to secondary natures; the former being denominated, according to *a privation of the mortal and corruptible* [κατα στερησιν του βροτου και φθαρτου]; but the latter, according to *a privation of the funeral and sepulchral* [κατα στερησιν του κηδους ηρεμενου και του ταφου]. And when the Gods are represented as energizing providentially, they are said to drink nectar. Thus Homer, in the beginning of the 4th book of the Iliad:

Οἱ δε θεοι παρ Ζηνι καθημενοι ηγορουντο
Χρυσεω εν δαπεδω, μετα δε σφισι ποτνια Ἡβη
Νεκταρ εωνοχοει· τοι δε χρυσεοις δεπαεσσι
Δειδεχατ' αλληλους, Τρωων πολιν εισοροωντες.

Now with each other, on the golden floor
Seated near Jove, the Gods converse; to whom
The venerable Hebe nectar bears,
In golden goblets; and as these flow round,
Th' immortals turn their careful eyes on Troy.

For then they providentially attend to the Trojans. The possession, therefore, of immutable providence by the Gods is signified by their drinking nectar; the exertion of this providence, by their beholding Troy; and their communicating with each other in providential energies, by receiving the goblets from each other.

too, in Orpheus, advises Jupiter to make use of honey as an artifice. For she says to him —

> When stretch'd beneath the lofty oaks you view
> Saturn, with honey by the bees produc'd,
> Sunk in ebriety [k], fast bind the God.

This, therefore, takes place, and Saturn being bound, is castrated in the same manner as Heaven; the theologist obscurely signifying by this, that divine natures become through pleasure bound, and drawn down into the realms of generation; and also that, when dissolved in pleasure, they emit certain seminal powers. Hence Saturn castrates Heaven, when descending to earth, through a desire of coition [l]. But the sweetness of honey signifies, with theologists, the same thing as the pleasure arising from copulation, by which Saturn, being ensnared, was castrated. For Saturn, and his sphere, are the first of the orbs that move contrary to the course of Cœlum, or the heavens. Certain powers, however, descend both from Heaven [or the inerratic sphere] and the planets. But Saturn receives the powers of Heaven,

---

[k] Ebriety, when ascribed to divine natures by ancient theologists, signifies a deific superessential energy, or an energy superior to intellect. Hence, when Saturn is said by Orpheus to have been intoxicated with honey or nectar, the meaning is, that he then energized providentially, in a deific and super-intellectual manner.

[l] Porphyry, though he excelled in philosophical, was deficient in theological knowledge; of which what he now says of the castrations of Saturn and Heaven, is a remarkable instance. For ancient theologists, by things preternatural, adumbrated the transcendent nature of the Gods; by such as are irrational, a power more divine than all reason; and by things apparently base, incorporeal beauty. Hence, in the fabulous narrations to which Porphyry now alludes, the genital parts must be considered as symbols of prolific power; and the castration of these parts as signifying the progression of this power into a subject order. So that the fable means that the prolific powers of Saturn are called forth into progression by Jupiter, and those of Heaven by Saturn; Jupiter being inferior to Saturn, and Saturn to Heaven.— See the Apology for the Fables of Homer, in vol. i. of my translation of Plato.

and Jupiter the powers of Saturn. Since, therefore, honey is assumed in purgations, and as an antidote to putrefaction, and is indicative of the pleasure which draws souls downward to generation; it is a symbol well adapted to aquatic Nymphs, on account of the unputrescent nature of the waters over which they preside, their purifying power, and their co-operation with generation. For water co-operates in the work of generation. On this account the bees are said, by the poet, to deposit their honey in bowls and amphoræ; the bowls being a symbol of fountains, and therefore a bowl is placed near to Mithra, instead of a fountain; but the amphoræ are symbols of the vessels with which we draw water from fountains. And fountains and streams are adapted to aquatic Nymphs, and still more so to the Nymphs that are souls, which the ancients peculiarly called bees, as the efficient causes of sweetness. Hence Sophocles does not speak unappropriately when he says of souls —

> In swarms while wandering, from the dead,
> A humming sound is heard.

8. The priestesses of Ceres, also, as being initiated into the mysteries of the terrene Goddess, were called by the ancients bees; and Proserpine herself was denominated by them *honied*. The moon, likewise, who presides over generation, was called by them a bee, and also a bull. And Taurus is the exaltation of the moon. But bees are ox-begotten. And this appellation is also given to souls proceeding into generation. The God, likewise, who is occultly connected with generation, is a stealer of oxen. To which may be added, that honey is considered as a symbol of death, and on this account, it is usual to offer libations of honey to the terrestrial Gods; but gall is considered as a symbol of life; whether it is obscurely signified by this, that the life of the soul dies through pleasure, but through bitterness the soul resumes its life, whence, also, bile is sacrificed to the Gods; or whether it is, because death liberates from molestation, but the pre-

sent life is laborious and bitter. All souls, however, proceeding into generation, are not simply called bees, but those who will live in it justly, and who, after having performed such things as are acceptable to the Gods, will again return [to their kindred stars]. For this insect loves to return to the place from whence it first came, and is eminently just and sober. Whence, also, the libations which are made with honey are called sober. Bees, likewise, do not sit on beans, which were considered by the ancients as a symbol of generation proceeding in a right line, and without flexure; because this leguminous vegetable is almost the only seed-bearing plant, whose stalk is perforated throughout without any intervening knots[m]. We must therefore admit, that honey-combs and bees are appropriate and common symbols of the aquatic Nymphs, and of souls that are married [as it were] to [the humid and fluctuating nature of] generation.

9. Caves, therefore, in the most remote periods of antiquity, were consecrated to the Gods, before temples were erected to them. Hence, the Curetes in Crete dedicated a cavern to Jupiter; in Arcadia, a cave was sacred to the Moon, and to Lycean Pan; and in Naxus, to Bacchus. But wherever Mithra was known, they propitiated the God in a cavern. With respect, however, to this Ithacensian cave, Homer was not satisfied with saying that it had two gates, but adds, that one of the gates was turned towards the north, but the other, which was more divine, to the south. He also says, that the northern gate was pervious to descent, but does not indicate whether this was also the case with the southern gate. For of this, he only says, " It is inaccessible to men, but it is the path of the immortals."

10. It remains, therefore, to investigate what is indi-

---

[m] Hence, when Pythagoras exhorted his disciples to abstain from beans, he intended to signify, that they should beware of a continued and perpetual descent into the realms of generation.

cated by this narration, whether the poet describes a cavern which was in reality consecrated by others, or whether it is an enigma of his own invention. Since, however, a cavern is an image and symbol of the world, as Numenius and his familiar Cronius assert, there are two extremities in the heavens, viz. the winter tropic, than which nothing is more southern, and the summer tropic, than which nothing is more northern. But the summer tropic is in Cancer, and the winter tropic in Capricorn. And since Cancer is nearest to us, it is very properly attributed to the Moon, which is the nearest of all the heavenly bodies to the earth. But as the southern pole, by its great distance, is invisible to us, hence Capricorn is attributed to Saturn, the highest and most remote of all the planets. Again, the signs from Cancer to Capricorn, are situated in the following order: and the first of these is Leo, which is the house of the Sun; afterwards Virgo, which is the house of Mercury; Libra, the house of Venus; Scorpius, of Mars; Sagittarius, of Jupiter; and Capricornus, of Saturn. But from Capricorn in an inverse order, Aquarius is attributed to Saturn; Pisces, to Jupiter; Aries, to Mars; Taurus, to Venus; Gemini, to Mercury; and, in the last place, Cancer to the Moon.

11. Theologists therefore assert, that these two gates are Cancer and Capricorn; but Plato calls them entrances. And of these, theologists say, that Cancer is the gate through which souls descend; but Capricorn that through which they ascend. Cancer is indeed northern, and adapted to descent; but Capricorn is southern, and adapted to ascent[n]. The northern parts, like-

---

[n] Macrobius, in the 12th chapter of his Commentary on Scipio's Dream, has derived some of the ancient arcana which it contains from what is here said by Porphyry. A part of what he has farther added, I shall translate, on account of its excellence and connexion with the above passage. "Pythagoras thought that the empire of Pluto began downwards from the milky way, because souls falling from thence appear to have already receded from the Gods. Hence he asserts, that the nutriment of milk is first offered to infants, because their first motion

wise, pertain to souls descending into generation. And the gates of the cavern which are turned to the north, are

commences from the galaxy, when they begin to fall into terrene bodies. On this account, since those who are about to descend are yet in *Cancer*, and have not left the milky way, they rank in the order of the Gods. But when, by falling, they arrive at the *Lion*, in this constellation they enter on the exordium of their future condition. And because, in the *Lion*, the rudiments of birth, and certain primary exercises of human nature, commence; but *Aquarius* is opposite to the *Lion*, and presently sets after the *Lion* rises; hence, when the sun is in *Aquarius*, funeral rites are performed to departed souls, because he is then carried in a sign which is contrary or adverse to human life. From the confine, therefore, in which the zodiac and galaxy touch each other, the soul, descending from a round figure, which is the only divine form, is produced into a cone by its defluxion. And as a line is generated from a point, and proceeds into length from an indivisible, so the soul, from its own point, which is a monad, passes into the duad, which is the first extension. And this is the essence which Plato, in the Timæus, calls impartible, and at the same time partible, when he speaks of the nature of the mundane soul. For as the soul of the world, so likewise that of man, will be found to be in one respect without division, if the simplicity of a divine nature is considered; and in another respect partible, if we regard the diffusion of the former through the world, and of the latter through the members of the body.

" As soon, therefore, as the soul gravitates towards body in this first production of herself, she begins to experience a material tumult, that is, matter flowing into her essence. And this is what Plato remarks in the Phædo, that the soul is drawn into body staggering with recent intoxication; signifying by this, the new drink of matter's impetuous flood, through which the soul, becoming defiled and heavy, is drawn into a terrene situation. But the starry *cup* placed between Cancer and the Lion, is a symbol of this mystic truth, signifying that descending souls first experience intoxication in that part of the heavens through the influx of matter. Hence oblivion, the companion of intoxication, there begins silently to creep into the recesses of the soul. For if souls retained in their descent to bodies the memory of divine concerns, of which they were conscious in the heavens, there would be no dissension among men about divinity. But all, indeed, in descending, drink of oblivion; though some more, and others less. On this account, though truth is not apparent to all men on the earth, yet all exercise their opinions about it; because *a defect of memory is the origin of opinion*. But these discover most who have drank least of oblivion, because they easily remember what they had known before in the heavens.

rightly said to be pervious to the descent of men; but the southern gates are not the avenues of the Gods, but

"The soul, therefore, falling with this first weight from the zodiac and milky way into each of the subject spheres, is not only clothed with the accession of a luminous body, but produces the particular motions which it is to exercise in the respective orbs. Thus in Saturn, it energizes according to a ratiocinative and intellective power; in the sphere of Jove, according to a practic power; in the orb of the Sun, according to a sensitive and imaginative nature; but according to the motion of desire in the planet Venus; of pronouncing and interpreting what it perceives in the orb of Mercury; and according to a plantal or vegetable nature, and a power of acting on body, when it enters into the lunar globe. And this sphere, as it is the last among the divine orders, so it is the first in our terrene situation. For this body, as it is the dregs of divine natures, so it is the first animal substance. And this is the difference between terrene and supernal bodies (under the latter of which I comprehend the heavens, the stars, and the more elevated elements,) that the latter are called upwards to be the seat of the soul, and merit immortality from the very nature of the region, and an imitation of sublimity; but the soul is drawn down to these terrene bodies, and is on this account said to die when it is enclosed in this fallen region, and the seat of mortality. Nor ought it to cause any disturbance that we have so often mentioned the death of the soul, which we have pronounced to be immortal. For the soul is not extinguished by its own proper death, but is only overwhelmed for a time. Nor does it lose the benefit of perpetuity by its temporal demersion. Since, when it deserves to be purified from the contagion of vice, through its entire refinement from body, it will be restored to the light of perennial life, and will return to its pristine integrity and perfection."

"The powers, however, of the planets, which are the causes of the energies of the soul in the several planetary spheres, are more accurately described by Proclus, in p. 260 of his admirable Commentary on the Timæus, as follows: ει δε βουλει και οτι των αγιωθεν πλανητων Σεληνη μεν αιτια τοις θνητοις της φυσεως, το αυτοφιον αγαλμα ουσα της πηγαιας φυσεως· Ηλιος δε δημιουργος των αισθησεων πασων, διοτι και του οραν και του ορασθαι αιτιος· Ερμης δε των της φαντασιας κινησεων αυτης γαρ της φαντασικης ουσιας, ως μιας ουσης αισθησεως και φαντασιας, Ηλιος υποστατης· Αφροδιτη δε των επιθυμητικων ορεξεων· Αρης δε των θυμοειδων κινησεων των κατα φυσιν εκασοις· κοινη δε των μεν ζωτικων πασων δυναμεων Ζευς, των δε γνωσ]ικων Κρονος, διηρυται γαρ παντα τα ειδη τα αλογα εις ταυτας, i. e. "If you are willing, also, you may say, that of the beneficent planets, the Moon is the cause to mortals of nature, being herself the visible statue of fontal nature. But the Sun is the Demiurgus of every thing sensible, in consequence of being the cause of sight and visibility. Mercury is the cause of the motions of the

of souls ascending to the Gods. On this account, the poet does not say that they are the avenues of the Gods, but of immortals; this appellation being also common to our souls, which are *per se*, or essentially, immortal. It is said, that Parmenides mentions these two gates in his treatise On the Nature of Things; as likewise, that they are not unknown to the Romans and Egyptians. For the Romans celebrate their Saturnalia when the Sun is in Capricorn; and during this festivity, slaves wear the shoes of those that are free, and all things are distributed among them in common; the legislator obscurely signifying by this ceremony, that through this gate of the heavens, those who are now born slaves will be liberated through the Saturnian festival, and the house attributed to Saturn, *i. e.* Capricorn, when they live again, and return to the fountain of life. Since, however, the path from Capricorn is adapted to ascent°, hence the Romans denominate that month in which the Sun, turning from Capricorn to the east, directs his course to the north, Januarius, or January, from *janua*, a gate. But with the Egyptians, the beginning of the year is not Aquarius, as with the Romans, but Cancer. For the star Sothis, which the Greeks call the Dog, is near to Cancer. And the rising of Sothis is the new moon with them, this being the principle of generation to the world. On this account, the gates of the Homeric cavern are not dedicated to the east and west, nor to the equinoctial signs, Aries and Libra, but to the north and south, and to those celestial signs which, towards the south, are most southerly, and, towards the north, are most northerly;

phantasy; for of the imaginative essence itself, so far as sense and phantasy are one, the Sun is the producing cause. But Venus is the cause of epithymetic appetites [or of the appetites pertaining to desire]; and Mars, of the irascible motions which are conformable to nature. Of all vital powers, however, Jupiter is the common cause; but of all gnostic powers, Saturn. For all the irrational forms are divided into these."

° For καταβασιν, in this place, it appears to me to be obviously necessary to read αναβασιν. For Porphyry has above informed us, that Capricorn is the gate through which souls ascend.

because this cave was sacred to souls and aquatic Nymphs. But these places are adapted to souls descending into generation, and afterwards separating themselves from it. Hence, a place near to the equinoctial circle was assigned to Mithra as an appropriate seat. And on this account he bears the sword of Aries, which is a martial sign. He is likewise carried in the Bull, which is the sign of Venus. For Mithra, as well as the Bull, is the demiurgus and lord of generation[p]. But he is placed near the equinoctial circle, having the northern parts on his right hand, and the southern on his left. They likewise arranged towards the south the southern hemisphere, because it is hot; but the northern hemisphere towards the north, through the coldness of the north wind.

12. The ancients, likewise, very reasonably connected winds with souls proceeding into generation, and again separating themselves from it, because, as some think, souls attract a spirit, and have a pneumatic essence. But the north wind is adapted to souls falling into generation; and, on this account, the northern blasts refresh those who are dying, and when they can scarcely draw their breath. On the contrary, the southern gales dissolve life. For the north wind, indeed, from its superior coldness, congeals [as it were, the animal life], and detains it in the frigidity of terrene generation. But the south wind being hot, dissolves this life, and sends it upward to the heat of a divine nature. Since, however, our terrene habitation is more northern, it is proper that souls which are born in it should be familiar with the north wind; but those that exchange this life for a better, with the south wind. This also is the cause why the north wind is at its commencement great; but the south

---

[p] Hence Phanes, or Protogonus, who is the paradigm of the universe, and who was absorbed by Jupiter, the Demiurgus, is represented by Orpheus as having the head of a *bull* among other heads with which he is adorned. And in the Orphic hymn to him, he is called *bull-roarer*.

wind, at its termination. For the former is situated directly over the inhabitants of the northern part of the globe; but the latter is at a great distance from them; and the blast from places very remote, is more tardy than from such as are near. But when it is coacervated, then it blows abundantly, and with vigour. Since, however, souls proceed into generation through the northern gate, hence this wind is said to be amatory. For, as the poet says,

> Boreas, enamour'd of the sprightly train,
> Conceal'd his godhead in a flowing mane.
> With voice dissembled, to his loves he neigh'd,
> And coursed the dappled beauties o'er the mead:
> Hence sprung twelve others of unrivall'd kind,
> Swift as their mother mares, and father wind ⁱ.

It is also said, that Boreas ravished Orithya ʳ, from

ⁱ Iliad, lib. xx. v. 223, &c.

ʳ This fable is mentioned by Plato in the Phædrus, and is beautifully unfolded as follows, by Hermias, in his Scholia on that Dialogue: " A twofold solution may be given of this fable; one from history, more ethical; but the other, transferring us [from parts] to wholes. And the former of these is as follows: Orithya was the daughter of Erectheus, and the priestess of Boreas; for each of the winds has a presiding deity, which the telestic art, or the art pertaining to sacred mysteries, religiously cultivates. To this Orithya, then, the God was so very propitious, that he sent the north wind for the safety of the country; and besides this, he is said to have assisted the Athenians in their naval battles. Orithya, therefore, becoming enthusiastic, being possessed by her proper God Boreas, and no longer energizing as a human being (for animals cease to energize according to their own peculiarities, when possessed by superior causes), died under the inspiring influence, and thus was said to have been ravished by Boreas. And this is the more ethical explanation of the fable.

" But the second, which transfers the narration to wholes, and does not entirely subvert the former, is the following: for divine fables often employ transactions and histories, in subserviency to the discipline of wholes. It is said then, that Erectheus is the God that rules over the three elements, air, water, and earth. Sometimes, however, he is considered as alone the ruler of the earth, and sometimes as the presiding deity of Attica alone. Of this deity Orithya is the daughter; and she is the prolific power of the Earth, which is indeed coextended with the

whom he begot Zetis and Calais. But as the south is attributed to the Gods, hence, when the Sun is at his meridian, the curtains in temples are drawn before the statues of the Gods; in consequence of observing the Homeric precept, "that it is not lawful for men to enter temples when the Sun is inclined to the south;" for this is the path of the immortals. Hence, when the God is at his meridian altitude, the ancients placed a symbol of mid-day and of the south in the gates of temples*; and, on this account, in other gates also, it was not lawful to speak at all times, because gates were considered as sacred. Hence, too, the Pythagoreans, and the wise men among the Egyptians, forbade speaking while passing through doors or gates; for then they venerated in silence that God who is the principle of wholes [and, therefore of all things].

13. Homer likewise knew that gates are sacred, as is

---

word *Erectheus*, as the unfolding of the name signifies. For it is *the prolific power of the Earth, flourishing and restored, according to the seasons*. But Boreas is the providence of the Gods, supernally illuminating secondary natures. For the providence of the Gods in the world is signified by Boreas, because this divinity blows from lofty places. And the elevating power of the Gods is signified by the south wind, because this wind blows from low to lofty places; and besides this, *things situated towards the south are more divine*. The providence of the Gods, therefore, causes the prolific power of the Earth, or of the Attic land, to *ascend*, and become visible.

"Orithya also may be said to be a soul aspiring after things above, from ορουω and θειω, according to the Attic custom of adding a letter at the end of a word, which letter is here an "ω." Such a soul, therefore, is ravished by Boreas supernally blowing. But if Orithya was hurled from a precipice, this also is appropriate, for such a soul dies a philosophic, not receiving a physical death, and abandons a life pertaining to her own deliberate choice, at the same time that she lives a physical life. And philosophy, according to Socrates in the Phædo, is nothing else than a meditation of death."

* In the original, ιστασαν ουν και συμβολον της μεσημβριας και του νοτου, επι τη θυρη, μεσημβριαζοντος του θεου, which Holstenius translates most erroneously as follows: "Austrum igitur meridiei symbolum statuunt; cum deus meridiano tempore ostio immineat."

evident from his representing Oeneus, when supplicating, shaking the gate:

> The gates he shakes, and supplicates the son [u].

He also knew the gates of the heavens which are committed to the guardianship of the Hours; which gates originate in cloudy places, and are opened and shut by the clouds. For he says,

> Whether dense clouds they close, or wide unfold [x].

And on this account, these gates emit a bellowing sound, because thunders roar through the clouds:

> Heaven's gates spontaneous open to the powers;
> Heaven's bellowing portals, guarded by the Hours [y].

He likewise elsewhere speaks of the gates of the Sun, signifying by these Cancer and Capricorn; for the Sun proceeds as far as to these signs, when he descends from the north to the south, and from thence ascends again to the northern parts. But Capricorn and Cancer are situated about the galaxy, being allotted the extremities of this circle; Cancer, indeed, the northern, but Capricorn the southern extremity of it. According to Pythagoras, also, the *people of dreams* [z], are the souls which are said to be collected in the galaxy, this circle being so called from the milk with which souls are nourished when they fall into generation. Hence, those who evocate departed souls, sacrifice to them by a libation of milk mingled with honey; because, through the allurements of sweetness, they will proceed into generation; with the birth of man, milk being naturally produced. Farther still, the southern regions produce small bodies; for it is usual with heat to attenuate them in the greatest degree. But all bodies generated in the north are large, as is

---

[u] Iliad, lib. xi. v. 579.   [x] Iliad, lib. viii. v. 395.
[y] Iliad, lib. viii. v. 393.

[z] The souls of the suitors are said by Homer, in the 24th book of the Odyssey (v. 11), to have passed, in their descent to the region of spirits, beyond *the people of dreams*.

evident in the Celtæ, the Thracians, and the Scythians; and these regions are humid, and abound with pastures. For the word Boreas is derived from Βορα, which signifies nutriment. Hence, also, the wind which blows from a land abounding in nutriment, is called Βορρας, as being of a nutritive nature. From these causes, therefore, the northern parts are adapted to the mortal tribe, and to souls that fall into the realms of generation. But the southern parts are adapted to that which is immortal[a], just as the eastern parts of the world are attributed to the Gods, but the western to dæmons. For, in consequence of nature originating from diversity, the ancients every where made that which has a twofold entrance to be a symbol of the nature of things. For the progression is either through that which is intelligible, or through that which is sensible. And if through that which is sensible, it is either through the sphere of the fixed stars, or through the sphere of the planets. And again, it is either through an immortal, or through a mortal progression. One centre, likewise, is above, but the other beneath the earth; and the one is eastern, but the other western. Thus, too, some parts of the world are situated on the left, but others on the right hand: and night is opposed to day. On this account, also, harmony consists of, and *proceeds*[b] through contraries. Plato also says, that there are two openings[c], one of which affords a passage to souls ascending to the heavens, but the other to souls descending to the earth. And, according to theologists, the Sun and Moon are the gates of souls, which ascend through the Sun, and descend through the Moon. With Homer, likewise, there are two tubs,

> From which the lot of every one he fills,
> Blessings to these, to those distributes ills[d].

[a] Hence, the southern have always been more favourable to genius, than the northern parts of the earth.

[b] In the original, τεξυει; but instead of it, I read ιτρευει.

[c] See my translation of the 10th book of his Republic.

[d] Iliad, xxiv. v. 528.

But Plato, in the Gorgias, by tubs intends to signify souls, some of which are malefic, but others beneficent, and some of which are rational, but others irrational*.

* The passage in the Gorgias of Plato, to which Porphyry here alludes, is as follows:— " Soc. But, indeed, as you also say, life is a grievous thing. For I should not wonder if Euripides spoke the truth when he says: 'Who knows whether to live is not to die, and to die is not to live?' And we, perhaps, are in reality dead. For I have heard from one of the wise, that we are now dead; and that the body is our sepulchre; but that the part of the soul in which the desires are contained, is of such a nature that it can be persuaded, and hurled upwards and downwards. Hence a certain elegant man, perhaps a Sicilian, or an Italian, denominated, mythologizing, this part of the soul a tub, by a derivation from the probable and the persuasive; and, likewise, he called those that are stupid, or deprived of intellect, uninitiated. He farther said, that the intemperate and uncovered nature of that part of the soul in which the desires are contained, was like a pierced tub, through its insatiable greediness."

What is here said by Plato is beautifully unfolded by Olympiodorus, in his MS. Commentary on the Gorgias, as follows:— " Euripides (in Phryxo) says, that to live is to die, and to die to live. For the soul coming hither, as she imparts life to the body, so she partakes [through this] of a certain privation of life; but this is an evil. When separated, therefore, from the body, she lives in reality: for she dies here, through participating a privation of life, because the body becomes the source of evils. And hence it is necessary to subdue the body.

"But the meaning of the Pythagoric fable, which is here introduced by Plato, is this: We are said to be dead, because, as we have before observed, we partake of a privation of life. The sepulchre which we carry about with us is, as Plato himself explains it, the body. But Hades is the unapparent, because we are situated in obscurity, the soul being in a state of servitude to the body. The tubs are the desires; whether they are so called from our hastening to fill them, as if they were tubs, or from desire persuading us that it is beautiful. The initiated, therefore, *i. e.* those that have a perfect knowledge, pour into the entire tub: for these have their tub full; or, in other words, have perfect virtue. But the uninitiated, viz. those that possess nothing perfect, have perforated tubs. For those that are in a state of servitude to desire always wish to fill it, and are more inflamed; and on this account they have perforated tubs, as being never full. But the sieve is the rational soul mingled with the irrational. For the [rational] soul is called a circle, because it seeks itself, and is itself sought; finds itself, and is itself found. But the irrational soul imitates a right line, since it does

Souls, however, are [analogous to] tubs, because they contain in themselves energies and habits, as in a vessel. In Hesiod too, we find one tub closed, but the other opened by Pleasure, who scatters its contents every where, Hope alone remaining behind. For in those things in which a depraved soul, being dispersed about matter, deserts the proper order of its essence; in all these, it is accustomed to feed itself with [the pleasing prospects of] auspicious hope.

14. Since, therefore, every twofold entrance is a symbol of nature, this Homeric cavern has, very properly, not one portal only, but two gates, which differ from each other conformably to things themselves; of which one pertains to Gods and good [dæmons[f]], but the other to mortals, and depraved natures. Hence, Plato took occasion to speak of bowls, and assumes tubs instead of amphoræ, and two openings, as we have already observed, instead of two gates. Pherecydes Syrus also mentions recesses and trenches, caverns, doors, and gates; and through these obscurely indicates the generations of souls, and their separation from these material realms. And thus much for an explanation of the Homeric cave, which we think we have sufficiently unfolded without adducing any farther testimonies from ancient philosophers and theologists, which would give a needless extent to our discourse.

15. One particular, however, remains to be explained,

---

not revert to itself like a circle. So far, therefore, as the sieve is circular, it is an image of the rational soul; but, as it is placed under the right lines formed from the holes, it is assumed for the irrational soul. Right lines, therefore, are in the middle of the cavities. Hence, by the sieve, Plato signifies the rational in subjection to the irrational soul. But the water is the flux of nature: for, as Heraclitus says, *moisture is the death of the soul.*"

In this extract the intelligent reader will easily perceive that the occult signification of the *tubs* is more scientifically unfolded by Olympiodorus than by Porphyry.

[f] In the original, και τας μεν, θεοις τε και τοις αγαθοις προσηκουσας. But after αγαθοις, I have no doubt we should insert δαιμοσι.

and that is the symbol of the olive planted at the top of the cavern ; since Homer appears to indicate something very admirable by giving it such a position. For he does not merely say that an olive grows in this place, but that it flourishes on the summit of the cavern.

> "High at the head a branching olive grows,
> Beneath, a gloomy grotto's cool recess."

But the growth of the olive in such a situation, is not fortuitous, as some one may suspect, but contains the enigma of the cavern. For since the world was not produced rashly and casually, but is the work of divine wisdom and an intellectual nature, hence an olive, the symbol of this wisdom, flourishes near the present cavern, which is an image of the world. For the olive is the plant of Minerva; and Minerva is wisdom. But this Goddess being produced from the head of Jupiter, the theologist has discovered an appropriate place for the olive, by consecrating it at the summit of the port; signifying by this, that the universe is not the effect of a casual event, and the work of irrational fortune, but that it is the offspring of an intellectual nature and divine wisdom, which is separated, indeed, from it [by a difference of essence], but yet is near to it, through being established on the summit of the whole port; [*i. e.* from the dignity and excellence of its nature governing the whole with consummate wisdom]. Since, however, an olive is ever-flourishing, it possesses a certain peculiarity in the highest degree adapted to the revolutions of souls in the world; for to such souls this cave [as we have said] is sacred. For in summer, the white leaves of the olive tend upward, but in winter, the whiter leaves are bent downward. On this account, also, in prayers and supplications, men extend the branches of an olive, ominating from this, that they shall exchange the sorrowful darkness of danger for the fair light of security and peace. The olive, therefore, being naturally ever-flourishing, bears fruit which is the auxiliary of labour [by being its reward]; it is also sacred to Minerva; supplies the victors in athletic labours with crowns; and affords a friendly branch to the suppliant petitioner. Thus, too, the world is governed by an intellectual nature, and is conducted by a wisdom eternal and ever-flourishing; by which the rewards of victory are conferred on the conquerors in the athletic race of life, as the reward of severe toil and patient perseverance. And the Demiurgus, who connects and contains the world [in ineffable comprehensions], invigorates miserable and suppliant souls.

16. In this cave, therefore, says Homer, all external possessions must be deposited. Here, naked, and assuming a suppliant habit, afflicted in body, casting aside every thing superfluous, and being averse to the energies of sense, it is requisite to sit at the foot of the olive, and consult with Minerva by what means we may most effectually destroy that hostile rout of passions which insidiously lurk in the secret recesses of the soul. Indeed, as it appears to me, it was not without reason that Numenius and his followers thought the person of Ulysses in the Odyssey represented to us a man, who passes in a regular manner over the dark and stormy sea of generation, and thus at length arrives at that region where tempests and seas are unknown, and finds a nation

"Who ne'er knew salt, or heard the billows roar."

17. Again, according to Plato, the deep, the sea, and a tempest, are images of a material nature. And on this account, I think, the poet called the port by the name of Phorcys. For he says, "It is the port of the ancient marine Phorcys⁵." The daughter, likewise, of this God is men-

---

⁵ Phorcys is one among the ennead of Gods who, according to Plato in the Timæus, fabricate generation. Of this deity, Proclus observes, "that as the Jupiter in this ennead causes the unapparent divisions and separation of forms made by Saturn to become apparent, and as Rhea calls them forth into motion and generation; so Phorcys inserts them in matter, produces sensible natures, and adorns the visible

tioned in the beginning of the Odyssey. But from Thoosa the Cyclops was born, whom Ulysses deprived of sight. And this deed of Ulysses became the occasion of reminding him of his errors, till he was safely landed in his native country. On this account, too, a seat under the olive is proper to Ulysses, as to one who implores divinity, and would appease his natal dæmon with a suppliant branch. For it will not be simply, and in a concise way, possible for any one to be liberated from this sensible life, who blinds this dæmon, and renders his energies inefficacious; but he who dares to do this, will be pursued by the anger[b] of the marine and material Gods, whom it is first requisite to appease by sacrifices, labours, and patient endurance; at one time, indeed, contending with the passions, and at another employing enchantments and deceptions, and by these, transforming himself in an all-various manner; in order that, being at length divested of the torn garments [by which his true person was concealed], he may recover the ruined empire of his soul. Nor will he even then be liberated from labours; but this will be effected when he has entirely passed over the raging sea, and, though still living, becomes so ignorant of marine and material works [through deep attention to intelligible concerns], as to mistake an oar for a corn-van.

18. It must not, however, be thought, that interpretations of this kind are forced, and nothing more than the conjectures of ingenious men; but when we consider the great wisdom of antiquity, and how much Homer excelled in intellectual prudence, and in an accurate knowledge of every virtue, it must not be denied that he has obscurely

---

essence, in order that there may not only be divisions of productive principles [or forms] in natures and in souls, and in intellectual essences prior to these; *but likewise in sensibles. For this is the peculiarity of fabrication.*

[b] "The anger of the Gods," says Proclus, " is not an indication of any passion in them, but demonstrates our inaptitude to participate of their illuminations."

indicated the images of things of a more divine nature in the fiction of a fable. For it would not have been possible to devise the whole of this hypothesis, unless the figment had been transferred [to an appropriate meaning] from certain established truths. But reserving the discussion of this for another treatise, we shall here finish our explanation of the present Cave of the Nymphs.

AUXILIARIES

TO THE

PERCEPTION OF INTELLIGIBLE NATURES.

SECTION I.

1. Every body is in place; but nothing essentially incorporeal, or any thing of this kind, has any locality.

2. Things essentially incorporeal, because they are more excellent than all body and place, are every where, not with interval, but impartibly.

3. Things essentially incorporeal, are not locally present with bodies, but are present with them when they please; by verging towards them so far as they are naturally adapted so to verge. They are not, however, present with them locally, but through habitude, proximity, and alliance.

4. Things essentially incorporeal, are not present with bodies, by hypostasis and essence; for they are not mingled with bodies. But they impart a certain power which is proximate to bodies, through verging towards them. For tendency constitutes a certain secondary power proximate to bodies.

5. Soul, indeed, is a certain medium between an impartible essence, and an essence which is divisible about bodies. But intellect is an impartible essence alone. And qualities and material forms are divisible about bodies.

6. Not every thing* which acts on another, effects

---

* In the original, Ου το ποιουν εις αλλο, πιλασει και αφη ποιει, α ποιει· κ. τ. λ. But it is evident, from the sense of the whole passage, that, for Ου το ποιουν, we should read, Ου παν το ποιουν, κ. τ. λ.

that which it does effect by approximation and contact; but those natures which effect any thing by approximation and contact, use approximation accidentally.

7. The soul is bound to the body by a conversion to the corporeal passions; and is again liberated by becoming impassive to the body.

8. That which nature binds, nature also dissolves: and that which the soul binds, the soul likewise dissolves. Nature, indeed, bound the body to the soul; but the soul binds herself to the body. Nature, therefore, liberates the body from the soul; but the soul liberates herself from the body.

9. Hence there is a twofold death; the one, indeed, universally known, in which the body is liberated from the soul; but the other peculiar to philosophers, in which the soul is liberated from the body. Nor does the one[b] entirely follow the other.

10. We do not understand similarly in all things, but in a manner adapted to the essence of each. For intellectual objects we understand intellectually; but those that pertain to soul rationally. We apprehend plants spermatically; but bodies idolically [*i. e.* as images]; and that which is above all these, super-intellectually and super-essentially[c].

---

[b] The article ο is wanting here in the original before ετερος.

[c] Knowledge subsists conformably to the nature by which it is possessed, and not conformably to the thing known. Hence it is either better than, or co-ordinate with, or inferior to the object of knowledge. Thus the rational soul has a knowledge of sensibles, which is superior to sensibles; but it knows itself with a co-ordinate knowledge; and its knowledge of divinity is inferior to the object of knowledge. Porphyry, therefore, is not correct in what he here says. This dogma respecting the conformity of knowledge to that which knows, rather than to the thing known, originated from the divine Iamblichus, as we are informed by Ammonius in his commentary on Aristotle's treatise De Interpretatione, and is adopted by Proclus (in Parmenid.). Boetius likewise employs it in his reasoning in lib. v. about the prescience of divinity. None of his commentators, however, have noticed the source from whence it was derived.

11. Incorporeal hypostases, in descending, are distributed into parts, and multiplied about individuals with a diminution of power; but when they ascend by their energies beyond bodies, they become united, and proceed into a simultaneous subsistence, through exuberance of power.

12. The homonymous is not in bodies only, but life also is among the number of things which have a multifarious subsistence. For the life of a plant is different from that of an animated being; the life of an intellectual essence differs from that of the nature which is beyond intellect; and the psychical differs from the intellectual life. For these natures live, though nothing which proceeds from, possesses a life similar to them.

13. Every thing which generates by its very essence, generates that which is inferior to itself[d]; and every thing generated, is naturally converted to its generator. Of generating natures, however, some are not at all converted to the beings which they generate; but others are partly converted to them, and partly not; and others are only converted to their progeny, but are not converted to themselves.

14. Every thing generated, possesses from that which is different from itself the cause of its generation, since nothing is produced without a cause. Such generated natures, however, as have their existence through composition, these are on this account corruptible. But such as, being simple and incomposite, possess their existence in a simplicity of hypostasis, these being indissoluble, are, indeed, incorruptible; yet they are said to be generated, not as if they were composites, but as being suspended from a certain cause. Bodies, therefore, are in a twofold respect generated; as being suspended from a certain producing cause; and as being composites. But soul and intellect are only generated as being suspended

---

[d] Because here the generator is that *primarily* which the thing generated is *secondarily*. See my translation of Proclus's Theological Elements.

from a cause, and not as composites. Hence bodies are generated, dissoluble and corruptible; but soul and intellect are unbegotten, as being without composition, and on this account indissoluble and incorruptible; yet they are generated so far as they are suspended from a cause.

15. Intellect is not the principle of all things; for intellect is many things; but, prior to *the many,* it is necessary that there should be *the one.* It is evident, however, that intellect is many things. For it always understands its conceptions, which are not one, but many; and which are not any thing else than itself. If, therefore, it is the same with its conceptions, but they are many, intellect also will be many things. But that it is the same with intelligibles [or the objects of its intellection], may be thus demonstrated. For, if there is any thing which intellect surveys, it will either survey this thing as contained in itself, or as placed in something else. And that intellect, indeed, contemplates or surveys, is evident. For, in conjunction with intellection, or intellectual perception, it will be intellect; but if you deprive it of intellection, you will destroy its essence. It is necessary, therefore, that, directing our attention to the properties of knowledge, we should investigate the perception of intellect. All the gnostic powers, then, which we contain, are universally sense, imagination, and intellect[*]. The power, however, which employs sense, surveys by projecting itself to externals, not being united to the objects which it surveys, but only receiving an impression of, by exerting its energies upon them. When,

[*] Porphyry here summarily comprehends the rational gnostic powers of the soul in intellect, because, being rational, they are expansions of intellect properly so called. But these powers, beginning from the lowest, are *opinion, dianoia,* and the summit of dianoia, which summit is the intellect of the human soul, and is that power, by the light of which we perceive the truth of axioms, it being intuitive perception. *Dianoia* is the discursive energy of reason; or it is that power which reasons scientifically, deriving the principles of its reasoning from intellect. And *opinion* is that power which knows *that* a thing is, but is ignorant of the cause of it, or *why* it is.

therefore, the eye sees a visible object, it is impossible that it should become the same with that which it perceives: for it would not see if there was not an interval between it and the object of its perception. And, after the same manner, that which is touched, if it was the same with that by which it is touched, would perish. From which it is evident that sense, and that which employs sense, must always tend to an external object, in order to apprehend something sensible. In like manner also, the phantasy, or imagination, always tends to something external, and by this extension of itself, gives subsistence to, or prepares an image; its extension to what is external, indicating that the object of its perception is a resemblance of something external. And such, indeed, is the apprehension of these two powers; neither of which verging to, and being collected into itself, perceives either a sensible or insensible form.

In intellect, however, the apprehension of its objects does not subsist after this manner, but is effected by converging to, and surveying itself. For by departing from itself, in order to survey its own energies, and become the eye of them, and the sight of essences, it will not understand any thing. Hence, as sense is to that which is sensible, so is intellect to that which is intelligible. Sense, however, by extending itself to externals, finds that which is sensible situated in matter; but intellect surveys the intelligible, by being collected into itself, and not extended outwardly[f]. On this account some are of opinion, that the hypostasis of intellect differs from that of the phantasy only in name. For the phantasy, in the rational animal, appeared to them to be intelligence. As these men, however, suspended all things from matter and a corporeal nature, it follows that they should also suspend from these intellect. But our intellect surveys

---

[f] In the original, ει δε μη εξω εκτεινομενος; but for ει δε μη, it appears to me to be obviously necessary to read ουδε μη.

both bodies and other essences. Hence it apprehends them situated somewhere. But as the proper objects of intellect have a subsistence out of matter, they will be no where[g] [locally]. It is evident, therefore, that intellectual natures are to be conjoined with intelligence. But if intellectual natures are in intellect, it follows that intellect, when it understands intelligibles, surveys both the intelligible and itself; and that proceeding into itself, it perceives intellectually, because it proceeds into intelligibles. If, however, intellect understands many things, and not one thing only, intellect also will necessarily be many. But *the one* subsists prior to the many; so that it is necessary that *the one* should be prior to intellect.

16. Memory is not the conservation of imaginations, but the power of calling forth *de novo* those conceptions which had previously occupied the attention of the mind[h].

17. Soul, indeed, contains the reasons [or forms] of all things, but energizes according to them, either being called forth to this energy by something else, or converting itself to them inwardly. And when called forth by something else, it introduces, as it were, the senses to externals, but when it enters into itself, it becomes occupied with intellectual conceptions. Hence some one may say, that neither the senses, nor intellectual perceptions, are without the phantasy; so that, as in the animal, the senses are not without the passive affection of the sen-

---

[g] In the original, ἔξω δε ὄντων ὕλης, οὐδαμοῦ ἂν εἴη ταῦτα; which Holstenius, wholly mistaking the meaning, most erroneously translates, "At si extra materiam sint, neutiquam id fieri poterit." Farther on, Porphyry asserts, that God, intellect, and soul, are no where, according to corporeal locality.

[h] In the original, ἡ μνήμη οὐκ ἐστι φαντασιῶν συντήρησις, αλλα τοῦ μελετηθέντων προβάλλεσθαι ἐκ νέας προβλήματα. But for προβλήματα, I read προλήμματα. This power, by which Porphyry characterizes memory, is of a stable nature. And hence memory is *stability of knowledge*, in the same manner as immortality is *stability of life*, and eternity *stability of being*.

sitive organs, in like manner intellections are not without the phantasy. Perhaps, however, it may be said, in answer to this, that, as an impression in the sensitive organ is the concomitant of the sensitive animal, so analogously a phantasm is the concomitant of the intellection of the soul in man, considered as an animal[i].

18. Soul is an essence without magnitude, immaterial, incorruptible, possessing its existence in life, and having life from itself.

19. The passivity of bodies is different from that of incorporeal natures. For the passivity of bodies is attended with mutation; but the adaptations and passions of the soul are energies; yet they are by no means similar to the calefactions and frigefactions of bodies. Hence, if the passivity of bodies is accompanied by mutation, it must be said that all incorporeal natures are impassive. For the essences which are separated from matter and bodies, are what they are in energy. But those things which approximate to matter and bodies, are themselves, indeed, impassive; but the natures in which they are surveyed are passive. For when the animal perceives sensibly, the soul [*i. e.* the rational soul] appears to be similar to separate harmony[k], of itself moving the chords adapted

---

[i] See the notes on the 3d book of my translation of Aristotle's treatise on the Soul, and also my translation of Plotinus on Felicity. "The phantasy," says Olympiodorus (in Platonis Phæd.) "is an impediment to our intellectual conceptions; and hence, when we are agitated by the inspiring influence of Divinity, if the phantasy intervenes, the enthusiastic energy ceases: for enthusiasm and the phantasy are contrary to each other. Should it be asked, whether the soul is able to energize without the phantasy? we reply, that its perception of universals proves that it is able. It has perceptions, therefore, independent of the phantasy; at the same time, however, the phantasy attends it in its energies, just as a storm pursues him who sails on the sea."

[k] The analogy of the soul to harmony, is more accurately unfolded as follows, by Olympiodorus, in his Commentary on the Phædo of Plato, than it is in this place by Porphyry: "Harmony has a triple subsistence. For it is either harmony itself, or it is that which is first harmonized, and which is such according to the whole of itself; or it is that which

to harmony; but the body is similar to the inseparable harmony in the chords, [*i.e.* to the harmony which cannot exist separate from the chords]. But the animal is the cause of the motion, because it is an animated being. It is, however, analogous to a musician, because it is harmonic; but the bodies which are struck through sensitive passion, are analogous to the harmonized chords of a musical instrument. For in this instance, also, separate harmony is not passively affected, but the chords. And the musician, indeed, moves according to the harmony which is in him; yet the chords would not be musically moved, even though the musician wished that they should, unless harmony ordered this to take place.

20. Incorporeal natures are not denominated like bodies, according to a participation in common of one and the same genus; but they derive their appellation from a mere privation with respect to bodies. Hence, nothing hinders some of them from having a subsistence as beings, but others as non-beings; some of them, from being prior to, and others posterior to bodies; some, from being separate, and others inseparable from bodies; some, from having a subsistence by themselves, but others from being indigent of things different from themselves, to their existence; some, from being the same through energies and self-motive lives, but others from subsisting together with lives, and energies of a certain quality. For they subsist according to a negation of the things which they are not, and not according to the affirmation of the things which they are.

21. The properties of matter, according to the an-

---

is secondarily harmonized, and which partially participates of harmony. The first of these must be assigned to intellect, the second to soul, and the third to body. This last, too, is corruptible, because it subsists in a subject; but the other two are incorruptible, because they are neither composites, nor dependent on a subject. Hence, the rational soul is analogous to a musician, but the animated body to harmonized chords; for the former has a subsistence separate, but the latter inseparable from the musical instrument."

cients, are the following: It is incorporeal; for it is different from bodies. It is without life; for it is neither intellect nor soul, nor vital from itself [*i. e.* essentially]. It is also formless, variable, infinite, and powerless. Hence, it is neither being, nor yet non-being. Not that it is non-being like motion, but it is true non-being, the image and phantasm of bulk, because it is that which bulk primarily contains. It is likewise powerless, and the desire of subsistence, has stability, but not in permanency, and always appears in itself to be contrary. Hence, it is both small and great, more and less, deficient and exceeding. It is always becoming to be, or rising into existence; abides not, and yet is unable to fly away; and is the defect of all being. Hence, in whatever it announces itself to be, it deceives; and though it should appear to be great, it is nevertheless small. For it resembles a flying mockery, eluding all pursuit, and vanishing into non-entity. For its flight is not in place, but is effected by its desertion of real being. Hence, also, the images which are in it, are in an image more unreal than themselves; just as in a mirror, where the thing represented is in one place, and the representation of it in another. It likewise appears to be full, yet contains nothing, though it seems to possess all things[1].

22. All passions subsist about the same thing as that about which corruption subsists; for the reception of passion is the path to corruption. And the thing that is the subject of passivity, is also the subject of corruption. Nothing incorporeal, however, is corrupted. But some of them either exist, or do not exist; so that they are not at all passive. For that which is passive, ought not to be a thing of this kind, but such as may be changed in quality, and corrupted by the properties of the things

---

[1] What Porphyry here says about matter, is derived from the treatise of Plotinus, *On the Impassivity of Incorporeal Natures*, to my translation of which I refer the reader.

that enter into it, and cause it to be passive. For the change in quality of that which is inherent, is not casually effected. Neither, therefore, does matter suffer; for it is of itself without quality. Nor do the forms which enter into, and depart from it, suffer; but the passion subsists about the composite from matter and form, the very being of which consists in the union of the two. For this, in the contrary powers and qualities of the things which enter and produce passion, is seen to be the subject of them. On which account, also, those things, the life of which is externally derived, and does not subsist from themselves, are capable of suffering both the participation and the privation of life. But those beings whose existence consists in an impassive life, must necessarily possess a permanent life; just as a privation of life, so far as it is a privation of it, is attended with impassivity. As, therefore, to be changed and to suffer pertain to the composite from matter and form, and this is body, but matter is exempt from this; thus also, to live and to die, and to suffer through the participation of life and death, is beheld in the composite from soul and body. Nevertheless, this does not happen to the soul; because it is not a thing which consists of life and the privation of life, but consists of life alone. And it possesses this, because its essence is simple, and the reason [or form] of the soul is self-motive[m].

23. An intellectual essence is so similar in its parts, that the same[n] things exist both in a partial and an all-perfect intellect. In an universal intellect, however, partial natures subsist universally; but in a partial intellect, both universals and particulars subsist partially.

24. Of that essence, the existence of which is in life, and the passions of which are lives, the death also consists in a certain life, and not in a total privation of life;

---

[m] See my translation of the before-mentioned treatise of Plotinus.

[n] For τα οντα here, I read τα αυτα.

PERCEPTION OF INTELLIGIBLE NATURES. 211

because, neither is the deprivation of life in this essence a passion, or a path which entirely leads to a non-vital subsistence.

25. In incorporeal lives, the progressions are effected while the lives themselves remain firm and stable, nothing pertaining to them being corrupted, or changed into the hypostasis of things subordinate to them. Hence, neither are the things to which they give subsistence produced with a certain corruption or mutation. Nor do these incorporeal lives subsist like generation, which participates of corruption and mutation. Hence, they are unbegotten and incorruptible, and on this account are unfolded into light without generation and incorruptibly.

26. Of that nature which is beyond intellect, many things are asserted through intellection, but it is surveyed by a cessation of intellectual energy better than with it[o]; just as with respect to one who is asleep, many things are asserted of him while he is in that state by those who are awake; but the proper knowledge and apprehension of his dormant condition, is only to be obtained through sleep. For the similar is known by the similar; because *all knowledge is an assimilation to the object of knowledge.*

27. With respect to that which is non-being, we either produce it, being ourselves separated from real being, or we have a preconception of it, as adhering to being. Hence, if we are separated from being, we have not an antecedent conception of the non-being which is above being, but our knowledge in this case is only that of a false passion, such as that which happens to a man when he departs from himself. For as a man may himself, and through himself, be truly elevated to the non-being which is above being, so, by departing from being,

---

[o] Hence, it is beautifully said in the Clavis of Hermes Trismegistus, " that the knowledge of *the good* [or the supreme principle of things], is a divine silence, and the quiescence of all the senses." See, also, on this subject, a most admirable extract from Damascius, περι αρχων, at the end of the 3d volume of my Plato.

he is led to the non-being which is a falling off from being.

28. The hypostasis of body is no impediment whatever to that which is essentially incorporeal, so as to prevent it from being where, and in such a way, as it wishes to be. For as that which is without bulk is incomprehensible by body, and does not at all pertain to it, so that which has bulk cannot impede or obscure an incorporeal nature, but lies before it like a non-entity. Nor does that which is incorporeal pervade locally, when it wishes to pass from one thing to another; for place is consubsistent with bulk. Nor is it compressed by bodies. For that which in any way whatever is connected with bulk, may be compressed, and effect a transition locally; but that which is entirely without bulk and without magnitude, cannot be restrained by that which has bulk, and does not participate of local motion. Hence, by a certain disposition, it is found to be there, where it is inclined to be, being with respect to place every where and yet no where[p]. By *a certain disposition*, therefore, it is either above the heavens, or is contained in a certain part of the world. When, however, it is contained in a certain part of the world, it is not visible to the eyes, but the presence of it becomes manifest from its works.

29. It is necessary that an incorporeal nature, if it is contained in body, should not be enclosed in it like a wild beast in a den; (for no body is able thus to enclose and comprehend it), nor is it contained in body in the same way as a bladder contains something liquid, or wind; but it is requisite that it should give subsistence to certain powers which verge to what is external, through its union with body; by which powers, when it descends, t becomes complicated with body. Its conjunction, therefore, with body, is effected through an ineffable

---

[p] For that which is truly incorporeal, is *every where* virtually, *i. e.* in power and efficacy, but is *no where* locally.

extension. Hence, nothing else binds it, but itself binds itself to body. Neither, therefore, is it liberated from the body, when the body is [mortally] wounded and corrupted, but it liberates itself, by turning itself from an adhering affection to the body.

30. None of the hypostases which rank as wholes, and are perfect, is converted to its own progeny; but all perfect hypostases are elevated to their generators as far as to the mundane body [or the body of the world]. For this body, being perfect, is elevated to its soul, which is intellectual: and on this account it is moved in a circle. But the soul of this body is elevated to intellect; and intellect, to the first principle of all things. All beings, therefore, proceed to this principle as much as possible, beginning from the last of things. The elevation, however, to that which is first, is either proximate or remote. Hence, these natures may not only be said to aspire after the highest God, but also to enjoy him to the utmost of their power. But in partial[q] hypostases, and which are able to verge to many things, there is also a desire of being converted to their progeny. Hence, likewise, in these there is error, in these there is reprehensible incredulity. These, therefore, matter injures, because they are capable of being converted to it, being at the same time able to be converted to divinity. Hence, perfection gives subsistence to secondary from primary natures, preserving them converted to the first of things; but imperfection converts primary[r] to posterior natures, and causes them to love the beings which have departed from divinity prior to themselves.

31. God is every where because he is no where: and this is also true of intellect and soul: for each of these is

---

[q] For μεριστaις here, I read, μερικαις. For Porphyry is here speaking of essences which are opposed to *such as rank as wholes*, as is evident from the whole of this paragraph.

[r] The primary natures of which Porphyry is now speaking, are rational partial souls, such as ours; for the natures superior to these, are never converted to beings posterior to themselves.

every where, because each is no where. But God indeed is every where, and no where, with respect to all things which are posterior to him; and he[s] alone is such as he is, and such as he wills himself to be. Intellect is in God, but is every where, and no where, with respect to the natures posterior to it. And soul is in God and intellect, and is every where and no where, in [or with respect to] body[t]. But body is in soul, and in intellect[u], and in God. And as all beings and non-beings are from and in God, hence, he is neither beings nor non-beings, nor subsists in them. For if, indeed, he was alone every where, he would be all things and in all, but since he is also no where, all things are produced through him, and are contained in him, because he is every where. They are, however, different from him, because he is no where. Thus, likewise, intellect being every where and no where, is the cause of souls, and of the natures posterior to souls; yet intellect is not soul, nor the natures posterior to soul, nor subsists in them; because it is not only every where, but is also no where, with respect to the natures posterior to it. And soul is neither body, nor in body, but is the cause of body; because being every where, it is also no where, with respect to body. And this progression of things in the universe extends as far as to that which is neither able to be at once every where, nor at once no where, but partially participates of each of these[x].

32. The soul does not exist on the earth [when it is conversant with terrene natures,] in the same manner

---

[s] For αυτου, *is thic*, I read, αυτος.

[t] In the original, και ψυχη εν νω τε και θεω πανταχου, και ουδαμου εν σωματι, but it appears to me to be necessary to read, και ψυχη εν νω τε και θεω, και πανταχου και ουδαμου εν σωματι.

[u] και εν νω, is omitted in the original, but ought to be inserted, as is evident from the version of Holstenius.

[x] The irrational life is a thing of this kind, which is partly separable and partly inseparable from body. Hence, so far as it is inseparable from body, it partakes of the *every where*; but, so far as it is separable, of the *no where*.

as bodies accede to the earth; but a subsistence of the soul on the earth, signifies its presiding over terrene bodies. Thus, also, the soul is said to be in Hades, when it presides over its image[y], which is naturally adapted to be in place, but possesses its hypostasis in darkness. So that if Hades is a subterranean dark place, the soul, though not divulsed from being, will exist in Hades, by attracting to itself its image. For when the soul departs from the solid body, the spirit accompanies it which it had collected from the starry spheres. But as from its adhering affection to the body, it exerts a partial reason, through which it possesses an habitude to a body of a certain quality, in performing the energies of life;— hence, from this adhesion to body, the form of the phantasy is impressed in the spirit, and thus the image is attracted by the soul. The soul, however, is said to be in Hades, because the spirit obtains a formless and obscure nature. And as a heavy and moist spirit pervades as far as to subterranean places, hence the soul is said to proceed under the earth. Not that this essence of the soul changes one place for another, and subsists in place, but it receives the habitudes of bodies which are naturally adapted to change their places, and to be allotted a subsistence in place; such-like bodies receiving it according to aptitudes, from being disposed after a certain manner towards it. For the soul, conformably to the manner in which it is disposed, finds an appropriate body. Hence, when it is disposed in a purer manner, it has a connascent body which approximates to an ethereal nature, and this is an ethereal body. But when it proceeds from reason to the energies of the phantasy; then its connascent body is of a solar-form nature. And when it becomes effeminate and vehemently excited by corporeal form, then it is connected with a lunar-form

---

[y] *i. e.* The animal spirit, or pneumatic soul, in which the rational soul suffers her punishments in Hades.

body. When, however, it falls into bodies which consist of humid vapours, then a perfect ignorance of real being follows, together with darkness and infancy.

Moreover, in its egress from the body, if it still possesses a spirit turbid from humid exhalations, it then attracts to itself a shadow, and becomes heavy; a spirit of this kind naturally striving to penetrate into the recesses of the earth, unless a certain other cause draws it in a contrary direction. As therefore the soul, when surrounded with this testaceous and terrene vestment, necessarily lives on the earth; so likewise when it attracts a moist spirit, it is necessarily surrounded with the image. But it attracts moisture when it continually endeavours to associate with nature, whose operations are effected in moisture, and which are rather under than upon the earth. When, however, the soul earnestly endeavours to depart from nature, then she becomes a dry splendour, without a shadow, and without a cloud, or mist. For moisture gives subsistence to a mist in the air; but dryness constitutes a dry splendour from exhalation.

33. The things which are truly predicated of a sensible and material nature, are these: that it has, in every respect, a diffused and dispersed subsistence; that it is mutable; that it has its existence in difference; that it is a composite; that it subsists by itself, [as the subject or recipient of other things;] that it is beheld in place, and in bulk: and other properties similar to these are asserted of it. But the following particulars are predicated of truly existing being, and which itself subsists from itself; viz. that it is always established in itself; that it has an existence perpetually similar and the same; that it is essentialized in sameness; that it is immutable according to essence, is uncompounded, is neither dissoluble, nor, in place, nor is dispersed into bulk; and is neither generated, nor capable of being destroyed: and other properties are asserted of it similar to these. To

which predications adhering, we should neither ourselves assert any thing repugnant to them, concerning the different nature of sensible and truly-existing beings, nor assent to those who do.

SECTION II.

34. There is one kind of virtues pertaining to the political character, and another to the man who tends to contemplation, and who, on this account, is called theoretic, and is now a beholder [of intellectual and intelligible natures]. And there are also other virtues pertaining to intellect, so far as it is intellect, and separate from soul. The virtues indeed of the political character, and which consist in the moderation of the passions, are characterized by following and being obedient to the reasoning about that which is becoming in actions. Hence, looking to an innoxious converse with neighbours, these virtues are denominated, from the aggregation of fellowship, political. And here prudence indeed subsists about the reasoning part; fortitude about the irascible part; temperance in the consent and symphony of the epithymetic[z] with the reasoning part; and justice, in each of these performing its proper employment with respect to governing and being governed. But the virtues of him who proceeds to the contemplative life, consist in a departure from terrestrial concerns. Hence, also, they are called purifications, being surveyed in the refraining from corporeal actions, and avoiding sympathies with the body. For these are the virtues of the soul elevating itself to true being. The political virtues therefore adorn the mortal man, and are the forerunners of purifications. For it is necessary that he who is adorned by the *cathartic* virtues, should abstain from doing any thing precedaneously in conjunction with body. Hence, in

---

[z] *i. e.* That part of the soul which is the source of all-various desires.

these purifications, not to opine with body, but to energize alone, gives subsistence to *prudence;* which derives its perfection through energizing intellectually with purity. But not to be similarly passive with the body, constitutes *temperance.* Not to fear a departure from body, as into something void, and non-entity, gives subsistence to *fortitude.* But when reason and intellect are the leaders, and there is no resistance [from the irrational part], *justice* is produced. The disposition therefore, according to the political virtues, is surveyed in the moderation of the passions; having for its end to live as man conformable to nature. But the disposition, according to the theoretic virtues, is beheld in apathy[a], the end of which is a similitude to God.

Since, however, of purification, one kind consists in purifying, but another pertains to those that are purified, the cathartic virtues are surveyed according to both these significations of purification. For the end of purification is to become pure. But since purification, and the being purified, are an ablation of every thing foreign, the good resulting from them will be different from that which purifies; so, that if that which is purified was good prior to the impurity with which it is defiled, purification is sufficient. That, however, which remains after purification, is good, and not purification. The nature of the soul also was not good [prior to purification], but is that which is able to partake of good, and is boniform. For if this were not the case, it would not have become situated in evil. The good therefore of the soul consists in being united to its generator, but its evil in an association with things subordinate to itself. Its evil also is twofold; the one arising from an association with terrestrial natures, but the other from doing this with an excess of the passions. Hence, all the political virtues which liberate the soul from one evil, may be denomi-

---

[a] This philosophic apathy is not, as is stupidly supposed by most of the present day, insensibility, but a perfect subjugation of the passions to reason.

nated virtues, and are honourable. But the cathartic are more honourable, and liberate it from evil, so far as it is soul. It is necessary therefore, that the soul, when purified, should associate with its generator. Hence, the virtue of it, after its conversion, consists in a scientific knowledge of [true] being; but this will not be the case, unless conversion precedes.

There is, therefore, another genus of virtues after the cathartic and political, and which are the virtues of the soul *energizing intellectually*. And here, indeed, wisdom and prudence consist in the contemplation of those things which intellect possesses. But *justice* consists in performing what is appropriate in conformity to, and energizing according to intellect. *Temperance* is an inward conversion of the soul to intellect. And *fortitude* is apathy, according to a similitude of that to which the soul looks, and which is naturally impassive. These virtues also, in the same manner as the others, alternately follow each other.

The fourth species of the virtues, is that of the paradigms subsisting in intellect: which are more excellent than the psychical virtues, and exist as the paradigms of these; the virtues of the soul being the similitudes of them. And intellect indeed is that in which all things subsist at once as paradigms. Here, therefore, prudence is science; but intellect that knows [all things] is wisdom. Temperance is that which is converted to itself. The proper work of intellect, is the performance of its appropriate duty, [and this is justice[b].] But fortitude is sameness, and the abiding with purity in itself, through an abundance of power. There are therefore four genera of virtues; of which, indeed, some pertain to intellect, concur with the essence of it, and are paradigmatic. Others pertain to soul now looking to intellect, and

[b] The words καὶ δικαιοσυν, are omitted in the original. But it is evident from the treatise of Plotinus " On the Virtues," that they ought to be inserted. For what Porphyry says in this Section about the virtues, is derived from that treatise.

being filled from it. Others belong to the soul of man, purifying itself, and becoming purified from the body, and the irrational passions. And others are the virtues of the soul of man, adorning the man, through giving measure and bound to the irrational nature, and producing moderation in the passions. *And he indeed, who has the greater virtues, has also necessarily the less; but the contrary is not true, that he who has the less, has also the greater virtues.* Nor will he who possesses the greater, energize precedaneously according to the less, but only so far as the necessities of the mortal nature require. The scope also of the virtues, is, as we have said, generically different in the different virtues. For the scope of the *political* virtues, is to give measure to the passions in their practical energies according to nature. But the scope of the *cathartic* virtues, is entirely to obliterate the remembrance of the passions ; and the scope of the rest subsists analogously to what has been before said. Hence, he who energizes according to the *practical* virtues, is a *worthy* man ; but he who energizes according to the *cathartic* virtues, is an *angelic man*, or is also *a good dæmon*. He who energizes according to the *intellectual* virtues alone is *a God;* but he who energizes according to the *paradigmatic* virtues, is *the father of the Gods*. We, therefore, ought especially to pay attention to the *cathartic* virtues, since we may obtain these in the present life. But through these, the ascent is to the more honourable virtues. Hence, it is requisite to survey to what degree purification may be extended : for it is a separation from body, and from the passive motion of the irrational part. But how this may be effected, and to what extent, must now be unfolded.

In the first place, indeed, it is necessary that he who intends to acquire this purification, should, as the foundation and basis of it, know himself to be a soul bound in a foreign thing, and in a different essence. In the second place, as that which is raised from this foundation, he should collect himself from the body, and as it were from different places, so as to be disposed in a manner perfectly impassive with respect to the body. For he who energizes uninterruptedly according to sense, though he may not do this with an adhering affection, and the enjoyment resulting from pleasure, yet, at the same time, his attention is dissipated about the body, in consequence of becoming through sense[c] in contact with it. But we are addicted to the pleasures or pains of sensibles; in conjunction with a promptitude, and converging sympathy; from which disposition it is requisite to be purified. *This, however, will be effected by admitting necessary pleasures, and the sensations of them, merely as remedies, or as a liberation from pain*[d], *in order that* [*the rational part*] *may not be impeded* [*in its energies*]. Pain also must be taken away. But if this is not possible, it must be mildly diminished. And it will be diminished, if the soul is not copassive with it. Anger, likewise, must as much as possible be taken away; and must by no means be premeditated. But if it cannot be entirely removed, deliberate choice must not be mingled with it, but the unpremeditated motion must be the impulse of the irrational part. *That however which is unpremeditated, is imbecile and small.* All fear likewise must be expelled. For he who is adapted to this purification, will fear nothing. Here, however, if it should take place, it will be unpremeditated. Anger therefore and fear must be used for the purpose of admonition. But the desire of every thing base must be exterminated. Such a one also, so far as he is a cathartic philosopher, will not desire meats and drinks [except so far as they are necessary]. Neither must there be the unpremeditated in natural venereal connexions; *but if this should take place, it must only be as far as to that precipitate imagination which*

[c] Instead of κατ' αυτην, here it is necessary to read, κατ' αισθησιν.

[d] Conformably to this, as we have before observed, Aristotle says in the 7th Book of his Nicomachean Ethics, " that corporeal pleasures are remedies against pain, and that they fill up the indigence of nature, but perfect no energy of the rational soul."

energizes in sleep. In short, the intellectual soul itself of the purified man must be liberated from all these [corporeal propensities]. He must likewise endeavour, that what is moved to the irrational nature of corporeal passions, may be moved without sympathy, and without animadversion; so that the motions themselves may be immediately dissolved, through their vicinity to the reasoning power. This, however, will not take place while the purification is proceeding to its perfection; but will happen to those in whom reason rules without opposition. Hence, in these, the inferior part will so venerate reason, that it will be indignant if it is at all moved, in consequence of not being quiet when its master is present, and will reprove itself for its imbecility. These, however, are yet only moderations of the passions, but at length terminate in apathy. For when copassivity is entirely exterminated, then apathy is present with him who is purified from this passivity. For passion becomes moved when reason imparts excitation, through verging [to the irrational nature].

35. Every thing which is situated somewhere, is there situated according to its own nature, and not preternaturally. For body, therefore, which subsists in matter and bulk, to be somewhere, is to be in place. Hence, for the body of the world, which is material and has bulk, to be every where, is to be extended with interval, and to subsist in the place of interval. But a subsistence in place, is not at all present with the intelligible world, nor, in short, with that which is immaterial, and essentially incorporeal, because it is without bulk, and without interval; so that the ubiquity of an incorporeal nature is not local. Hence, neither will one part of it be here, but another there; for if this were the case, it would not be out of place, nor without interval; but wherever it is, the whole of it is there. Nor is it indeed in this, but not in another place; for thus it would be comprehended by one place, but separated from another. Nor is it remote from this thing, but near to that; in the same manner as

remoteness and nearness are asserted of things which are adapted to be in place, according to the measures of intervals. Hence, the sensible is present, indeed, with the intelligible world, according to interval, but [a truly] incorporeal nature is present with the world impartibly, and unaccompanied by interval. The impartible, likewise, when it is in that which has interval, is wholly in every part of it, being one and the same in number [in every part of it]. That which is impartible, therefore, and without multitude, becomes extended into magnitude, and multiplied, when intimately connected with that which is naturally multitudinous, and endued with magnitude; and thus the latter receives the former in such a way as it is adapted to receive it, and not such as the former truly is. But that which is partible and multitudinous, is received by that which is naturally impartible and without multitude, impartibly and non-multitudinously, and after this manner is present with it; *i.e.* the impartible is present impartibly, without plurality, and without a subsistence in place, conformably to its own nature, with that which is partible, and which is naturally multitudinous, and exists in place. But that which is partible, multiplied, and in place, is present with the impartible essence, partibly, multitudinously, and locally. Hence, it is necessary, in the survey of these natures, to preserve and not confound the peculiarities of each; or rather, we should not imagine or opine of that which is incorporeal, such properties as pertain to bodies, or any thing of the like kind. For no one would ascribe to bodies the peculiarities of a genuinely incorporeal essence. For all of us are familiar with bodies; but the knowledge of incorporeal natures is attainable by us with great difficulty; because, through not being able to behold them intuitively, we are involved in doubt about their nature; and this takes place as long as we are under the dominion of imagination.

Thus, therefore, you should say, If that which is in place, is out of, or has departed from itself, through having proceeded into bulk, that which is intelligible is not in place, and is in itself, because it has not proceeded into corporeal extension. Hence, if the former is an image, the latter is an archetype. And the former, indeed, derives its being through the intelligible; but the latter subsists in [and through] itself. For every [physical] image is the image of intellect. It is also requisite that, calling to mind the peculiarities of both these, we should not wonder at the discrepance which takes place in their congress with each other; if, in short, it is proper on this occasion to use the word congress. For we are not now surveying the congress of bodies, but of things which are entirely distinct from each other, according to peculiarity of hypostasis. Hence, also, this congress is different from every thing which is usually surveyed in things essentially the same. Neither, therefore, is it temperament, or mixture, or conjunction, or apposition, but subsists in a way different from all these; appearing, indeed, in all the mutual participations of consubstantial natures, in whatever way this may be effected; but transcending every thing that falls under the apprehension of sense. Hence, an intelligible essence is wholly present without interval, with all the parts of that which has interval, though they should happen to be infinite in number. Nor is it present distributed into parts, giving a part to a part; nor being multiplied, does it multitudinously impart itself to multitude; but it is wholly present with the parts of that which is extended into bulk, and with each individual of the multitude, and all the bulk impartibly, and without plurality, and as numerically one. But it pertains to those natures to enjoy it partibly, and in a distributed manner, whose power is dissipated into different parts. And to these it frequently happens, that through a defect of their own nature, they counterfeit an intelligible essence; so that doubts arise respecting that essence, which appears to have passed from its own nature into theirs.

36. Truly-existing being is neither great nor small,

for magnitude and parvitude are properly the peculiarities of bulk. But true being transcends both magnitude and parvitude; and is above the greatest, and above the least; and is numerically one and the same, though it is found to be simultaneously participated by every thing that is greatest, and every thing that is least. You must not, therefore, conceive of it as something which is greatest; as you will then be dubious how, being that which is greatest, it is present with the smallest masses, without being diminished or contracted. Nor must you conceive of it as something which is least; since you will thus again be dubious how, being that which is least, it is present with the greatest masses, without being multiplied or increased, or without receiving addition. But at one and the same time receiving into the greatest magnitude that which transcends the greatest bulk, and into the least magnitude that which transcends the least *, you will be able to conceive how the same thing, abiding in itself, may be simultaneously seen in any casual magnitude, and in infinite multitudes and corporeal masses. For according to its own peculiarity, it is present with the magnitude of the world impartibly and without magnitude. It also antecedes the bulk of the world, and comprehends every part of it, in its own impartibility; just as, *vice versa*, the world, by its multitude of parts, is multifariously present, as far as it is able, with truly-existing being, yet cannot comprehend it, neither with the whole of its bulk, nor the whole of its power; but meets with it in all its parts as that which is infinite, and cannot be passed beyond; and this both in other respects, and

---

* In the original, αλλα το εκδεχομενος των μεγιστων ογκοι, εις το μεγιστον, και των ελαχιστων εις το ελαχιστον, αμα λαβων, κ.τ.λ. This Holstenius most erroneously translates, "Verum id quod maximam molem intervallo maximo, et minimam minimo excedit simul sumens, &c." For a truly incorporeal nature, such as that of which Porphyry is now speaking, has nothing to do with interval, and, therefore, does not by interval surpass either the greatest or the least corporeal mass; but is received transcendently by the greatest and the least magnitude.

because truly-existing being is entirely free from all corporeal extension.

37. That which is greater in bulk, is less in power, when compared, not with things of a similar kind, but with those that are of a different species, or of a different essence. For bulk is, as it were, the departure of a thing from itself, and a division of power into the smallest parts. Hence, that which transcends in power, is foreign from all bulk. For power proceeding into itself, is filled with itself, and, by corroborating itself, obtains its proper strength; on which account, body proceeding into bulk through a diminution of power, is as much remote from truly-incorporeal being, as that which truly exists is from being exhausted by bulk; for the latter abides in the magnitude of the same power, through an exemption from bulk. As, therefore, truly-existing being is, with reference to a corporeal mass, without magnitude and without bulk; thus also, that which is corporeal is, with reference to truly-existing being, imbecile and powerless. For that which is greatest by magnitude of power, is exempt from all bulk; so that the world existing every where, and, as it is said, meeting with real being which is truly every where, is not able to comprehend the magnitude of its power. It meets, however, with true being, which is not partibly present with it, but is present without magnitude, and without any definite limitation. The presence, therefore, of truly-existing being with the world, is not local, but assimilative, so far as it is possible for body to be assimilated to that which is incorporeal, and for that which is incorporeal to be surveyed in a body assimilated to it. Hence, an incorporeal nature is not present with body, so far as it is not possible for that which is material to be assimilated to a perfectly immaterial nature; and it is present, so far as a corporeal can be assimilated to an incorporeal essence. Nevertheless, this is not effected through reception; since, if it were, each would be corrupted. For the material, indeed, in receiving the immaterial nature, would be corrupted;

through being changed into it; and the immaterial essence would become material. Assimilations, therefore, and participations of powers, and the deficiency of power, proceed into things which are thus different in essence from each other, into each other. The world, therefore, is very far from possessing the power of real being; and real being is very remote from the imbecility of a material nature. But that which subsists between these, assimilating and being assimilated, and conjoining the extremes to each other, becomes the cause of deception about the extremes, in consequence of applying, through the assimilation, the one to the other.

38. Truly-existing being is said to be many things, not by a subsistence in different places, nor in the measures of bulk, nor by coacervation, nor by the circumscriptions or comprehensions[f] of divisible parts, but by a difference which is immaterial, without bulk, and without plurality, and which is divided according to multitude. Hence, also, it is one; not as one body, nor as in one place; nor as one bulk; nor as one which is many things; because it is different so far as it is one, and its difference is both divided and united. For its difference is not externally acquired, nor adscititious, nor obtained through the participation of something else, but it is many things from itself. For, remaining one, it energizes with all energies, because, through sameness, it constitutes all difference; not being surveyed in the difference of one thing with respect to another, as is the case in bodies. For, on the contrary, in these, unity subsists in difference; because diversity has in them a precedaneous existence; but the unity which they contain is externally and adscititiously derived. For in truly existing being, indeed, unity and sameness precede; but difference is generated, from this unity being energetic. *Hence, true being is multiplied in impartibility; but body is united in multitude and bulk.* The

---

[f] For διαληψιν, here, I read καταληψιν, and Holstenius also has in this place *comprehensionibus*.

former also is established in itself, subsisting in itself according to unity; but the latter is never in itself, because it receives its hypostasis in an extension of existence. The former, therefore, is an all-energetic one; but the latter is an united multitude. Hence, it is requisite to explore how the former is one and different; and again, how the latter is multitude and one. Nor must we transfer the peculiarities of the one to those which pertain to the other.

39. It is not proper to think that the multitude of souls was generated on account of the multitude of bodies; but it is necessary to admit that, prior to bodies, there were many souls, and one soul [the cause of the many]. Nor does the one and whole soul prevent the subsistence in it of many souls; nor do the multitude of souls distribute by division the one soul into themselves. For they are distinct from, but are not abscinded from the soul, which ranks as a whole; nor do they distribute into minute parts this whole soul into themselves. They are also present with each other without confusion; nor do they produce the whole soul by coacervation. For they are not separated from each other by any boundaries; nor, again, are they confused with each other; just as neither are many sciences confused in one soul [by which they are possessed]. For these sciences do not subsist in the soul like bodies, as things of a different essence from it; but they are certain energies of the soul. For the nature of soul possesses an infinite power. Every thing also that occurs in it is soul; and all souls are [in a certain respect] one; and again, the soul which ranks as a whole, is different from all the rest. For as bodies, though divided to infinity, do not end in that which is incorporeal, but alone receive a difference of segments according to bulk; thus also soul, being a vital form, may be conceived to consist of forms *ad infinitum*. For it possesses specific differences, and the whole of it subsists together with, or without these. For, if there is in the soul that which is as it were a part divided from the

rest of the parts, yet, at the same time that there is difference, the sameness remains. If, however, in bodies, in which difference predominates over sameness, nothing incorporeal when it accedes cuts off the union, but all the parts remain essentially united, and are divided by qualities and other forms; what ought we to assert, and conceive of a specific incorporeal life, in which sameness is more prevalent than difference; to which nothing foreign to form is subjected, and from which the union of bodies is derived? Nor does body, when it becomes connected with soul, cut off its union, though it is an impediment to its energies in many respects. But the sameness of soul produces and discovers all things through itself, through its specific energy, which proceeds to infinity; since any part of it whatever is capable of effecting all things, when it is liberated and purified from a conjunction with bodies; just as any part of seed possesses the power of the whole seed. As, however, seed, when it is united with matter, predominates over it, according to each of the productive principles which the seeds contain; and all the seed, its power being collected into one, possesses the whole of its power in each of the parts; thus also, in the immaterial soul, that which may be conceived as a part, has the power of the whole soul. But that part of it which verges to matter, is vanquished, indeed, by the form to which it verges, and yet is adapted to associate with immaterial form, though it is connected with matter, when withdrawing itself from a material nature, it is converted to itself. Since, however, through verging to matter, it becomes in want of all things, and suffers an emptiness of its proper power; but when it is elevated to intellect, is found to possess a plenitude of all its powers; hence those who first obtained a knowledge of this plenitude of the soul, very properly indicated its emptiness by calling it *poverty*, and its fulness by denominating it *satiety*.

SECTION III.

40. The ancients, wishing to exhibit to us the peculiarity of incorporeal being, so far as this can be effected by words, when they assert that it is one, immediately add, that it is likewise all things; by which they signified that it is not some one[s] of the things which are known by the senses. Since, however, we suspect that this incorporeal one is different from sensibles, in consequence of not perceiving this total one, which is all things according to one, in a sensible nature, and which is so because this one is all things:—hence the ancients added, that *it is one so far as one;* in order that we might understand that what is all things in truly existing being, is something uncompounded, and that we might withdraw ourselves from the conception of a coacervation. When likewise they say that it is every where, they add that it is no where. When also they assert that it is in all things, they add, that it is no where in every thing. Thus, too, when they say, that it is in all things, and in every divisible nature which is adapted to receive it, they add, that it is a whole in a whole. And, in short, they render it manifest to us, through contrary peculiarities; at one and the same time assuming these, in order that we may exterminate, from the apprehension of it, the fictitious conceptions which are derived from bodies, and which obscure the cognoscible peculiarities of real being.

41. When you have assumed an eternal essence, infinite in itself according to power, and begin to perceive intellectually an hypostasis unwearied, untamed, and never-failing, but transcending in the most pure and

---

[s] In the original, καθο εν τι των κατ' αισθησιν συνεγνωσμενων; but it appears to me to be necessary, after καθο, to insert the words ουκ εστιν. For incorporeal being is not like some one of the things which are known by the senses, because no one of these is one, and, at the same time, all things. Holstenius did not perceive the necessity of this emendation, as is evident from his version of the passage.

genuine life, and full from itself; and which is likewise established in itself, satisfied with, and seeking nothing but itself:—to this essence, if you add a subsistence in place, or a relation to a certain thing, at the same time that you [appear to] diminish it, by ascribing to it an indigence of place, or a relative condition of being, you do not [in reality] diminish this essence, but you separate yourself from the perception of it, by receiving as a veil the phantasy which runs under your conjectural apprehension of it. For you cannot pass beyond, or stop, or render more perfect, or effect the least change in a thing of this kind, because it is impossible for it to be in the smallest degree deficient. For it is much more neverfailing than any perpetually flowing fountain can be conceived to be. If, however, you are unable to keep pace with it, and to become assimilated to the intelligible all, you should not investigate any thing pertaining to real being; or, if you do, you will deviate from the path that leads to it, and will look to something else. But if you investigate nothing else, being established in yourself and your own essence, you will be assimilated to the intelligible universe, and will not adhere to any thing posterior to it. Neither, therefore, should you say, I am of a great magnitude. For, omitting this greatness, you will become universal; though you were universal prior to this. But, together with the universal, something else was present with you, and you became less by the addition; because the addition was not from truly-existing being. For to that you cannot add any thing. When, therefore, any thing is added from non-being, a place is afforded to Poverty as an associate, accompanied by an indigence of all things. Hence, dismissing non-being, you will then become sufficient to yourself[h]. For he will not return properly to himself who does not dismiss things

---

[h] Immediately after this something is wanting in the original, (as is evident from the asterisks,) which, as it appears to me, no conjecture can appropriately supply.

of a more vile and abject nature, and who opines himself to be something naturally small, and not to be such as he truly is. For thus he, at one and the same time, departs both from himself, and from truly-existing being. When, also, any one is present with that which is present in himself, then he is present with true being, which is every where. But when you withdraw from yourself, then, likewise, you recede from real being;—of such great consequence is it, for a man to be present with that which is present with himself, [*i. e.* with his rational part], and to be absent from that which is external to him.

If, however, true being is present with us, but non-being is absent, and real being is not present with us in conjunction with other things [of a nature foreign to it]; it does not accede in order that it may be present, but we depart from it, when it is not present [with things of a different nature]. And why should this be considered as wonderful? For you when present are not absent from yourself; and yet you are not present with yourself, though present. And you are both present with and absent from yourself when you survey other things, and omit to behold yourself. If, therefore, you are thus present, and yet not [in reality] present with yourself, and on this account are ignorant of yourself, and in a greater degree discover all things, though remote from your essence, than yourself, with which you are naturally present, why should you wonder if that which is not present is remote from you who are remote from it, because you have become remote from yourself? For, by how much the more you are [truly] present with yourself, though it is present, and inseparably conjoined with you, by so much the more will you be present with real being, which is so essentially united to you, that it is as impossible for it to be divulsed from you, as for you to be separated from yourself. So that it is universally possible to know what is present with real being, and what is absent from it, though it is every where present, and again is also no where. For those who are able to proceed into their own essence intellectually, and to obtain a knowledge of it, will, in the knowledge itself, and the science accompanying this knowledge, be able to recover or regain themselves, through the union of that which knows with that which is known. And with those, who are present with themselves, truly-existing being will also be present. But from such as abandon the proper being of themselves to other things,—from these, as they are absent from themselves, true being will also be absent. If, however, we are naturally adapted to be established in the same essence, to be rich from ourselves, and not to descend to that which we are not; in so doing becoming in want of ourselves, and thus again associating with Poverty, though Porus[1] [or Plenty] is present;—and if we are cut off from real being, from which we are not separated either by place, or essence, nor by any thing else, through our conversion to non-being, we suffer as a just punishment of our abandonment of true being, a departure from, and ignorance of ourselves. And again, by a proper attention to, we recover ourselves, and become united to divinity. It is, therefore, rightly said, that the soul is confined in body as in a prison, and is there detained in chains like a fugitive slave[k]. We should, however, [earnestly] endeavour to be liberated from our bonds. For, through being converted to these sensible objects, we desert ourselves, though we are of a divine origin, and are, as Empedocles says,

Heaven's exiles, straying from the orb of light.

[1] In the original, και δια τουτων παλιν τη πενια συνιται, καιπερ παροντος αυτω; but for αυτω, I read πορου; as it appears to me that Porphyry is here alluding to what is said by Diotima, in the Banquet of Plato, concerning the parents of Love, viz. that they are *Poverty* and *Porus*, or *Plenty*.

[k] See the Phædo of Plato. But something is here wanting in the original, as is evident not only from the asterisks, but from the want of connexion in the words themselves.

So that every depraved life is full of servitude; and on this account is without God and unjust, the spirit in it being full of impiety, and consequently of injustice. And thus, again, it is rightly said, that justice is to be found in the performance of that which is the province of him who performs it. The image also of true justice consists in distributing to each of those with whom we live, that which is due to the desert of each.

42. That which possesses its existence in another [i. e. in something different from itself], and is not essentialized in itself, separably from another, if it should be converted to itself, in order to know itself, without that in which it is essentialized, withdrawing itself from it; would be corrupted by this knowledge, in consequence of separating itself from its essence. But that which is able to know itself without the subject in which it exists, and is able to withdraw itself from this subject, without the destruction of itself, cannot be essentialized in that, from which it is capable of converting itself to itself, without being corrupted, and of knowing itself by its own energies. Hence, if sight, and every sensitive power, neither perceives itself, nor apprehends or preserves itself by separating itself from body; but intellect, when it separates itself from body, then especially perceives intellectually, is converted to itself, and is not corrupted;—it is evident that the sensitive powers obtain the power of energizing through the body; but that intellect possesses its energies and its essence not in body, but in itself.

43. Incorporeal natures are properly denominated, and conceived to be what they are, according to a privation of body; just as, according to the ancients, matter, and the form which is in matter, and also natures and [physical] powers, are apprehended by an abstraction from matter. And after the same manner place, time, and the boundaries of things, are apprehended. For all such things are denominated according to a privation of body. There are likewise other things which are said to be incorporeal improperly, not according to a privation of

body, but, in short, because they are not naturally adapted to generate body[1]. Hence those of the former signification subsist in bodies; but those of the second are perfectly separated from bodies, and from those incorporeal natures which subsist about bodies. For bodies, indeed, are in place, and boundaries are in body. But intellect, and intellectual reason, neither subsist in place nor in body; nor proximately give existence to bodies, nor subsist together with bodies, or with those incorporeal natures which are denominated according to a privation of bodies. Neither, therefore, if a certain incorporeal vacuum should be conceived to exist, would it be possible for intellect to be in a vacuum. For a vacuum may be the recipient of body; but it is impossible that it should be the recipient of intellect, and afford a place for its energy. Since, however, the genus of an incorporeal nature appears to be twofold, one of these the followers of Zeno do not at all admit, but they adopt the other; and perceiving that the former is not such as the latter, they entirely subvert it, though they ought rather to conceive that it is of another genus, and not to fancy that, because it is not the latter, it has no existence.

44. Intellect and the intelligible are one thing, and sense and that which is sensible another. And the intelligible, indeed, is conjoined with intellect, but that which is sensible with sense. Neither, however, can sense by itself apprehend itself * * *. But the intelligible, which

---

[1] i. e. They are not adapted to be the immediate causes of body, because they are perfectly separated from it. The original is, ου δε τ' αλλα καταχρηστικως λεγομενα ασωματα, ου κατα στερησιν σωματος, κατα δε ολως μη πεφυκεναι γενναν σωμα. Holstenius, not understanding what is here said by Porphyry, translates the words κατα δε ολως μη πεφυκεναι γενναν σωμα, "sed quod nullum omnino corpus generare possunt." For Porphyry, as is evident from what immediately follows, is here speaking of natures which are perfectly separated from bodies, and which are, therefore, not naturally adapted to be the immediate generators of them, not through any deficiency, but through transcendency of power.

is conjoined with intellect, and intellect, which is conjoined with the intelligible, by no means fall under the perception of sense. Intellect, however, is intelligible to intellect. But if intellect is the intelligible object of intellect, intellect will be its own intelligible object. If, therefore, intellect is an intellectual and not a sensible object, it will be intelligible. But if it is intelligible to intellect, and not to sense, it will also be intelligent. The same thing, therefore, will be that which is intelligent, or intellectually perceives, and which is intellectually perceived, or is intelligible; and this will be true of the whole with respect to the whole; but not as he who rubs, and he who is rubbed. Intellect, therefore, does not intellectually perceive by one part, and is intellectually perceived by another: for it is impartible, and the whole is an intelligible object of the whole. It is likewise wholly intellect, having nothing in itself which can be conceived to be deprived of intelligence. Hence one part of it does not intellectually perceive, but not another part of it [m]. For, so far as it does not intellectually perceive, it will be unintelligent. Neither, therefore, departing from this thing, does it pass on to that. For of that from which it departs, it has no intellectual perception. But if there is no transition in its intellections, it intellectually perceives all things at once. If, therefore, it understands all things at once, and not this thing now, but another afterwards, it understands all things instantaneously and always * * * [n].

Hence, if all things are instantaneously perceived by it, its perceptions have nothing to do with the past and

---

[m] In the original, διο ουχι τοδε μεν εαυτου νοει, τοδε δε ου νοει, which Holstenius erroneously translates, " Ideoque non quidem unam sui partem intelligit, alteram vero non intelligit." For Porphyry is not here speaking of intellect surveying its parts, but of its being *wholly* intellective. This is evident from what immediately follows.

[n] The asterisks in the original denote something is wanting. Nevertheless, what immediately follows them, is evidently connected with what immediately precedes.

the future, but subsist in an indivisible untemporal *now;* so that the simultaneous, both according to multitude, and according to temporal interval, are present with intellect. Hence, too, all things subsist in it according to one, and in one, without interval, and without time. But if this be the case, there is nothing discursive or transitive in its intellections, and consequently they are without motion. Hence, they are energies according to one, subsisting in one, and without increase or mutation, or any transition. If, however, the multitude subsists according to one, and the energy is collected together at once, and without time, an essence of this kind must necessarily always subsist in [an intelligible] one. But this is eternity. Hence, eternity is present with intellect. That nature, however, which does not perceive intellectually according to one, and in one, but transitively, and with motion, so that in understanding it leaves one thing and apprehends another, divides and proceeds discursively,— this nature [which is soul] subsists in conjunction with time. For with a motion of this kind, the future and the past are consubsistent. But soul, changing its conceptions, passes from one thing to another; not that the prior conceptions depart, and the posterior accede in their place, but there is, as it were, a transition of the former, though they remain in the soul, and the latter accede, as if from some other place. They do not, however, accede in reality from another place; but they appear to do so in consequence of the self-motion of the soul, and through her eye being directed to a survey of the different forms which she contains, and which have the relation of parts to her whole essence. For she resembles a fountain not flowing outwardly, but circularly scattering its streams into itself. With the motion, therefore, of soul, time is consubsistent; but eternity is consubsistent with the permanency of intellect in itself[o]. It is not, however, divided

[o] See the fourth book of my translation of Proclus, on the Timæus of Plato, in which the nature of time and eternity is most admirably

from intellect in the same manner as time is from soul; because in intellect the consubsistent essences are united. But that which is perpetually moved, is the source of a false opinion of eternity, through the immeasurable extent of its motion producing a conception of eternity. And that which abides [in one,] is falsely conceived to be the same with that which is [perpetually] moved. For that which is perpetually moved, evolves the time of itself in the same manner as *the now* of itself, and multiplies it, according to a temporal progression. Hence, some have apprehended that time is to be surveyed in permanency no less than in motion; and that eternity, as we have said, is infinite time; just as if each of these imparted its own properties to the other; time, which is always moved, adumbrating eternity by the perpetuity of itself, and the sameness of its motion; and eternity, through being established in sameness of energy, becoming similar to time, by the permanency of itself arising from energy. In sensibles, however, the time of one thing is distinct from that of another. Thus, for instance, there is one time of the sun, and another of the moon, one time of the morning-star, and another of each of the planets. Hence, also, there is a different year of different planets. The year, likewise, which comprehends these times, terminates as in a summit in the motion of the soul [of the universe,] according to the imitation of which the celestial orbs are moved. The motion of this soul, however, being of a different nature from that of the planets, the time of the former also is different from that of the latter. For the latter subsists with interval, and is distinguished from the former by local motions and transitions.

unfolded. See, also, my translation of Plotinus, on Eternity and Time. In these works, what both these divine men have said of eternity, and what the former has said of time, contains, as it appears to me, the *ne plus ultra* of philosophical investigation on these most abstruse subjects.

APPENDIX.

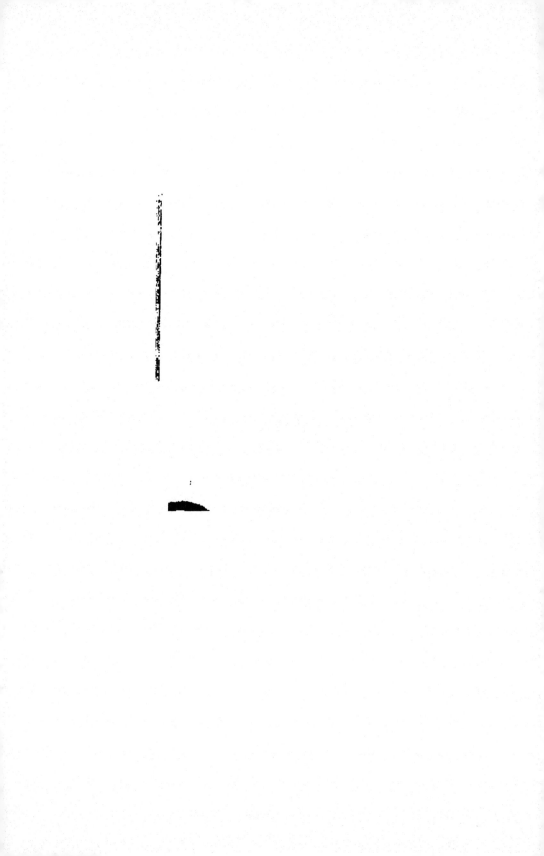

APPENDIX.

ON

THE WANDERINGS OF ULYSSES.

In my History of the Restoration of the Platonic Theology [see Vol. II. of my Proclus on Euclid,] and in a note accompanying my translation of the treatise of Porphyry, on the Cave of the Nymphs, in that work, I attempted, from the hints afforded by Porphyry, and the work of an anonymous Greek writer, De Ulyxis Erroribus, to unfold the latent meaning of the wanderings of Ulysses, as narrated by Homer. But as, from my continued application to the philosophy of Plato for upwards of forty years, I now know much more of that philosophy than I then did, a period of thirty-five years having elapsed from that to the present time, I shall again attempt to explain those wanderings, rejecting some things, and retaining others which I had adopted before.

In the first place, it is necessary to observe, that Ulysses does not rank among the first heroic characters, or in other words, he was not one of those heroes who descend into the regions of mortality at certain periods, not only in compliance with that necessity through which all partial souls such as ours descend periodically, but also for the purpose of benefiting others, and leading them back to their pristine state of perfection. Hence, he was by no means such an exalted hero as Hercules, or Pythagoras, or Socrates, or Plato; for they largely benefited others; but he only benefited himself. For all his companions perished prior to his arrival at Ithaca. So that he was able to save himself, but not others. "Hence," says Olympiodorus, in his MS. Scholia on the Gorgias of Plato, "it is said, that Ulysses wandered on the sea by the will of Neptune. For by this it is signified that the Odyssean life was neither terrestrial, nor yet celestial, but between these. Since, therefore, Neptune is the lord of the middle natures, on this account it is said, that Ulysses wandered through the will of Neptune, because he had a Neptunian allotment. Thus, also, theologists speak of the sons of Jupiter, Neptune, and Pluto; regarding the allotment of each. For we say, that he who has a divine and celestial polity, is the son of Jupiter; that he who has a terrestrial polity, is the son of Pluto; and he is the son of Neptune, whose polity or allotment is between these*." Hence Ulysses, from his Neptunian allotment, was a man who ranked among the middle class of characters that transcend the majority of mankind.

In the next place, in order to understand accurately the recondite meaning of the wanderings of Ulysses, it is requisite to know what the most divine and theological poet Homer indicates by the Trojan war in the Iliad. For Homer, by combining fiction with historical facts, has delivered to us some very occult, mystic, and valuable information, in those two admirable poems, the Iliad and Odyssey. Hence, by those who directed their attention to this recondite information, he was said, conformably to the tragical mode of speaking, which was usual with the most ancient writers, to have been blind, because, as

---

* Δια τοι τουτο, και τον Οδυσσεα λεγουσι κατα θαλατταν πλανασθαι βουλη του Ποσειδωνος· σημαινουσι γαρ την Οδυσσειον ζωην, οτι ουδε χθονια ην, αλλ' ουδε μην ετι ουρανια, αλλα μεση· επει ουν ο Ποσειδων του μεταξυ κυριος εστι, δια τουτο και τον Οδυσσεα φασι βουλη Ποσειδωνος [supple πλανασθαι·] επειδη τον κληρον του Ποσειδωνος ειχεν· ουτω γουν και τους μεν φασι Διος υιους, τους δε Ποσειδωνος, τους δε Πλουτωνος, προς τους κληρους εκαστου· τον μεν γαρ εχοντα θειαν και ουρανιαν πολιτειαν Διος φαμεν υιον, τον δε χθονιαν, Πλουτωνος, τον δε την μεταξυ Ποσειδωνος.

Proclus observes[b], he separated himself from sensible beauty, and extended the intellect of his soul to invisible and true harmony. He was said, therefore, to be blind, because *that* intellectual beauty to which he raised himself cannot be perceived by corporeal eyes. Thus, too, Orpheus is tragically said to have been lacerated in an all-various manner, because men of that age *partially* participated of his mystic doctrine. The *principal part* of it, however, was received by the Lesbians; and on this account, his *head*, when separated from his body, is said to have been carried to Lesbos. Hence, the Platonic Hermeas, conformably to this opinion of the occult meaning of the Iliad, beautifully explains as follows the Trojan war, in his Scholia on the Phædrus of Plato:

" By *Ilion*, we must understand the generated and material place, which is so denominated from *mud and matter* (παρα την ιλυν και την υλην,) and in which there are war and sedition. But the Trojans are material forms, and all the lives which subsist about bodies. Hence, also, the Trojans are called *genuine* (ιθαγενεις). For all the lives which subsist about bodies, and irrational[c] souls, are favourable and attentive to their proper matter. On the contrary, the Greeks are rational souls, coming from Greece, *i. e.* from the intelligible into matter. Hence, the Greeks are called *foreigners* (επηλυδες,) and vanquish the Trojans, as being of a superior order. But they fight with each other about the image of Helen, as the poet says [about the image of Eneas].

Around the phantom Greeks and Trojans fight[d].

Helen signifying intelligible beauty, being a certain *vessel* (ελενοη τις ουσα,) attracting to itself intellect. An efflux, therefore, of this intelligible beauty is imparted to matter

---

[b] In Plat. Polit. p. 398.

[c] Instead of αναλογοι ψυχαι, in this place, it is necessary to read αλογοι ψυχαι.

[d] Iliad, V. v. 451.

through Venus; and about this efflux of beauty the Greeks fight with the Trojans [*i. e.* rational with irrational lives [e]]. And those, indeed, that oppose and vanquish matter, return to the intelligible world, which is their true country; but those who do not, as is the case with the multitude, are bound to matter. As, therefore, the prophet, in the tenth book of the Republic, previously to the descent of souls, announces to them how they may return [to their pristine felicity], according to periods of a thousand and ten thousand years; thus, also, Calchas predicts to the Greeks their return in ten years, the number ten being the symbol of a perfect period. And as, in the lives of souls, some are elevated through philosophy, others through the amatory art, and others through the royal and warlike disciplines; so with respect to the Greeks, some act with rectitude through prudence, but others through war or love, and their return is different [according to their different pursuits]."

The first obviously fabulous adventure, then, of Ulysses, is that of the Lotophagi, which Homer beautifully narrates, and whose narration Pope very elegantly translates as follows:

> The trees around them all their fruit produce,
> Lotos the name, and dulcet is the juice [f]!
> (Thence call'd Lotophagi) which, whoso tastes,
> Insatiate riots in the sweet repasts,
> Nor other home, nor other care intends,
> But quits his house, his country, and his friends.

---

[e] Conformably to this, Proclus, in Plat. Polit. p. 398, says, "that all the beauty subsisting about generation [or the regions of sense], from the fabrication of things, is signified by Helen; about which there is a perpetual battle of souls, till the more intellectual having vanquished the more irrational forms of life, return to the place from whence they originally came." For the beauty which is in the realms of generation, is an efflux of intelligible beauty.

[f] This second line is, in Pope's version, "Lotos the name, divine, nectarious juice!" which I have altered as above, as being more conformable to the original.

> The three we sent from off th' enchanting ground
> We dragg'd reluctant, and by force we bound;
> The rest in haste forsook the pleasing shore,
> Or, the charm tasted, had return'd no more ᵍ.

Plato, in the 8th book of his Republic, has admirably unfolded to us what the *lotos* occultly indicates, viz. that it signifies " false and arrogant reasonings and opinions:" for daily experience shows that nothing is more enchanting and delicious than these to such as have made no solid proficiency in virtue, and who, like some of the companions of Ulysses, being fascinated by erroneous conceptions, consign their true country and true kindred to oblivion, and desire to live for ever lost in the intoxication of fallacious delight.

The next adventure of Ulysses is that of the Cyclops, whom he deprived of sight, and irritated by reproaches. But according to Porphyry, in the above-mentioned excellent treatise, this is no other than the natal dæmon of Ulysses, or the dæmon to whose protecting power he became subject, as soon as he was born[h]. In order, however, to understand perfectly the arcane meaning of this fable, it is necessary to observe, that according to the ancient theology, those souls that in the present life will speedily return to their pristine felicity in the intelligible world, have not the essential dæmon, or the dæmon which is inseparable from the essence of the soul, different from the dæmon that presides over the birth; for they are one and the same. But the case is otherwise with more imperfect souls; as the natal is in these different from the *essential* dæmon[i]. As Ulysses, therefore,

[g] Lib. ix. l. 94, &c.

[h] Vid. Censoris, De Die Natali, cap. iii.

[i] This is evident from the following passage in the Commentary of Proclus, on the First Alcibiades of Plato : Ταις μεν ουν αποκαταστατικως ζωσαις ψυχαις ο αυτος εστιν ανω κανταυθα δαιμων· ταις δε ατελεσ]εραις αλλος μεν ο κατ' ουσιαν δαιμων, αλλος δε ο κατα τον προβεβλημενον βιον. p. 37, Edit. Creuz. But for a copious account of the essential dæmon, and of the different orders and offices of dæmons, see the notes accompanying my translation of the First Alcibiades, Phædo, and Gorgias of Plato.

does not rank among the more perfect heroic characters, and was not one who in the present life is immediately ascending to his kindred star, or, in Platonic language, to the paternal port, the soul's true paradise of rest; but was a man who, prior to this, had many laborious wanderings to accomplish, and many difficulties and dangers of no common magnitude to sustain, his *natal* was not the same with his *essential* dæmon. As he is, however, departing from a sensible to an intellectual life, though circuitously and slowly, he is represented in so doing as blinding and irritating his *natal* dæmon. For he who blinds the eye of sense, and extinguishes its light, after his will has profoundly assented to its use, must expect punishment for the deed; as necessary ultimately to his own peculiar good, and the general order of the universe. Indeed, troubles and misfortunes resulting from such undertakings, not only contribute to appease the anger of their authors, but likewise purify and benefit the subjects of their revenge. According to the Greek theology, therefore, he who, in the present life, while he is in the road of virtue, and is eagerly searching for wisdom, perceives that there is a great resemblance between his destiny and that of Ulysses, may safely conclude, that either here, or in a prior state of existence, he has voluntarily submitted to the power of his natal dæmon, and has now deprived him of sight; or in other words, has abandoned a life of sense; and that he has been profoundly delighted with the nature of matter, and is now abrogating the confessions which he made. This, too, is insinuated in the beautiful story of Cupid and Psyche, by Apuleius, when the terrestrial Venus sends Mercury with a book in which her name is inscribed, to apprehend Psyche as a fugitive from her mistress. For this whole story relates to the descent of the soul into this terrene body, and its wanderings and punishments, till it returns to its true country and pristine felicity[k].

[k] See the note (p. 90) accompanying my translation of the Metamorphosis of Apuleius.

In the next fable, which is that of Æolus, the poet appears to me to signify that providence of divinity which is of an elevating and guardian nature, the influence of which, when properly received by the subjects of it, enables them to pass with security over the stormy sea of life to their native land; but when this influence is neglected through the sleep of reason, the negligence is followed by a temporary destruction of hope. This providence also of the Gods is not only one, but *all-various*, which Homer appears to indicate by Æolus; the word αιολος signifying various and manifold. As the advancement, therefore, of Ulysses in the virtues is as yet imperfect, extending no farther than to the *ethical* and *political*, which are but adumbrations of the *true* virtues, the cathartic and theoretic[1], he is said to have fallen asleep, and to have been thereby disappointed of his wishes, his soul not being at that time in a truly vigilant state, as not having yet elevated its eye to real being from objects of sense which resemble the delusions of dreams.

By the adventure of the Lestrigons, which follows in the next place, Homer represents to us Ulysses flying from voracity, and fierce and savage manners; a flight indispensably necessary, as preparatory to his attainment of the higher virtues.

In the next adventure, which contains the beautiful allegory of Circe, we shall find some deep arcana of philosophy contained, exclusive of its connexion with Ulysses. By the Æean isle, then, in which the palace of Circe was situated, the region of sorrow and lamentation is signified, as is evident from the name of the island itself. And, by Circe, we must understand the Goddess of sense. For thus Porphyry, in Stobæus, p. 141: " Homer calls the period and revolution of regeneration in a circle, Circe, the daughter of the Sun, who perpetually connects and combines all corruption with genera-

---

[1] For an accurate account of the gradation of the virtues, see Porphyry's Auxiliaries to Intelligibles, p. 217.

tion, and generation again with corruption." And this is asserted still more explicitly by Proclus, in his Scholia on the Cratylus of Plato. For he says, " Circe is that divine power which weaves all the life contained in the four elements, and, at the same time, by her song harmonizes the whole sublunary world. But the shuttle with which she weaves, is represented by theologists as golden, because her essence is intellectual, pure, immaterial, and unmingled with generation; all which is signified by the shuttle being golden. And her employment consists in *separating*[m] stable things from such as are in motion, according to divine diversity." And he also informs us, " that Circe ranks among the divinities who preside over generation, or the regions of sense." Homer, too, with great propriety, represents Circe, who rules over the realms of generation, as waited on by Nymphs sprung from fountains; for Nymphs, says Hermias (in Plat. Phædrum,) are Goddesses who preside over regeneration, and are the attendants of Bacchus, the son of Semele. On this account, they are present with water; that is, they ascend, as it were, into, and rule over generation. But this Dionysius, or Bacchus, supplies the regeneration of every sensible nature."

Hence we may observe, that the Æean isle, or this region of sense, is, with great propriety, called the abode of trouble and lamentation. In this region, then, the companions of Ulysses, in consequence of being very imperfect characters, are changed, through the incantations of the Goddess, into brutes, *i. e.* into unworthy and irrational habits and manners. Ulysses, however, as one who is returning, though slowly, to the proper perfection of his nature, is, by the assistance of Mercury, or reason, prevented from destruction. Hence intellect, roused by its impassive power, and at the same time armed with prudent anger, and the plant moly, or temperance, which is able to repel the allurements of pleasure, wars on

---

[m] For the shuttle is a symbol of separating power.

sensible delight, and prevents the effects of its transforming power. Ulysses, also, though he was not able to lead his companions back to their native land, the paternal port of the soul, yet saves them from being transformed, through the enchantments of sense, into an irrational life.

After this follows the allegory respecting the descent of Ulysses into *Hades*, which occultly signifies, that he still lived a life according to sense, and not according to intellect, and that, in consequence of not having yet vanquished a terrestrial life, he was involved in *obscurity*. For ancient wise men universally considered Hades as commencing in the present state of existence, and that sense is nothing more than the energy of the dormant soul, and a perception, as it were, of the delusions of dreams, as I have abundantly proved in my treatise on the Mysteries. The secret meaning, also, of what Ulysses saw in Hades, is no less beautiful than profound, as the following extract from the manuscript Commentary of Olympiodorus, on the Gorgias of Plato, abundantly evinces: " Ulysses," says he, " descending into Hades, saw, among others, Sysiphus, and Tityus, and Tantalus. And Tityus he saw lying on the earth, and a vulture devouring his liver; the liver signifying that he lived solely according to the *epithymetic* part of his nature [or that part of the soul which is the source of desires,] and that through this, indeed, he was, indeed, internally prudent; but earth signifying the terrestrial condition of his prudence. But Sysiphus, living under the dominion of ambition and anger, was employed in continually rolling a stone up an eminence, because it perpetually descended again; its descent implying the vicious government of himself; and his rolling the stone, the hard, refractory, and, as it were, rebounding condition of his life. And, lastly, he saw Tantalus extended by the side of a lake, and that there was a tree before him, with abundance of fruit on its branches, which he desired to gather, but it vanished from his view. And this indeed indicates, that he lived under the dominion of the phantasy; but his hanging over the lake, and in vain attempting to drink, denotes the elusive, humid, and rapidly-gliding condition of such a life."

We must now, however, view Ulysses passing from sense to imagination; in the course of which voyage he is assailed by various temptations of great power, and destructive effect. We shall perceive him victorious in some of these, and sinking under others; but struggling against the incursions of all. Among the first of these is the enchanting melody of the Sirens,

> Whose song is death, and makes destruction please.

But what is occultly signified by the Sirens, is beautifully unfolded by Proclus, on the Cratylus of Plato, as follows: "The divine Plato knew that there are three kinds of Sirens; the *celestial,* which is under the government of Jupiter; *that which is effective of generation,* and is under the government of Neptune; and *that which is cathartic,* and is under the government of Pluto. It is common to all these, to incline all things through an harmonic motion to their ruling Gods. Hence, when the soul is in the heavens, they are desirous of uniting it to the divine life which flourishes there. But it is proper that souls living in generation should sail beyond them, like the Homeric Ulysses, that they may not be allured by generation, of which the sea is an image. And when souls are in Hades, the Sirens are desirous of uniting them through intellectual conceptions to Pluto. So that Plato knew that in the kingdom of Hades there are Gods, dæmons, and souls, who dance, as it were, round Pluto, allured by the Sirens that dwell there." Ulysses, therefore, as now proceeding to a life which is under the dominion of imagination, but which is superior to a life consisting wholly in sensitive energies, abandons those alluring and fraudulent pleasures of sense, which charm the soul with flattering and mellifluous incantations. Hence he closes with divine reasons and energies, as with wax, the impulses of desire and the organs of sense; so that every passage being barred from access, they may in vain warble the song of ecstasy, and expect to ruin the soul by the enchanting strain. He also restrains the corporeal assaults by the bands of morality, and thus employs the senses without yielding to their impetuous invasions; and experiences delight without resigning the empire of reason to its fascinating control.

Ulysses, having escaped the dangers of the Sirens, passes on to the rocks of Scylla and Charybdis, of terrific appearance and irresistible force. By these two rocks the poet seems to signify the passions of anger and desire, and their concomitants, that compress human life on both sides; and which every one must experience who proceeds, like Ulysses, in a regular manner to an intellectual state of existence. Some of these are, like Scylla, of a lofty malignity; fraudulent, yet latent and obscure, as being concealed in the penetration of the soul. And such is revenge, and other passions of a similar kind. In these recesses a dæmon, the prince of such passions, resides. For the Chaldean oracles assert that terrestrial dæmons dwell in the soul, which is replete with irrational affections[n]. This dæmon also may justly be denominated a dire and enraged dog, who partly exposes his own malice, and partly hides it in impenetrable obscurity. Hence he is capable of producing mischief in a twofold respect. For he privately hurts by malignant stratagems, openly ravishes the soul on the lofty rock of fury, and rends it with the triple evil of deadly teeth, viz. dereliction of duty, hatred of humanity, and self-conceit. Indeed, a dæmon of this kind will be perpetually vigilant in endeavouring to destroy, at one

---

[n] And this is the meaning of the Chaldaic oracle, —

Σον αγfειον θηρες χθονος οικησουσιν.

i. e. "The wild beasts of the earth shall inhabit thy vessel." For, as Psellus well observes, by *the vessel*, the composite temperature of the soul is signified, and by the wild beasts of the earth, terrestrial dæmons.

time the whole, and at another time a part of the soul of one, struggling, like Ulysses, against passion, and yielding reluctantly to its invasions.

But the other affections which pertain to desire are of a more corporeal nature, and are more conspicuously depraved. A wild fig-tree, *i. e.* the will, is produced on the top of this rock; wild, indeed, on account of its free nature, but sweet in fruition; and under which, often through the day, the impetuosities of the boiling body are accustomed to absorb and destroy the man, agitating upwards and downwards inflamed desire; so that mighty destruction, both to soul and body, is produced by their mutual consent. But it is highly proper that a rock of this last kind should be anxiously avoided by one, who, like Ulysses, is labouring to return to his true country and friends. Hence, if necessity requires, he will rather expose himself to the other: for there the energy of thought, and of the soul's simple motions, is alone necessary to be exerted, and it is easy to recover the pristine habit of the soul. In short, the poet seems to represent, by this allegory of the two rocks, as well the dangers which spontaneously arise from the irascible part of the soul, as those which are the effect of deliberation, and are of a corporeal nature; both of which must be sustained, or one at least, by a necessary consequence. For it is impossible that neither of them should be experienced by one who is passing over the stormy ocean of a sensible life.

After this succeeds the allegory of the Trinacrian isle, containing the herds sacred to the God of day, which were violated by the companions of Ulysses; but not without the destruction of the authors of this impiety, and the most dreadful danger to Ulysses. By the result of this fable, the poet evidently shows that punishment attends the sacrilegious and the perjured; and teaches us that we should perpetually reverence divinity, with the greatest sanctity of mind, and be cautious how we commit any thing in divine concerns contrary to piety of manners and purity of thought. But Homer, by attributing sense to the flesh and hides of the slain herds, manifestly evinces that every base deed universally proclaims the iniquity of its author; but that perjury and sacrilege are attended with the most glaring indications of guilt, and the most horrid signatures of approaching vengeance and inevitable ruin. We may here, too, observe, that the will of Ulysses was far from consenting to this impious deed; and that, though his passions prevailed at length over his reason, it was not till after frequent admonition had been employed, and great diligence exerted, to prevent its execution. This, indeed, is so eminently true, that his guilt was the consequence of surprise, and not of premeditated design; which Homer appears to insinuate by relating that Ulysses was asleep when his associates committed the offence.

In the next fable we find Ulysses, impelled by the southern wind towards the rocks of Scylla and Charybdis; in the latter of which he found safety, by clinging to the fig-tree which grew on its summit, till she refunded the mast, on which he rode after the tempest. But the secret meaning of the allegory appears to me to be as follows: — Ulysses, who has not yet taken leave of a life according to sense, is driven by the warmth of passion, represented by the southern gales, into the dire vortex of insane desires, which frequently boiling over, and tossing on high the storms of depraved affections, plunges into ruin the soul obnoxious to its waves. However, perceiving the danger to which he is exposed, when the base storms begin to swell, and the whirlpools of depravity roar, he seizes the helm of temperance, and binds himself fast to the solid texture of his remaining virtue. The waves of desire are, indeed, tempestuous in the extreme; but before he is forcibly merged, by the rage of the passions, into the depths of depravity, he tenaciously adheres to his unconsenting will, seated, as it were, on the lofty summit of terrene desire. For this, like the wild fig-tree, affords the best refuge to the soul struggling with the billows of base perturbations. Hence he thus recovers the integrity which he had lost, and afterwards swims without danger over the waves of temptation; ever watchful and assiduous, while he sails through this impetuous river of the flesh, and is exposed to the stormy blasts of heated passion and destructive vice. Hence, too, while he is thus affected, and anxious lest the loss from unworthy affections should return upon himself, he will escape being lacerated by the teeth of Anger, though she should terribly and fiercely bark in the neighbourhood of Desire, and endeavour, like Scylla, to snatch him on her lofty rock. For those who are involuntarily disturbed, like Ulysses, by the billows of Desire, suffer no inconvenience from the depraved rock of Wrath; but considering the danger of their present situation, they relinquish the false confidence produced by rage for modest diffidence and anxious hope.

Hitherto we have followed Ulysses in his voyage over the turbulent and dangerous ocean of sense; in which we have seen him struggling against the storms of temptation, and in danger of perishing through the tempestuous billows of vice. We must now attend him in the region of imagination, and mark his progress from the enchanted island, till he regains the long-lost empire of his soul. That the poet then, by Calypso, occultly signifies the phantasy or imagination, is, I think, evident from his description of her abode. For she is represented as dwelling in a cavern, illuminated by a great fire; and this cave is surrounded with a thick wood, is watered by four fountains, and is situated in an island, remote from any habitable place, and environed by the mighty ocean. All which particulars correspond with the phantasy, as I presume the following observations will evince. In the first place, the primary and proper vehicle of the phantasy, or, as it is called by the Platonic philosophers, *the imaginative spirit*, is attenuated and ethereal, and is therefore naturally luminous. In the next place, the island is said to be surrounded with a thick wood, which evidently corresponds to a material nature, or this body, with which the phantasy is invested. For υλη, or *matter*, also signifies *a wood*. But the four fountains, by which the cave is watered, occultly signify the four gnostic powers of the soul, *intellect, the discursive energy of reason, opinion, and sense;* with all which the phantasy, being also a gnostic power, communicates; so that it receives images, like a mirror, from all of them, and retains those which it receives from the senses, when the objects by which they were produced are no longer present. Hence the imagination, or the phantasy, [φαντασια,] is denominated from being των φανεντων στασις, *the permanency of appearances*. And, in the last place, the island is said to be environed by the ocean; which admirably accords with a corporeal nature, for ever flowing, without admitting any periods of repose. And thus much for the secret agreement of the cavern and island with the region of imagination.

But the poet, by denominating the Goddess Calypso, and the island Ogygia, appears to me very evidently to confirm the preceding exposition. For Calypso is derived from καλυπτω, which signifies *to cover as with a veil;* and Ogygia is from ωγυγιος, ancient. And as the imaginative spirit is the primary vehicle of the rational soul, which it derived from the planetary spheres, and in which it descended to the sublunary regions, it may with great propriety be said to cover the soul as with a fine garment or veil; and it is no less properly denominated *ancient*, when considered as the first vehicle of the soul.

In this region of the phantasy, then, Ulysses is represented as an involuntary captive, continually employed in bewailing his absence from his true country, and ardently longing to depart from the fascinating embraces of the Goddess. For thus his situation is beautifully described by the poet:

> But sad Ulysses, by himself apart,
> Pour'd the big sorrows of his swelling heart;

> All on the lonely shore he sat to weep,
> And roll'd his eyes around the restless deep;
> Tow'rd his lov'd coast he roll'd his eyes in vain,
> Till dimm'd with rising grief they stream'd again [o].

His return, however, is at length effected through Mercury, or reason, who prevails on the Goddess to yield to his dismission. Hence, after her consent, Ulysses is, with great propriety, said to have placed himself on the throne on which Mercury had sate: for reason then resumes her proper seat when the reasoning power is about to abandon the delusive and detaining charms of imagination. But Homer appears to me to insinuate something admirable when he represents Ulysses, on his departure from Calypso, sailing by night, and contemplating the order and light of the stars, in the following beautiful lines:

> And now, rejoicing in the prosperous gales,
> With beating heart Ulysses spread his sails;
> Plac'd at the helm he sate, and mark'd the skies,
> Nor clos'd in sleep his ever watchful eyes.
> There viewed the Pleiads, and the northern team,
> And great Orion's more refulgent beam;
> To which around the axle of the sky
> The Bear, revolving, points his golden eye;
> Who shines exalted on the ethereal plain,
> Nor bathes his blazing forehead in the main [p].

For what he here says of Ulysses, is perfectly conformable to what is said by Plato in the 7th book of his Republic, respecting the man who is to be led from the cave, which he there describes, to the light of day, *i. e.* from a sensible to an intellectual life, viz. " that he will more easily see what the heavens contain, and the heavens themselves, by *looking in the night to the light of the stars and the moon,* than by day looking on the sun, and the light of the sun." For by this, as Proclus well

---

[o] Odyss. lib. v. 82, &c. The translation by Pope.
[p] Ibid. lib. v. 269, &c.

observes, "Plato signifies the contemplation of intelligibles, of which the stars and their light are imitations, so far as all of them partake of the form of the sun, in the same manner as intelligibles are characterized by the nature of *the good*. These, then, such a one must contemplate, that he may understand their essence, and those summits of their nature, by which they are deiform processions from the ineffable principle of things." Ulysses, therefore, who is hastening to an intellectual life, contemplates these lucid objects with vigilant eyes, rejoicing in the illuminations and assistance they afford him while sailing over the dark ocean of a sensible life.

But as he is now earnestly engaged in departing from sense, he must unavoidably be pursued by the anger of Neptune, the lord of generation and a sensible life, whose service he has forsaken, and whose offspring he has blinded by stratagem, and irritated by reproach. Hence, in the midst of these delightful contemplations, he is almost overwhelmed by the waves of misfortune, roused by the wrath of his implacable foe. He is, however, through divine assistance, or Leucothea, enabled to sustain the dreadful storm. For, receiving from divinity the immortal fillet of true fortitude, and binding it under his breast, (the proper seat of courage,) he encounters the billows of adversity, and bravely shoots along the boisterous ocean of life. It must, however, be carefully observed, that the poet is far from ascribing a certain passion to a divine nature, when he speaks of the anger of Neptune: for, in thus speaking, he, as well as other theologists, intended only to signify our inaptitude to the participation of its beneficent influence.

Ulysses therefore, having with much difficulty escaped the dangers arising from the wrath of Neptune, lands at length on the island of Phæacia, where he is hospitably received, and honourably dismissed. Now, as it is proper that he who, like Ulysses, departs from the delusions of imagination, should immediately betake himself to the more intellectual light of the rational energy of the soul, the land of Phæacia ought to correspond to our intellectual part, and particularly to that portion of it which is denominated in Greek *dianoia*, and which is characterized by the power of reasoning scientifically, deriving the principles of its discursive energy from intellect. And that it has this correspondence, the following observations will, I persuade myself, abundantly evince. In the first place, then, this island is represented by the poet as enjoying a perpetual spring, which plainly indicates that it is not any terrestrial situation. Indeed, the critical commentators have been so fully convinced of this, that they acknowledge Homer describes Phæacia as one of the Fortunate Islands; but they have not attempted to penetrate his design, in such a description. If, however, we consider the perfect liberty, unfading variety, and endless delight, which our intellectual part affords, we shall find that it is truly the Fortunate Island of the soul, in which, by the exercise of the theoretic virtues, it is possible for a man, even in the present life, to obtain genuine felicity, though not in that perfection as when he is liberated from the body. With respect to the Fortunate Islands, their occult meaning is thus beautifully unfolded by Olympiodorus, in his MS. commentary on the Gorgias of Plato: Δει δε ειδεναι οτι αι νησοι υπερκυπτουσι της θαλασσης ανωτερω ουσαι, την ουν πολιτειαν την υπερκυψασαν του βιου και της γενησεως, μακαρων νησους καλουσι· ταυτον δε εστι και το ηλυσιον πεδιον. δια τοι τουτο και ο Ηρακλης τελευταιον αθλον, εν τοις εσπεριοις μερεσιν εποιησατο, αντι κατηγωνισατο τον σκοτεινον και χθονιον βιον, και λοιπον εν ημερα, ο εστιν εν αληθεια και φωτι εξη: *i. e.* "It is necessary to know that islands are raised above, being higher than the sea. A condition of being, therefore, which transcends this corporeal life and generation, is denominated the islands of the blessed; but these are the same with the Elysian fields. And on this account, Hercules is reported to have accomplished his last labour in the Hesperian regions; signifying by this, that having vanquished an obscure and terrestrial life, he afterwards lived in open day, that is, in truth and resplendent light."

In the next place, the poet, by his description of the palace of Alcinous, the king of this island, admirably indicates the pure and splendid light of the energy of reason. For he says of it:

> The front appear'd with radiant splendours gay,
> Bright as the lamp of night, or orb of day.
> The walls were massy brass: the cornice high
> Blue metals crown'd in colours of the sky.
> Rich plates of gold the folding doors incase;
> The pillars silver on a brazen base.
> Silver the lintels deep projecting o'er,
> And gold the ringlets that command the door.
> Two rows of stately dogs on either hand,
> In sculptur'd gold, and labour'd silver, stand.
> These Vulcan form'd intelligent to wait
> Immortal guardians at Alcinous' gate [q].

And he represents it as no less internally luminous by night.

> Refulgent pedestals the walls surround,
> Which boys of gold with flaming torches crown'd;
> The polish'd ore, reflecting ev'ry ray,
> Blaz'd on the banquets with a double day.

Indeed Homer, by his description of the outside of this palace, sufficiently indicates its agreement with the planet Mercury, the deity of which presides over the rational energy. For this God, in the language of Proclus[r], "unfolds into light intellectual gifts, fills all things with divine *reasons* [*i. e.* forms, and productive principles,] elevates souls to intellect, wakens them as from a profound sleep, converts them through investigation to themselves, and by a certain obstetric art and invention of pure intellect, brings them to a blessed life." According to astronomers, likewise, the planet Mercury is resplendent with the colours of all the other planets. Thus Baptista Porta in Cœlest. Physiog. p. 88. "Videbis in eo Saturni luridum, Martis ignem, Jovis candidum,

---

[q] Odyss. lib. vii. 84, &c. The translation by Pope.
[r] In Euclid. Element. lib. i. p. 14.

Veneris flavum, necnon utriusque nitor, hilaritasque, et ob id non peculiaris formæ, sed eorum formam capit, cum quibus associatur, ob id in describendo ejus colore astrologi differunt." *i. e.* " You may perceive in this planet the pale colour of Saturn, the fire of Mars, the whiteness of Jupiter, and the yellow of Venus; and likewise the brilliancy and hilarity of each. On this account it is not of a peculiar form, but receives the form of its associates, and thus causes astrologers to differ in describing its colour."

But that the island of Phæacia is the dominion of reason, is, I think, indisputably confirmed by Homer's account of the ships fabricated by its inhabitants. For of these, he says:

> So shalt thou instant reach the realm assign'd,
> In wond'rous ships self-mov'd, instinct with mind.
> No helm secures their course, no pilot guides,
> Like man intelligent they plough the tides,
> Conscious of ev'ry coast and ev'ry bay,
> That lies beneath the sun's all-seeing ray;
> And veil'd in clouds impervious to the eye,
> Fearless and rapid through the deep they fly [a].

For it is absurd to suppose that Homer would employ such an hyperbole, in merely describing the excellency of the Phæacian ships. Hence, as it so greatly surpasses the bounds of probability, and is so contrary to the admirable prudence which Homer continually displays, it can only be admitted as an allegory, pregnant with latent meaning, and the recondite wisdom of antiquity. The poet likewise adds respecting the Phæacians:

> These did the ruler of the deep ordain
> To build proud navies, and command the main;
> On canvas wings to cut the wat'ry way,
> No bird more light, *no thought more swift than they.*

The last of which lines so remarkably agrees with the preceding explanation, that I presume no stronger confirm-

[a] Odyss. lib. viii. 556, &c.

ation can be desired. Nor is the original less satisfactory:

των νηες ωκειαι ωσει πτερον ηε νοημα¹,

i. e. "*The ships of these men are swift as a wing, or as a conception of the mind.*" But the inhabitants of the palace are represented as spending their days in continual festivity, and unceasing mirth; in listening to the harmony of the lyre, or in forming the tuneful mazes of the joyful dance. For to the man who lives under the guidance of reason, or to the good man, every day, as Diogenes said, is a festival. Hence, such a one is constantly employed in tuning the lyre of recollection, in harmonious revolutions about an intelligible essence, and the never-satiating and deifying banquet of intellect.

And here we may observe how much the behaviour of Ulysses, at the palace of Alcinous, confirms the preceding exposition, and accords with his character, as a man passing in a regular manner from the delusions of sense, to the realities of intellectual enjoyment. For as he is now converted to himself, and is seated in the palace of reason, it is highly proper that he should call to mind his past conduct, and be afflicted with the survey; and that he should be wakened to sorrow by the lyre of reminiscence, and weep over the follies of his past active life. Hence, when the divine bard Demodocus, inspired by the fury of the Muses, sings the contention between Ulysses and Achilles, on his golden lyre, Ulysses is vehemently affected with the relation. And when the inhabitants of the palace, *i. e.* the powers and energies of the rational soul, transported with the song, demanded its repetition,

> Again Ulysses veil'd his pensive head,
> Again, unmann'd, a shower of sorrow shed.

For to the man who is making a proficiency in virtue, the recollection of his former conduct is both pleasing and painful; pleasing, so far as in some instances it was attended with rectitude, but painful so far as in others it was erroneous.

¹ Odyss. lib. vii. 33.

Ulysses, also, is with the greatest propriety represented as relating his past adventures in the palace of Alcinous. For as he now betakes himself to the intellectual light of the reasoning power, it is highly necessary that he should review his past conduct, faithfully enumerate the errors of his life, and anxiously solicit a return to true manners, and perfect rectitude of mind. As likewise he is now on his passage, by the pure energy of reason to regain the lost empire of his soul, he is represented as falling into so profound a sleep in his voyage, as to be insensible for some time of its happy consummation; by which the poet indicates his being separated from sensible concerns, and wholly converted to the energies of the rational soul. Nor is it without reason that the poet represents Ithaca, as presenting itself to the mariners' view, when the bright morning star emerges from the darkness of night. For thus he sings:

> But when the morning star, with early ray,
> Flam'd in the front of heav'n and promis'd day;
> Like distant clouds, the mariner descries
> Fair Ithaca's emerging hills arise [u].

Since it is only by the dawning beams of intellect, that the discursive energy of reason can gain a glimpse of the native country and proper seat of empire of the soul.

Ulysses therefore, being now converted to the energies of the rational soul, and anxious to commence the cathartic virtues, recognizes, through the assistance of Minerva, or wisdom, his native land: and immediately enters into a consultation with the Goddess, how he may effectually banish the various perturbations and inordinate desires, which yet lurk in the penetralia of his soul. For this purpose, it is requisite that he should relinquish all external possessions, mortify every sense, and employ every stratagem, which may finally destroy these malevolent foes. Hence, the garb of poverty, the wrinkles of age, and the want of the necessaries of life, are symbols

---

[u] Odyss. lib. xiii. 93, &c.

of mortified habits, desertion of sensible pursuits, and an intimate conversion to intellectual good. For the sensitive eye must now give place to the purer sight of the rational soul; and the strength and energies of the corporeal nature must yield to the superior vigour of intellectual exertion, and the severe exercise of cathartic virtue. And this, Homer appears most evidently to indicate in the following beautiful lines:

> Now seated in the olive's sacred shade,
> Confer the hero and the martial maid.
> The Goddess of the azure eyes began:
> Son of Laertes! much experienc'd man!
> The suitor train thy earliest care demand,
> Of that luxurious race to rid the land.
> Three years thy house their lawless rule has seen,
> And proud addresses to the matchless queen[x];
> But she thy absence mourns from day to day,
> And inly bleeds, and silent wastes away;
> Elusive of the bridal hour, she gives
> Fond hopes to all, and all with hopes deceives[y].

Hence:

> It fits thee now to wear a dark disguise,
> And secret walk unknown to mortal eyes;
> For this my hand shall wither ev'ry grace,
> And ev'ry elegance of form and face,
> O'er thy smooth skin a bark of wrinkles spread,
> Turn hoar the auburn honours of thy head,
> Disfigure every limb with coarse attire,
> And in thine eyes extinguish all the fire;
> Add all the wants and the decays of life,
> Estrange thee from thy own; thy son, thy wife;
> From the loath'd object ev'ry sight shall turn,
> And the blind suitors their destruction scorn [z].

After this follows the discovery of Ulysses to Telemachus, which is no less philosophically sublime than

---

[x] *i. e.* Philosophy; for of this Penelope is an image.
[y] Odyss. lib. xiii. 373, &c.
[z] Odyss. lib. xiii. 397, &c. The translation of the above, and likewise of all the following passages from the Odyssey, is by Pope.

poetically beautiful. For, by Telemachus, we must understand *a true scientific conception of things;* since this is the legitimate offspring of the energy of the rational soul, in conjunction with philosophy. Hence Ulysses, while employed in the great work of mortification, recognizes his genuine offspring, and secretly plans with him the destruction of his insidious foes. And hence we may see the propriety of Telemachus being represented as exploring his absent father, and impatient for his return. For the rational soul then alone associates with a true conception of things, when it withdraws itself from sensible delights, and meditates a restoration of its fallen dignity and original sway.

And now Ulysses presents himself to our view in the habits of mortification, hastening to his long deserted palace, or the occult recesses of his soul, that he may mark the conduct and plan the destruction of those baneful passions which are secretly attempting to subvert the empire of his mind. Hence, the poet very properly and pathetically exclaims:

> And now his city strikes the monarch's eyes,
> Alas! how chang'd! a man of miseries;
> Propt on a staff, a beggar, old and bare,
> In tatter'd garments, flutt'ring with the air[a].

However, as this disguise was solely assumed for the purpose of procuring ancient purity and lawful rule, he divests himself of the torn garments of mortification, as soon as he begins the destruction of occult desires; and resumes the proper dignity and strength of his genuine form. But it is not without reason that Penelope, who is the image of philosophy, furnishes the instrument by which the hostile rout of passions are destroyed. For what besides the arrows of philosophy can extirpate the leading bands of impurity and vice? Hence, as soon as he is furnished with this irresistible

---

[a] Odyss. lib. xvii. 201, &c.

weapon, he no longer defers the ruin of his insidious foes, but

> Then fierce the hero o'er the threshold strode;
> Stript of his rags, he blaz'd out like a God.
> Full in their face the lifted bow he bore,
> And quiver'd deaths a formidable store;
> Before his feet the rattling show'r he threw,
> And thus terrific to the suitor crew [b].

But Homer represents Penelope as remaining ignorant of Ulysses, even after the suitors are destroyed, and he is seated on the throne of majesty, anxious to be known, and impatient to return her chaste and affectionate embrace. For thus he describes her:

> Then gliding through the marble valves in state,
> Oppos'd before the shining fire she sate.
> The monarch, by a column high enthron'd,
> His eye withdrew, and fixed it on the ground,
> Anxious to hear his queen the silence break:
> Amaz'd she sate, and impotent to speak;
> O'er all the man her eyes she rolls in vain,
> Now hopes, now fears, now knows, then doubts again [c].

By which Homer indicates, that Philosophy, through her long absence from the soul, and the foreign manners and habits which the soul had assumed, is a stranger to it, so that it is difficult for her to recognize the union and legitimate association which once subsisted between them. However, in order to facilitate this discovery, Ulysses renders all pure and harmonious within the recesses of his soul; and, by the assistance of Minerva, or wisdom, resumes the garb and dignity which he had formerly displayed.

> Then instant to the bath (the monarch cries,)
> Bid the gay youth and sprightly virgins rise,

[b] Odyss. lib. xxii. 1, &c.   [c] Odyss. lib. xxiii. 88, &c.

> Thence all descend in pomp and proud array,
> And bid the dome resound the mirthful lay;
> While the sweet lyrist airs of raptures sings,
> And forms the dance responsive to the strings [d].

And afterwards, Ulysses is described as appearing, through the interposition of Minerva, *like one of the immortals.*

> So Pallas his heroic form improves,
> With bloom divine, and like a God he moves [e].

For, indeed, he who, like Ulysses, has completely destroyed the domination of his passions, and purified himself, through the cathartic virtues, from their defiling nature, no longer ranks in the order of mortals, but is assimilated to divinity. And now, in order that he may become entirely known to Philosophy, that chaste Penelope of the soul, it is only requisite for him to relate the secrets of their mystic union, and recognize the bower of intellectual love. For then perfect recollection will ensue; and the anxiety of diffidence will be changed into transports of assurance, and tears of rapturous delight.

And thus we have attended Ulysses in his various wanderings and woes, till, through the *cathartic* virtues, he recovers the ruined empire of his soul. But, as it is requisite that he should, in the next place, possess and energize according to the theoretic or contemplative virtues, the end of which is a union with deity, as far as this can be effected by man in the present life, Homer only indicates to us his attainment of this end, without giving a detail of the gradual advances by which he arrived at this consummate felicity. This union is occultly signified by Ulysses first beholding, and after-

---

[d] Odyss. lib. xxiii. 131, &c.
[e] Odyss. lib. xxiii. 163, &c.

wards ardently embracing his father with ecstatic delight. With most admirable propriety, also, is Ulysses represented as proceeding, in order to effect this union, by himself *alone*, to his father who is also *alone*.

> *Alone* and unattended, let me try
> If yet I share the old man's memory [f],

says Ulysses. And afterwards it is said,

> But all *alone* the hoary king he found [g].

For a union with the ineffable *one* of the Demiurgus, the true father of the soul, can only be accomplished by the soul recurring to its own *unity;* and having for this purpose previously dismissed and abandoned every thing foreign to it. This occurrence, indeed, of the soul with deity, is, as Plotinus divinely says, φυγη μονου προς μονον [h], *a flight of the alone to the alone*, in which most beautiful expression I have no doubt he alludes to this mystic termination of the wanderings of Ulysses, in the embraces of his father. Proclus also, in a no less admirable manner, alludes to this union in his Commentaries on the Timæus of Plato [i]. The allusion is in his comment on the words, " It is difficult, therefore, to discover the maker and father of this universe; and, when found, it is impossible to speak of him to all men." On this passage Proclus observes: " It is necessary that the soul, becoming an intellectual world, and being as much as possible assimilated to the whole intelligible world, should introduce herself to the maker of the universe; and from this introduction, should, in a certain respect, become familiar with him through a continued intel-

---

[f] Odyss. lib. xxiv. 215, &c.   [g] Ibid. lib. xxiv. 225.
[h] These are the concluding words of the last book of his last Ennead.
[i] See vol. i. p. 254, of my translation of that work.

lectual energy. For uninterrupted energy about any thing calls forth, and resuscitates our dormant ideas. But through this familiarity, becoming stationed at the door of the father, it is necessary that we should be united to him. For discovery is this, to meet with him, to be united to him, *to associate alone with the alone,* and to see him himself, the soul hastily withdrawing herself from every other energy to him. For, being present with her father, she then considers scientific discussions to be but words[k], banquets together with him on the truth of real being, and in pure splendour is purely initiated in entire and stable visions. Such, therefore, is the discovery of the father, not that which is doxastic [or pertaining to opinion]; for this is dubious, and not very remote from the irrational life. Neither is it scientific; for this is syllogistic and composite, and does not come into contact with the intellectual essence of the intellectual Demiurgus. But it is that which subsists according to intellectual vision itself, a contact with the intelligible, and a union with the demiurgic intellect. For this may properly be denominated difficult, either as hard to obtain, presenting itself to souls after every evolution of life, or as the true labour of souls. For, after the wandering about generation, after purification, and the light of science, intellectual energy and the intellect which is in us shine forth, placing the soul in the father as in a port, purely establishing her in demiurgic intellections, and conjoining light with light; not such as that of science, but more beautiful, more intellectual, and partaking more of the nature of *the one* than this. *For this is the paternal port, and the discovery of the father, viz. an undefiled union with him.*"

With great beauty also, and in perfect conformity to the most recondite theology, is the father of Ulysses

---

[k] This is in consequence of a union with the Demiurgus being so much superior to scientific perception.

represented as coarsely clothed, and occupied in botanical labours:

> But all alone the hoary king he found;
> His habit coarse, but warmly wrapt around;
> His head, that bow'd with many a pensive care,
> Fenc'd with a double cap of goatskin hair;
> His buskins old, in former service torn,
> But well repair'd; and gloves against the thorn.
> In this array the kingly gard'ner stood,
> And clear'd a plant, encumber'd with its wood[l].

For this simplicity, and coarseness of the garb of Laertes, considered as an image of the true father of Ulysses, is, in every respect, conformable to the method adopted by ancient mythologists in their adumbrations of deity. For they imitated the transcendency of divine natures by things preternatural; a power more divine than all reason by things irrational; and, by apparent deformity, a beauty which surpasses every thing corporeal. This array, therefore, of the father of Ulysses, is, in the language of Proclus, indicative " of an essence established in the simplicity of *the one,* and vehemently rejoicing, as some one of the piously wise says, in an unadorned privation of form, and extending it to those who are able to survey it[m]." And the botanical labours of Laertes are an image of the providential attention of the Demiurgus to the immediate ramifications and blossoms of his own divine essence, in which they are ineffably rooted, and from which they eternally germinate.

Though Ulysses, however, is placed through the theoretic virtues in the paternal port, as far as this is possible to be effected in the present life, yet we must remember, according to the beautiful observation of Por-

---

[l] Odyss. lib. xxiv. 225, &c.

[m] τα μεν γαρ εςι θεια και εν τη απλοτητι του ενος ιδρυμενα την ακαλλοπιστον ευμορφιαν (lege αμορφιαν) ως φησι τις των τα οσια σοφων, διαφεροντως αγαπωντα, και προτεινοντα τοις εις αυτα βλεπειν δυναμενοις.— Procl. in Parmenid. lib. i., p. 38. 8vo. Parisiis, 1821.

phyry, that he is not freed from molestation, till he has passed over the raging sea of a material nature; *i. e.* has become impassive[n] to the excitations of the irrational life, and is entirely abstracted from external concerns. For,

> Then heav'n decrees in peace to end his days,
> And steal himself from life by slow decays;
> Unknown to pain, in age resign his breath,
> When late stern Neptune points the shaft of death;
> To the dark grave retiring as to rest;
> His people blessing, by his people blest[o].

I shall only observe farther, that Plotinus also considered the wanderings of Ulysses as a fabulous narration containing a latent meaning, such as that which we have above unfolded. This is evident from the following extract from his admirable treatise *on the Beautiful:* " It is here, then, [in order to survey the beautiful itself] that we may more truly exclaim,

> Haste, let us fly and all our sails expand,
> To gain our dear, our long-lost native land [p].

But by what leading stars shall we direct our flight, and by what means avoid the magic power of Circe, and the detaining charms of Calypso? For thus the fable of Ulysses obscurely signifies, which feigns him abiding an unwilling exile, though pleasant spectacles

---

[n] This impassivity, or perfect subjugation of the passions to reason, which is the *true apathy* of the Stoics and Platonists, is indicated by Ulysses finding a nation

" Who ne'er knew salt or heard the billows roar."

[o] Odyss. lib. xxiii. 281, &c. By *the people,* in these lines, the inferior parts or powers of the soul are indicated.

[p] Iliad, lib. ii. 140, and lib. ix. 27.

were continually presented to his sight; and every thing was proffered to invite his stay, which can delight the senses and captivate the heart. But our true country, like that of Ulysses, is from whence we came, and where our father lives[q]."

[q] See my paraphrased translation of this treatise, p. 37, &c.

THE END.

CPSIA information can be obtained
at www.ICGtesting.com
Printed in the USA
LVOW13s1453190717
541845LV00028BA/919/P